Seeking Connections

Seeking Connections

An Interdisciplinary Perspective on Music Teaching and Learning

JANET REVELL BARRETT

OXFORD
UNIVERSITY PRESS

Oxford University Press is a department of the University of Oxford. It furthers the University's objective of excellence in research, scholarship, and education by publishing worldwide. Oxford is a registered trade mark of Oxford University Press in the UK and certain other countries.

Published in the United States of America by Oxford University Press
198 Madison Avenue, New York, NY 10016, United States of America.

© Oxford University Press 2023

All rights reserved. No part of this publication may be reproduced, stored in a retrieval system, or transmitted, in any form or by any means, without the prior permission in writing of Oxford University Press, or as expressly permitted by law, by license, or under terms agreed with the appropriate reproduction rights organization. Inquiries concerning reproduction outside the scope of the above should be sent to the Rights Department, Oxford University Press, at the address above.

You must not circulate this work in any other form
and you must impose this same condition on any acquirer.

Library of Congress Cataloging-in-Publication Data
Names: Barrett, Janet R., author.
Title: Seeking connections : an interdisciplinary perspective on music teaching and learning / Janet Revell Barrett.
Description: New York, NY : Oxford University Press, 2023. |
Includes bibliographical references and index. |
Contents: Adopting an interdisciplinary perspective—Interdisciplinarity from the inside out—Multidimensionality as a springboard for connections : the Facets Model—The musics of our time—The foundations of an interdisciplinary pedagogy—Triptych play—Bridges of inspiration : synergy between music and art—Connecting contexts : music and history—Assessing the strength of connections—The music curriculum in an interdisciplinary landscape.
Identifiers: LCCN 2022058579 (print) | LCCN 2022058580 (ebook) |
ISBN 9780197511282 (paperback) | ISBN 9780197511275 (hardback) |
ISBN 9780197511305 (epub)
Subjects: LCSH: Music—Instruction and study. | Interdisciplinary approach in education. | Music teachers—Training of.
Classification: LCC MT1.B326 S44 2023 (print) | LCC MT1.B326 (ebook) |
DDC 780.71—dc23/eng/20221209
LC record available at https://lccn.loc.gov/2022058579
LC ebook record available at https://lccn.loc.gov/2022058580

DOI: 10.1093/oso/9780197511275.001.0001

Paperback printed by Marquis Book Printing, Canada
Hardback printed by Bridgeport National Bindery, Inc., United States of America

*To John Robert, Jane Ruth, Camden Edward, and Porter Alexander—
May your lives be filled with wonderment*

Contents

Preface ix
Acknowledgments xvii
Note on Sources xix
Orienting Questions xxi

1. Adopting an Interdisciplinary Perspective 1
2. Interdisciplinarity from the Inside Out 19
3. Multidimensionality as a Springboard for Connections: The Facets Model 36
4. The Musics of Our Time 67
5. The Foundations of an Interdisciplinary Pedagogy 86
6. Triptych Play 108
7. Bridges of Inspiration: Synergy between Music and Art 134
8. Connecting Contexts: Music and History 162
9. Assessing the Strength of Connections 186
10. The Music Curriculum in an Interdisciplinary Landscape 208

Notes 217
References 223
Index 231

Preface

The primary goals of an interdisciplinary approach to the music curriculum are to foster students' sense-making and to encourage lifelong engagement in music and the arts. *Seeking Connections: An Interdisciplinary Perspective on Music Teaching and Learning* provides a well-structured rationale for interdisciplinarity in the music curriculum, principles for meaningfully connected music teaching and learning, and examples of strong alignments between music and other fields of study. It is my hope that this book will contribute to these valuable ends through the principled work of music teachers who find an interdisciplinary approach compelling and worthy of their time and consideration.

This book has been decades in preparation, born of a yearning for greater attention to the power of the arts in the lives of young persons. The project is rooted in the potential of school experience to instill values of curiosity and connectedness, and the promise of teachers, especially music teachers, to foster students' thinking accordingly. My own teaching career has spanned over four decades, beginning in elementary and middle school settings before I transitioned to teacher education at the university level. During these years, I have noticed how the magnetic pull of routines and traditions, an ever-present fear of program cuts and reductions, and an often unquestioned acceptance of narrow policies and platforms for school reform have compromised teachers' imaginative curriculum-making and sense of agency. It is unsurprising that many music educators hesitate to promote the correspondence of music to other subject matters when they are trying so valiantly to protect its place in the school curriculum. It is understandable when these teachers hold tight to precious hours of interaction with students by striving to be as efficient in their instruction, and singularly focused on music, as possible. It makes sense that music teachers feel compelled to align their music programs with various mandates from local, state, and national entities. It is equally urgent for music educators to think otherwise, freeing the curriculum to take inspiration from the way music moves in realms beyond schools. It is my hope that by entertaining a generous view of the music curriculum and its impact on students' engagement with the arts, teachers may push against narrowing tendencies and increasingly conservative forces. In "teaching against the grain" (Cochran-Smith, 1991), music educators may see themselves as agents of change, powered by the "social, intellectual, ethical, and political activity of teaching" (p. 279), and in this instance, fueled as well by artistic voices and visions.

I have been fortunate to witness this openness in the work of pre-service teachers, graduate students, and in-service teachers who welcome students' interpretations, ideas, and curiosities by loosening the reins of predictability and control. I have appreciated the various ways that these teachers have put integrated principles into practice—from a trial balloon of a curricular unit to ambitious proposals for entire courses. I am profoundly grateful to those who have given permission for me to describe their excursions in this book. The settings for these projects have ranged from elementary school music classes to secondary ensembles to college courses to professional development seminars to professional chamber ensembles. With imagination, flexibility, and attention to the particular needs of students in particular contexts, these teachers have exercised wide latitude in deciding how to explore, adapt, and branch out as they draw from the heuristics we have considered. I pay tribute to their adventurous grasp of possibilities through curricular profiles and examples that sample from what I have been privileged to witness as they have shared their work with me.

The term *interdisciplinary* calls for explanation as it appears in the subtitle. Depending upon one's taxonomy of choice, some might view these curricular proposals as multidisciplinary, transdisciplinary, or cross-curricular. Terminology is further complicated when you add other common labels heard in schools—such as curriculum integration, integrated arts, related arts, or arts-infused curriculum, to name a few. I have found these terms to be used liberally in educational circles, while simultaneously lacking much conceptual clarity. Interdisciplinarity typically refers to the combination of two or more disciplines in the academic curriculum. I argue that this definition limits educators' focus on school-based patterns of organization and instruction rather than personal attributes of mind or broad realms of understanding. In other words, these terms most frequently point to patterns of school organization rather than the experiences students may have with music and closely related arts. I ask the reader to set aside the tangled set of taxonomies, definitions, claims, and controversies that surround multiple versions of the connected curriculum to consider a more personalized or even phenomenological view of the interrelations of music with other realms of human study, accomplishment, and expression.

Interdisciplinarity, in the way I have framed it here, can be viewed more broadly then as a capacity held by teachers, students, artists, and others to seek meaningful connections across varied domains and aspects of experience. These relationships can be found both within the subject matter of music itself, across disciplines, and, most important, as means to integrate musical understanding into lived experience. In other words, interdisciplinarity can be viewed as a perspective, stance, or preferred way that individuals (in this instance, teachers and students) think, in contrast to its typical use as an organizational scheme for partitioning the school schedule and units of study. Such a capacity is fueled by curiosity, a willingness to push beyond the familiar, and the spirit of risk-taking when facing the limits of one's expertise. At heart, this project is about the potential of the music curriculum to enliven experience. In this sense, the term *interdisciplinary* used in this more elastic sense seems to be the wisest choice to convey this generous reach of possibility.

Teachers of any subject or level who adopt an interdisciplinary perspective strive for breadth and depth of understanding that builds on grounded knowledge of specific disciplines while seeking the dynamic interplay of ideas that accompanies a well-rounded, or humanistic, stance toward education. In this way, specialization does not stand in the way of an expansive view of knowledge. By contrast, expert knowledge of one area, such as music, can be used as a bridge to other areas of study, such as history, cultural studies, visual art, literature, theater, dance, or closely related fields. These bridges are highlighted in this book, beckoning students and teachers who are willing to cross over and back again. Growth awaits those who are open to traveling back and forth across boundaries.

Well-roundedness is currently in short supply in schools, which have been driven in recent decades toward a race for academic achievement defined narrowly as the attainment of high test scores in a small range of subject areas, primarily reading and math. High-stakes decisions based on these scores have led to school closings, reductions in the teaching force, and serious challenges to arts education, as the precious commodities of instructional time and resources are co-opted in the service of test preparation. Claims about the potential of music to "make children smarter" or programs that use music to prompt learning in other subjects while shortchanging musical content are of grave concern to music teachers, who understandably resist compromising musical goals by using music in trivial and superficial ways as curricular window dressing, what Bresler (1995) identified as a subservient approach. External pressure on the school curriculum to raise test scores threatens arts education, which in turn triggers protectiveness and entrenchment within the school as teachers "dig in" to preserve music programs and to shore up the walls that divide subject matters from other areas of the curriculum.

Yet music, as a vibrant field, is not sealed off from the dynamic interchanges of contemporary life. Outside of its packaging as a school subject, music moves more freely. In its most fluid and organic sense, music is a permeable field of expression, influenced by other fields and factors, domains and disciplines, issues and inspirations. In turn, music influences other forms of thought and action. This permeability is one of the central premises of this book. An interdisciplinary stance toward music education supports an expansive curricular vision that fosters strong relationships of music to personal experience, diverse subject matters, and contemporary society. Music thus becomes integral to the overall curriculum of the school, contributing to the magnanimous aim of educating students for current and future enjoyment of music while valuing music for what it can bring to lived experience. Additionally, when the music curriculum is sufficiently comprehensive, the study of music is rigorous ("disciplined" in the best sense) and extensive, which invites ongoing exploration. Music teachers and students develop an integrated view of diverse musical styles *within* music, and an integrated view of music's correspondence to closely related fields and disciplines *outside*. Building these integrated webs of understanding requires an emphasis on the ways that understanding moves across categorical boundaries, inviting plentiful opportunities for relational thinking.

Organization of the Book

Chapter 1 introduces three visual metaphors to prompt thinking about music's relation to other subject matters in the curriculum. Disciplinary, interdisciplinary, and emancipatory aims are described in support of the primary principle at the heart of the book—that of music's permeability in relation to other forms of human experience. After tracing curricular stances, I raise the question of validity or integrity in integrated curriculum and suggest aims to guide sound curriculum making. The chapter ends by describing various realms for relational thinking to enable meaningful connections in the music curriculum. The nature of experience is the topic of Chapter 2, both from the students' perspective as they engage in an *educative* experience, and from the role of music teachers as disciplinary specialists who wish to broaden the comprehensive nature of the curriculum. In this chapter, etudes for the reader are introduced as brief ruminations on their own educational experiences in schools, or the breadth of their "lateral knowledge" as it intersects with music.

Multidimensionality—the notion that any particular work of art can be encountered from multiple stances or "angles"—focuses Chapter 3. After establishing the notion that works of art can be viewed as touchstones, catalysts, or cases, a heuristic model, the Facets Model, is presented in a newly revised form (from its previous introduction in Barrett, McCoy, and Veblen, 1997). The iconic anthem of freedom created by James Weldon Johnson and his brother, J. Rosamond Johnson, "Lift Every Voice and Sing," illustrates this multidimensional approach.

Chapter 4 begins with a virtual visit to an extraordinary garden that inspired an equally fascinating composition, *The Garden of Cosmic Speculation*. The visit launches an expansive search for musical expression through varied styles and genres, featuring a profile of a contemporary chamber musician whose work on behalf of new sonic landscapes is described. This chapter also introduces stretching exercises that encourage teachers to search for contemporary repertoire with multidimensional potential.

The quest for heuristics—general rules of thumb or strategies—to guide interdisciplinary planning and pedagogy occupies Chapter 5. A profile features the flexible approach of a music educator whose pedagogy enlivens students' musical explorations in an urban magnet high school. After critiquing common frameworks for curriculum planning and instruction, I offer key ideas that move toward more fluid and flexible models. These ideas are illustrated in Chapter 6 through a strategy involving sets of three works spanning three art forms. Paintings, poetry, and musical examples are related to one another in playfully engaging triptychs.

The interplay of music and visual art is the subject of Chapter 7. Following the triptychs inspired by multiple artists, poets, and composers, this exploration highlights the artistic output and musical fascinations of the Swiss artist Paul Klee. As a further illustration of the pedagogical principles outlined in Chapter 5, a panoramic curriculum project is provided that encourages interpretation, creativity, and student engagement.

Chapter 8 highlights two cases of practice. A project designed to foster historical empathy involving upper elementary students in a unit focused on the Underground Railroad is described. The path of inquiry taken by the music teacher in this project prompts an extended discussion of the ways that children's literature and music both support the teaching of historical content, including the "hard history" of enslavement. A second case centers on a large-scale performance and curricular project undertaken by a graduate student who engaged singers and instrumentalists in a series of experiences that attend to one day in the life of a US president. The cases open up questions for inquiry, and avenues for more informed alignment of the contextual nature of music and the ways history informs musical understanding.

The assessment of students' relational thinking opens up a Pandora's box of quandaries and questions. In Chapter 9, I suggest that teachers' professional judgment, keen respect for their students' thinking, and capabilities for description and reflection may be paramount in approaching the responsibilities of assessment in revitalized ways. I also provide an overview of different forms of understanding that warrant different strategies for assessment, illustrating the close alignment of curriculum, instruction, and assessment through a metaphor of a braid. Two further examples of practice—one from a high school choral setting and the other from a professional development seminar commemorating an historical figure—exemplify these alignments.

The final chapter steps back to consider how an interdisciplinary perspective sits within the broader landscape of schooling. For the field at large, I address avenues for strengthening professional development for teachers as well as approaches for fostering creative curriculum-making in music teacher education. For music teachers, the chapter ends with some guiding ideas for taking on an interdisciplinary perspective in elementary and secondary school settings.

Setting Forth

Throughout *Seeking Connections*, I have embedded frequent moments for reflection and contemplation. Before the first chapter, you will find a series of orienting questions for consideration or discussion, intended to engage your thinking about the purpose, scope, and critical appraisal of integrated approaches to the curriculum. I have also included opportunities to respond to *etudes*, personal reflections on experience; and *stretching exercises*, strategies for branching out to less familiar realms and situations. Integrated throughout the book is a frequent invitation to PAUSE, prompting moments of engagement with the works being described in the text by accessing them in whatever ways you have at hand. The musical examples, poetry, and art works so identified are catalysts for experience; lingering with them will enhance your understanding of their qualities as well as their potential for imaginative interdisciplinary curriculum. I also hope that you can explore these ideas and examples in class settings or professional discussion groups, which will strengthen creative and critical thinking about the aims and promises of this curricular stance. Ultimately, the resonance of an interdisciplinary perspective will only be realized through educative experiences that reach toward an even grander aim—the melding of artistic relationships with human relationships. May this be so.

Champaign, Illinois
February 2022

Acknowledgments

In what now seems like long ago and far away, Claire McCoy, Kari Veblen, and I started this journey. Claire's poetic presence and Kari's generous worldview have stayed with me ever since. Claire's voice was silenced too soon, but her vibrant spirit carries through these pages.

I am so grateful to the music teachers who have embraced this work, and to Northwestern University and the University of Illinois at Urbana-Champaign for granting me the honor of devoting entire courses to these pursuits. What a privilege to witness the myriad ways these thoughtful music educators have brought creativity, curiosity, and student-focused dedication to this work.

Special recognition to graduate students Tim Caskin, Stephen Dowling, Graham Heise, Julianna Karvelius, Paul Meiste, Rachel Palmer, and Melissa Plaskota for their contributions to this project. Channing Paluck, Jon Schaller, Jennifer Thomas, and Erich Weiger were kind enough to read and respond to various drafts in progress, and better yet, to discuss these ideas as they took shape.

Several individuals agreed to be interviewed for the book, and to have their work profiled. For their time and thoughtful perspectives, I gratefully acknowledge Miles Comiskey, Melissa Ngan, Katherine Seybert, and Alex Underwood. Thanks as well to Jerry L. Jaccard for his reflections on Paul Klee, and to Jason Thompson for sending marvelous musical sources for arrangements of "Lift Every Voice and Sing."

Editor Norm Hirschy's support and patience guided this project through many phases and stages, especially through the long isolation of the pandemic. Chelsea Hogue's assistance was invaluable in seeing the manuscript through to completion. Kirsten Dennison's keen eye and aesthetic sense guided the graphic design of figures in this book.

What a privilege it is to lead a scholar's life with ready access to the writings of luminaries such as Maxine Greene, Randall Allsup, Bennett Reimer, Elliot Eisner, and John Dewey. What joy it is to spend a morning deeply immersed in reading and thinking about the arts and education. How marvelous it is to pile books of poetry and art all around my desk, with any music I desire just a click away. I am grateful beyond measure for such treasures.

Throughout my career, I have also been surrounded by colleagues, friends, and collaborators who have inspired and encouraged my scholarly pursuits. For so many reasons, I thank Jeffrey Sposato, Jeff Magee, Eunice Boardman, Steve Demorest, Nancy Rasmussen, Herb Dick, Joanna Cortright, Laura Krider, John Nuechterlein, John Heim, Janet Robbins, Sandy Stauffer, Carol Scott-Kassner, Diane Persellin, Mary Goetze, Nancy Boone-Allsbrook, Lizabeth Bradford Wing, Mark Robin Campbell, Linda Thompson, Crystal McDonough, Louise Knight, Amy Gwinn-Becker, Karen Tollenaar Demorest, Samia Amamoo, Maud Hickey, Fred Muhlsteff, Peter Webster, Bennett Reimer, and so many others. Of course, the love of my family is my greatest joy—Alex, Anna, Paige, Nick, Mark, Winston, and my precious grandchildren.

Note on Sources

Thanks to the American Composers Forum for permission to reproduce the dashboard from the BandQuest curriculum. Sections of Chapter 5 were first presented at the Research in Music Education (RIME) conference at the University of Exeter (2013); other excerpts were published in the *Mountain Lake Reader: Conversations on the Study and Practice of Music Teaching* (2006). My thanks to editor Sandra L. Stauffer for permission to reprint these passages. Sections of Chapter 9 were published in Barrett, J. R. (2008). Assessing the strength of interdisciplinary connections in the music curriculum. In T. S. Brophy (Ed.), *Integrating curriculum, theory, and practice: Proceedings of the 2007 Florida Symposium on Assessment in Music Education* (pp. 103–113). GIA. These excerpts are used with permission.

Orienting Questions

In the spirit of engagement, of seeking connections rather than reproducing them, I invite readers to spend time discussing or reflecting on these orienting questions.

- What comes to mind when you think of the current state of the music curriculum?
- If the music curriculum deserves to be revitalized, in what ways might the curriculum be transformed in bold, dynamic, and relevant directions?
- How do you approach curriculum-making?
- Where do you turn for ideas and examples to inspire vibrant curricular work?
- When do you notice students making connections between music and other areas of their lives? How do you make teaching for connections a priority in your classroom?
- How can you make teaching for connections—supporting students' relational thinking—more likely and visible in your classroom?
- How does the curriculum embrace the musics of our time, draw on the pedagogies of our time, and reflect the issues of our time?
- What is the potential of an interdisciplinary approach to the music curriculum to address the aims and aspirations of social justice in school settings?
- What is the potential of an interdisciplinary approach to foster creative thinking in music?
- What are some starting places for interdisciplinary connections that uphold the integrity of the music curriculum while branching out to other disciplines in ways that uphold their integrity as well?
- In your view and from your experience, which subject areas are most likely to inspire meaningful curricular connections with music?

- What conditions in schools free music teachers to use their curricular imagination?
- What do you hope to take from your reading and reflection as you move forward to create meaningful connections in the music curriculum?
- What vibrant educational experiences do you hope to create for the students in your charge?

1
Adopting an Interdisciplinary Perspective

Three Metaphors

In your mind's eye, conjure up three images. The first, a brick wall, each brick firmly held into place by thick mortar. The second, the paint-splattered floor of an art studio covered in kaleidoscopic layers of colorful pigment. The third, a cell suspended in plasma, its darker nucleus visible as it floats through the bloodstream surrounded by other cells. You may wonder what these images have to do with music, with curriculum, with interdisciplinarity. I employ these visual metaphors to point to different stances on music in the curriculum, and to introduce an idea that animates this project as an interdisciplinary perspective on music teaching and learning (see Figures 1.1–1.3).

> PAUSE to think about these three images, generating your own explanations and interpretations.

Visual metaphors communicate relationships between and among ideas quickly and directly. The Greek root of metaphor is *metaphora*, which has to do with carrying something across or bearing it from one place to another. In this case, what is carried across is *meaning*. When a metaphor works well, it enables us to understand a concept or idea with relative ease, although we often need to work through the details of the resemblances between the word (or image) itself and the thing to which it refers. In this instance, the three visual metaphors of brick wall, atelier floor, and cell convey concepts of knowledge, of subject matters, of disciplines and their relationships to the entirety of what can be known or understood.

Although you may have generated plausible explanations for these metaphors on your own, consider these interpretations. In the first image, if any given brick is seen to represent music, we might think of the ways that music is taught, learned, and experienced as a school subject in and of itself. The mortar surrounding the brick separates the subject from others around

2 SEEKING CONNECTIONS

Figure 1.1 A brick wall
istock.com/CatLane

it. The metaphor conveys a situation in which music is walled off, sequestered, isolated. What does it mean to think of music as a discrete and self-contained discipline? Music certainly has distinctive ways of knowing and feeling; becoming a musician certainly involves cultivation of distinctive skills, understandings, and dispositions. What is lost, though, if an overly narrow focus on this development or inhospitable circumstances essentially

Figure 1.2 Floor of an art studio
istock.com/TommL

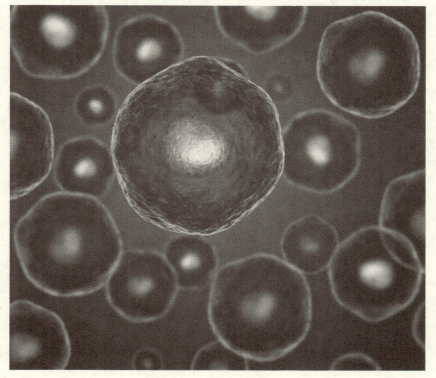

Figure 1.3 Cell wall
istock.com/TommL

separate music as a school subject from the rest of the school, from contexts beyond the school, and from reaching more students? Being surrounded by mortar is all too insular.

The second metaphor of the atelier floor eliminates borders altogether in a grand "mash-up" of disciplinary ideas. It conveys the way subject matters freely intermingle just as the colors blend and overlap. This metaphor illustrates a common rationale for interdisciplinary work that calls for dissolving subject matter boundaries, seen as necessary for addressing the pressing challenges of contemporary life. In this view, teachers—regardless of their particular field of expertise or educational background—encourage students to tackle complex problems from any angle that might be germane to a possible solution. Adopting this stance suggests that disciplinary categories or distinctions matter less than the usefulness of the discipline to address the overall problem at hand. Music's role in the educational scheme of things becomes primarily instrumental in the sense of how it functions to bring about solutions, or support other subject matters in the search for solutions. What is lost, though, in this instrumentality?

The third image of the cell might call up memories from high school in which your biology teacher emphasized that the walls of a cell function as a permeable membrane, allowing substances essential to the cell to be filtered in, and others to filter out. Although the relationship between biology and music is not a primary focus in these pages, the visual metaphor of the cell captures a vital premise for those interested in more connected fields of study. It suggests that music as an expressive way of knowing is central to students' lives, to the work of music teachers who seek to bring its generous benefits to young persons, and to school communities that value music and the arts as essential to a comprehensive education. The cell and its nucleus stand in this metaphor for the fullness of experience possible through music. The wall of the cell, though, is indeed permeable. In conversation and collaboration with other ways of knowing—both in the arts and subject matters outside the arts—music's presence in students' lives is strengthened. Music's reach is broadened beyond the music classroom. The relationships between music and these areas of understanding, each deserving its own focus as well, influence what can be taught and learned. In the very soundest instances, influences or meanings pass back and forth through the borders of the subject areas, while still retaining the important qualities, traditions, and affordances of each area. Although the metaphor is relatively simple to describe, its implications are profound for music teachers, the curricula they create, and the students whose growth these curricula seek to foster.

The overarching principle to be explored in *Seeking Connections* reflects this permeability: *Music influences, and is influenced by, other ways of knowing.*

An Invitation and an Overview

Reflect on ways that you have experienced permeability, tracing the ways that music's influence has been woven through multiple settings and instances that make up your educational history as a student and teacher. Search for moments when music has aligned with other aspects of your life. Call to mind times when you have been surprised by a student's comment that demonstrated how they were making sense by relating music to something beyond the topic of the moment. Catalogue the moments when you planned to open spaces for meaningful connections, and as a result of that opening, found new avenues of student curiosities. Take note of projects you have longed to launch, or ones you want to revisit with a renewed sense of purpose.

This introductory chapter acknowledges the complexities of teaching music in ways that uphold its validity in educational settings while stretching its capacities to contribute to comprehensive programs of study. The opening metaphors set the stage for thinking about disciplinary, interdisciplinary, and emancipatory aims for music education. To hold these aims as possible, as interdependent aims for music teachers' curriculum-making, requires creative and critical thinking. How do music teachers do this work well? If the argument for an interdisciplinary perspective is compelling, what guiding ideas inform an interdisciplinary stance?

Music as a Discipline; Music Teachers as Specialists; Thinking about Walls

The notion of a *discipline* has a fairly stable meaning, but it still deserves interrogating. Disciplines are characteristic ways of thinking about realms of human knowledge, and thus probing the meaning of a discipline can direct us toward the domain of epistemology, the study of the structure and function of knowledge, as well as aesthetics, which explores the special properties of the arts in experience. Think of the community of performers, composers, conductors, scholars, improvisers, teachers, audiences, aficionados, and critics—all who work and collaborate within this domain. Heidi Hayes Jacobs defines a discipline in a way that links it directly to school subjects as a "specific body of teachable knowledge with its own background of education, training, procedures, methods, and content areas" (1989, p. 7).[1]

In my view, Jacobs's description more aptly fits the *field* of music education, a branch of the all-encompassing parent discipline of music in all its manifestations. Her characterization is helpful, though, in thinking about the curricular elements of sound, practices, skills, instructional materials, works, and musical dispositions that constitute teachers' specialized understandings. This body of knowledge is far from fixed, however, since music educators continually consider the question of *whose musics* we study, perform, and seek to understand. The expansion of new genres, styles, and ways of making music leads teachers to redefine what it means to know music, as it also prompts them to expand their own capabilities.

Disciplinary affiliations go far deeper than the acquisition of professional knowledge, though. They also stem from the way that teachers see themselves, wrapped in professional identities, personal history, lived experiences. The composer Libby Larsen captures the intensity many teachers feel about music and their desires to lead lives immersed in music:

> Music is so blindingly beautiful and completely generous that I wonder if what propels us as musicians to study, practice, perform, and create it, is an intense loneliness in knowing that we are not music—yet born to make music, we yearn to *be* it.[2]

Passion for music, and dedication to share that passion with the young, compels persons to pursue professional paths as music teachers. Speaking with teachers and reading their autobiographies attest to their yearning to be involved in as much music as possible, to *be* it, while igniting that passion in others.

The path of music teaching fueled by that yearning often branches off in an increasingly specialized direction. When asked to describe their work, many teachers define themselves as band, choir, orchestra, or general music teachers, alongside a growing cadre of music teachers who are developing new strains of expertise in digital production, composition, hip-hop, and other promising curricular variations. To pursue various "sub-specialties" requires additional education, socialization with like-minded others, and avenues for professional recognition and advancement. Of these variations, the gloriously ambiguous term *general music* most likely resists specialization more than the others, although within that category sit communities of teachers bound through affiliation to particular approaches to teaching music. Is it possible to become too narrowly oriented toward a particular type of music teaching, too singularly focused, so passionate about one's area that others are neglected? And, critical to the discussion, does increasing specialization also tend to draw borders and boundaries around what can be taught and learned?

Perhaps another tendency familiar to music teachers results from responding to inhospitable conditions for music programs in schools, which require teachers to adopt a defensive position so they can maintain precious contact time or resources. The intense demands of their teaching responsibilities—such as meeting the needs of large numbers of students, preparing for frequent public performances, teaching multiple classes or courses, or traveling between school buildings—complicate efforts to coordinate the curriculum. The music area may be physically isolated from other areas in the building to minimize sound transfer, which further isolates the music program. Music teachers may be called upon repeatedly to advocate for their programs through persistent cycles of budget reductions that impact their work. To face these programmatic threats, they become more astute in defending the case for music as essential on its own terms. The defense of music programs often depends upon an argument that music's presence in the school is justified on the basis of its singularity—that it does what no other school subject can do for students. When circumstances reach this point, music teachers may become hesitant to speak about music's interrelationships with other subject areas for fear of losing curricular ground, at risk of being displaced or even replaced.

I find it helpful to step back, acknowledging that subject areas are both socially constructed and politically maintained, a view explained by art educator Michael Parsons. His perspective on interdisciplinarity may be more prevalent in university settings than in elementary and secondary schools, but his main point, that defined boundaries stand in the way of deeply coherent thought, still applies to the specialized, departmental nature that characterizes school curricula. Parsons explains how disciplines are perpetuated and upheld:

> Disciplines are more often thought of as "fields" or "domains," as having boundaries in the way that kingdoms and other domains do, boundaries that are historically arrived at, are somewhat arbitrary and reveal the exercise of power. We are more aware that the academic disciplines are the constructions of self-promoting and powerful elites that require varied acts of exclusion for their maintenance. And, in a further step, boundaries like this are likely to be impediments to knowledge, just as boundaries to real domains are obstacles to travel. Meaning, the metaphor suggests, is as likely to be found in crossing borders as in remaining in the center. (Parsons, 2004, p. 785)

Consider moments during which you have witnessed teachers patrolling the boundaries of their teaching specialties, pushing against initiatives that seek greater integration. In what ways might this fierce devotion to "acts of exclusion" stand in the way of meaningful connections that might be lurking right at the borders of the subject matter? What boundaries in teaching contexts loom as obstacles to travel? As I read Parsons's last sentence about crossing borders, I think of permeability, and the flow between and among subject areas that calls us to meaning.

An Interdisciplinary Spirit in the Arts and Higher Education

In a commencement address for Northwestern University's Bienen School of Music,[3] I first heard the flutist Claire Chase, who also founded the International Contemporary Ensemble, a groundbreaking ensemble on the "new music" scene. She argued that classical music is just now being born, encouraging graduates to take their place in an ever-shifting musical landscape that requires new forms of invention. Listening with my interdisciplinary mindset, I made note of Chase's prediction: "if the twentieth century was the century of specialization, the twenty-first century is the century of integration—a new renaissance in which lines between disciplines, fields, and aesthetic frames dissolve."[4]

As a creative force in contemporary music, Chase's rich musical life intersects and interacts with collaborators in other art forms and in settings such as museums, art festivals, and turbine halls, as well as ice floes in Greenland and boats on the Amazon. Her forward-thinking ensemble, like other innovative arts groups, is but one sign of this renaissance of flourishing art forms reaching new audiences and pushing music beyond worn categories and genres. She stands with her colleagues at the intersection of many inventive sources of energy, witnessing how fluidly and facilely artists move from one form to another.

The bright spirit shown by these performers, composers, directors, animators, dancers, choreographers, filmmakers, videographers, and others permeates the landscape of contemporary art-making in this century. Within this milieu of creative fluidity (think, for example, of the MacArthur Foundation "genius" grant recipients), artists frequently thrive by making bold leaps from one area of expertise to another, mirroring calls in interdisciplinary communities for dissolving barriers and demolishing disciplinary walls.

In higher education, the integration of knowledge and the construction of meaning within and across disciplinary fields provokes animated discussion and debate, while a renaissance of activity in interdisciplinary teaching, scholarship, and programmatic offerings climbs toward a zenith. Higher education has pursued the goal of knowledge integration and synthesis in general education programs throughout most of the twentieth century and beyond. One of the most compelling and common arguments for interdisciplinarity purports that such efforts bring many streams of expertise and deep networks of knowledge to bear on complex problems that cannot be thoroughly investigated using the methods of inquiry, knowledge bases, and resources of single disciplines alone.

Scholarly communities reflect this cross-fertilization of traditional research areas in journal publications, hiring patterns, grant applications, and professional conferences. The proliferation of cross-disciplinary units, projects, centers, and areas such as cultural studies, gender studies, and a host of other contemporary hybrids is a hallmark of postmodern life in academe. I think, for example, of musicology, in which there are special interest groups such as ecomusicology and medical ethnomusicology; or music theory, which offers special interest groups for persons interested in dance and movement, or investigating what mathematics brings to complex analyses of music.

Outcroppings of interdisciplinary alignments surround me in the academy—dancers pairing with engineers to study the kinetics of the human body and ways that new technologies can provide movement capabilities for persons with physical impairments; social scientists collaborating with lawyers to tackle problems of poverty and access to housing; material scientists working with architects to design environmentally sustainable buildings. In the university, interdisciplinary expertise is set in motion under the auspices of research centers and consortia founded to solve complex physical, social, and environmental problems.

Rather than breaking down walls that also dilute expertise, however, specialists also work across, within, and around problems in tandem with other specialists as they jointly tackle these richly compelling projects. As evidence of this commitment to joint work, my university recently opened a Design Center intended to be used by students, faculty, and the broader community to foster technological capabilities that have yet to be invented. Rather than belonging to a particular unit on the campus, the center is open to anyone and welcomes participation from all disciplines.[5] On many campuses, students can propose their own interdisciplinary version of a major program of study by combining coursework and concentrations across domains and departments. Although many university scholars and administrators still fiercely patrol the boundaries of disciplines in the way that Parsons described, interdisciplinarity in higher education seems to be thriving.

When I think of these initiatives and partnerships that sit at the nexus of expertise, I am fascinated by possibilities. As Chase put it, the intellectual spirit of the times seems to favor and even depend upon integration. But I pause to consider whether education in the arts, and especially music education in elementary and secondary education, can persist in a "new renaissance in which lines between disciplines, fields, and aesthetic frames dissolve." Thinking of the atelier floor, I cannot imagine the "frames" of school music actually dissolving. I suspect other music educators would agree with this concern. How, though, might the energies of integration in contemporary life vibrate in school music programs?

The Quest for More Interdisciplinarity in Schools

Elementary and secondary schools have long aspired to promote interdisciplinary thinking, often promoted as a vital plank of school reform.

Disappointingly, many of the rationales for these initiatives are entangled in claims about "preparing students for the world of work," essentially reducing the possibilities for interdisciplinary capacities to whatever they contribute to economic well-being and vocational training. Closely related is the ever-present and misguided expectation that the arts should do their part in raising students' test scores in reading and math. Burton, Horowitz, and Abeles (2000) call this an unfortunate "leitmotif of arts education" (p. 228). Many of these projects aim in only one direction, using the arts in a subservient manner while prioritizing other goals (Bresler, 1995). Very little, if any, attention is dedicated to the question, What are the benefits of studying other subjects to the study of arts, or music in particular?

Some educational scholars note that overly ambitious schemes to break down the walls of traditional school subjects via interdisciplinary paths have been thwarted again and again, particularly given robust curricular patterns that seem fixed and immutable in schools. As Wineburg and Grossman observe, "subject matters represent deep institutional structures that, like the arms of a starfish, have a way of regenerating soon after amputation" (2000, p. 2). Reba Page describes unfortunate outcomes for plans that go awry: "Putting two subject matters together is no easy task and, rather than a generative hybrid that has its own integrity . . . most often, integrated curriculum is simply a 'conglomerate' in which opposing ideas, set side by side, cancel each other out and, thus, contribute to students' sense that there is little knowledge to learn in school" (2006, p. 59).

Another misguided pattern places many subject matters together with a central theme as a hub, quickly rotating through subject areas in ways that remind me of a carousel, or speed dating. This scheme skims and scans, which might be useful for teachers' brainstorming, but if the carousel never stops long enough for students to experience depth and wonder with any of its features, superficial exposure is more likely than deep understanding.

If disciplinary ways of thinking are socialized into the very fabric of school life, and are not likely to be eradicated, then what promise does an interdisciplinary stance on music learning and teaching hold? If interdisciplinary projects typically end up in an unsatisfying conglomerate of confusing and contested ideas, then what initiatives are salvageable? Investigating the multiple meanings, diverse aims, underlying premises, and instructional patterns of the integrated curriculum in elementary and secondary schools is in itself a daunting undertaking (Hargreaves, Earl, Moore, & Manning, 2001), yet teachers must be alert to varied claims and promises.

Grossman, Wineburg, and Beers caution against asking: "Which kind of curriculum, traditional subject-based or interdisciplinary, is better?" This question leads us on a false search for an answer by forcing us to think in dichotomous terms. Instead, they maintain: "Intellectual connectedness and integration go on in both traditional disciplinary classrooms and in innovative interdisciplinary ones. The larger problem for students is too often that they go on in neither" (2000, p. 14).

Sorting out the tensions of turf and territory, overlap and oversight, surface and depth, calls for critical and creative thought. What insights offer paths forward if music teachers intend to uphold the integrity of their subject matter while also creating space for connections?

Toward Permeability in the Curriculum

The notion of an interdisciplinary approach to music teaching and learning might seem paradoxical in that music education has evidently functioned for centuries as a field unto itself. How can a particular school subject claim to foster both disciplinary and interdisciplinary growth? The educational philosopher Philip Phenix addresses this conundrum in *Realms of Meaning* (1964). Although he does not name the arts specifically, his general claim obtains:

> Every discipline is to some degree integrative in nature. Every discipline makes use of materials from other disciplines. They do not exist in watertight compartments. Some disciplines by their very logic are strongly integrative. This is true of the synoptic disciplines [which Phenix names chiefly as history, philosophy, and religion], but also of others, such as geography and literature. Hence, practice in crossing discipline lines is available even in the study of individual disciplines. (p. 320)

Phenix's notion of the inherently integrative nature of disciplines parallels the ideas of musicologist Claire Detels, whose book *Soft Boundaries: Revisioning the Arts and Aesthetics in American Education* speaks primarily to the context of music in higher education, with implications for elementary and secondary schools. She calls for stronger integration of music history and aesthetic philosophy in schools of music, advocating for "soft boundaries" within those walls. A tangible benefit of softened borders is the way they would make the arts more accessible and relevant to citizens outside universities, thereby strengthening their societal value. "Soft boundaries," Detels writes, "mean more interdisciplinary contact among teachers and students in the separate disciplines of the arts and aesthetics and more contact and communication with the wider public" (1999, p. 29). In moving across boundaries, concepts become "permeable—continually open to redefinition and change as additional experience in received and examined" (p. 28). Detels's notion embraces work in the center and at the edges of a field. Her argument opens the door for specialization and interdisciplinarity to coexist, particularly if teachers and scholars reframe their thinking about borders and boundaries.

Seeing the disciplines as inherently interdisciplinary requires a profound shift in thinking for many teachers. Such a view complements a strong subject-matter orientation while expanding avenues for study, inquiry, and experience. To rephrase the principle of permeability prompted by the visual metaphor of the cell: *Disciplines (and their corollary school subjects) are influenced by other disciplines. In turn, any particular discipline may influence other realms of thought.* At the risk of introducing another metaphor—once you accept this premise, the interdisciplinary gate swings open. Furthermore, it swings in both directions.

Rather than completely dissolving the boundaries between disciplines, this mediated stance of permeability needs different verbs—softening, bending, elasticizing, overlapping, expanding, breaking open. The *Oxford English Dictionary* reminds us of the word's Latin roots, "*permeabilis, that can be passed through.*" An interdisciplinary perspective on music teaching and learning, therefore, concentrates on the extent to which music as a subject matter is integrative, and also to the curricular and instructional ramifications of teaching music as an integrative subject. The approach depends upon an acknowledgment of permeable boundaries and on a commitment to the pursuit of relationships between music and other forms of experience. In terms of the music curriculum, disciplinary and interdisciplinary stances can be considered as complementary to, not in competition with, one another. Teaching and learning music while keeping both stances in mind results in strong groundings within the discipline while also keeping the discipline relevant to its dynamic surroundings.

Toward an Interdisciplinary Perspective as Music Educators

Perspective is key here, as a stance, an orientation, a mindset, if you will. In the words of the brilliant composer, conductor, and teacher Leonard Bernstein: "The best way to 'know' a thing is in the context of another discipline" (1965, p. 3). Bernstein made this statement as he was paying tribute to one of his philosophy professors, David Prall, who was a keen influence on his worldview. Bernstein credited Prall for instilling interdisciplinary dispositions and values that inspired him to draw from poetry, philosophy, and physics as he examined the structures and workings of music.[6] Bernstein's intellectual zest for expanding his frame of reference deepened his capacity in turn to explain his remarkably fertile thinking about music. I think of this phenomenon as *lamination*, as insights from "outside" fold back and layer to deepen understandings of music. Although few persons would be so bold as to compare themselves with Bernstein's genius, he personifies an interdisciplinary perspective and exemplifies its benefits to music.

It may seem paradoxical, then, but a valid starting point for developing this disposition, if it is not already well practiced, is to search within music itself. Finding meaningful connections between and among musical works, styles, performers, and genres is fundamental to building a well-integrated base of musical knowledge, and for strengthening a relational stance. Tracing the roots and branches of musical repertoires as well as their rhizomatic outcroppings is an *intra*disciplinary practice. For music teachers and their students, this search traces relationships through musical borrowing, the processes of transmission, honoring traditions as well as bending them.

Going "outside" may not require traveling to far destinations. Taking inventory of hybrid and blended forms of expression also provides access to permeability. Inherently synthetic forms such as musical theater and opera rely on the symbiotic interplay of sound, gesture, image, and narrative, for example. Drawing attention to the interplay as an integral part of a classroom experience is a natural complement to their study. As another example, the creation, performance, interpretation, and appreciation of songs rely on the melding of poetic text in expressive forms. The arts often take inspiration from one another; the interplay of music, painting, dance, theater, literature, sculpture, architecture, and other media offers fertile ground for study and experience. The imprints of time and place on creative activity expand possibilities for understanding the origins, transmissions, and multiple meanings of art works as they are situated in history and culture. These initial ideas can lead to substantive and satisfying educational encounters. Once you take this stance, the permeability of music, its eclectic influences and their hold on experience, springs to the foreground of your attention, and in many instances leads to ideas that multiply and branch out in fascinating directions.

Toward Doing This Work Well

I have met music teachers who resist this focus on music's interdisciplinary dimensions, and in conversation, they express justifiable hesitations having been compelled to participate in projects they felt diminished music's role in the curriculum, trivialized its importance, or used music in subservient ways toward irrelevant ends. All too often, they have been disappointed when stated promises fall short of satisfactory realizations. Each time I hear these regrettable stories, they strengthen my desire to provide stronger arguments for evaluating the soundness of proposed programs, as well as creating one's own. I return to premises about curricular integrity outlined in *Sound Ways of Knowing* (Barrett, McCoy, & Veblen, 1997), which have held fast in large part, with some modifications. I think of Reba Page's statement that such putting subjects together should result in a "generative hybrid that has its own integrity" (2006, p. 59) and the equation often quoted by the late Claire McCoy that interdisciplinary projects "work" when "$1 + 1 > 2$," when the whole is greater than the sum of the parts.

I hold that judging the quality of an interdisciplinary example, curriculum, or program involves exercising multiple criteria, which, as Eisner recommends, "invite inquiry; they do not close it off" (2002, p. 176). These include appraising the curricular proposal for its *disciplinary validity*, the goodness of fit with the content, processes, and dispositions of music study, and the practices of its members; its *interdisciplinary validity*, the goodness of fit with the content, processes, and dispositions of the related disciplines, as informed by its practitioners; its *mutuality*, the shared benefit of combining two or more disciplines in complementary fashion; and especially its *generativity*, the way that meanings enable students to create, analyze, produce, evaluate, and pursue additional knowledge, understanding, and experience. It is through generativity that the curriculum can be judged as *emancipatory* as well, as the curriculum releases persons to attend to their own growth and becoming, to address the pressing challenges of our time, and to enable the expressive lives of persons and the artistic vibrancy of communities.

Criteria such as these inform the work of those who consider themselves both specialists and interdisciplinarians, described as persons who seek to develop disciplinary depth and interdisciplinary breadth in order to pursue meaningful connections across related ways of knowing, and doing so with purpose and care. Teachers who adopt an interdisciplinary perspective also attend to the forms of understanding, means of instruction, and insightful evaluation of the strength and validity of these connections.

Toward Aims of Interdisciplinarity for the Music Curriculum

John Dewey emphasizes that aims in education provide purposeful direction for teachers, guiding an intentional path. They enable teachers "to act with meaning" (1916/1944, p. 104). Holding aims in view enables teachers to create conditions that will in turn enable students' learning. One of the distinguishing attributes that draws me to Dewey's thinking is his notion that aims should be flexible. While holding thoughtful aims in view, teachers can adapt and modify the search toward those aims as circumstances develop. This attribute is especially congruent with an interdisciplinary perspective, which encourages discovery throughout the educational process, avoiding the dual problems of being too fixed at the outset or too tethered to measurements at the endpoint. Dewey holds that the journey—the path toward the aim—should also feel fulfilling and satisfying along the way. In other words, relationships—both subject-oriented and social—are noted, encouraged, and fostered within an educational context.

I encourage you to hold the following aims as provisional while considering the principles, strategies, examples, and recommendations that will follow in this volume. "The more general ends we have, the better. One statement will emphasize what another slurs over. What a plurality of hypotheses does for the scientific investigator, a plurality of stated aims may do for the instructor" (Dewey, 1916/1944, p. 110). In that regard, I propose that some of the aims of interdisciplinarity in the music curriculum are to:

- Foster students' sense-making and enhance their understanding of music as it relates to other areas of schooling and their lives;
- Make educative experiences more likely in music classrooms, especially through multidimensional encounters with works of art;
- Broaden the comprehensiveness of the music curriculum by encompassing both disciplinary and interdisciplinary relationships—as music education becomes more comprehensive, it necessarily becomes more interdisciplinary in nature;
- Emphasize creative imagination, interpretation, and relational thinking;
- Strengthen music education's commitment to social justice through contextual understanding;
- Invite teachers' pedagogical creativity, inquiry, flexibility, and professional judgment;
- Encourage lifelong engagement with music and the arts, and curiosity about music and the arts outside of the realm of schooling;
- Enliven music classrooms and school communities through integrating subject matters and enhancing social interaction.

Broadly construed, the purpose of an interdisciplinary perspective is to foster relational thinking. Consider four realms in which meaningful connections might be made, including:

- Connections *within* an arts discipline, so that students understand how the processes, works, styles, and ways of thinking within an arts domain are related through *intradisciplinary relationships*;
- Connections *across* the arts, so that students understand how the expressive forms, functions, and processes of the arts share commonalities and sources of inspiration, while also accentuating their distinctive modes of participation and expression;
- Connections *across* the arts to subjects outside the arts, which lead students to realize how the arts are influenced by, and in turn influence, other realms of human experience; and
- Connections that *transcend* disciplinary boundaries altogether, allowing students to see the world more clearly and to situate themselves within that world.

These realms, and ultimately, their interrelationships, are represented in Figure 1.4.

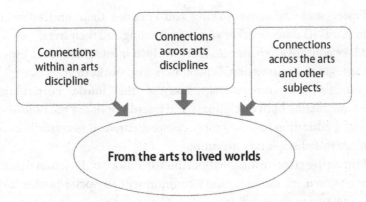

Figure 1.4 Realms of relational thinking

The realms of relational thinking map out territories for exploration. They point toward intriguing and compelling educational landscapes. For music teachers willing to travel outside the boundaries to meet students in their lived worlds, these realms multiply possibilities for meaning making; they open up pathways for growth; they call for new visions of curriculum.

2
Interdisciplinarity from the Inside Out

Music teachers hold bold aims in view for the students in their charge. These aims serve as a compass, guiding teachers' decisions as they infuse daily classroom encounters with purpose and care. As teachers reflect on the way that any given class or rehearsal forwards students' growth, their thoughts inevitably turn to the nature of experience—both from their perspective as teachers, and as much as possible, from the standpoint of their students.

We tend to use the term *experience* casually and liberally in everyday speech. It frequently refers to commonplace events and felt paths of daily life, and perhaps even occasionally to chronicle long-lasting engagement with the world. Whatever the scope, we recognize implicitly that not all experiences are qualitatively equivalent to others, especially when we step back to consider particular moments of our lives in schools. Some stand out. Others sink in. Many dissipate. A few are etched in our identities. This type, which we may even call *formative*, or significant in shaping our identities, may even set teachers or students toward previously unimagined horizons. The educational philosophy John Dewey used *experience* in this especially consequential way: "Every experience is a moving force. Its value can be judged only on the ground of what it moves toward and into" (1938, p. 38). In Dewey's view of educative experiences, *an* experience (distinguished with the indefinite article to set it apart from the everyday) is dynamic, propelling individuals *toward* or *into* other experiences.

Educators who seek to create these dynamic experiences draw from a fund of experiential knowledge of their own. As Dewey develops this idea, he challenges teachers to summon their personal insights as they guide students' paths accordingly to their teacherly responsibilities. "The greater maturity of experience which should belong to the adult as educator puts [them][1] in a position to evaluate each experience of the young in a way in which the one having the less maturity of experience cannot do" (1938, p. 38). Taking stock of this maturity of experience is a crucial responsibility. In thinking about music teachers who adopt an interdisciplinary stance, taking stock means taking inventory of life experiences with music, other arts, and disciplines outside the arts, as well as reflecting on the range and richness of these experiences. An arts-filled life deepens this storehouse as teachers seek out avenues for continual learning.

The phrase "from the inside out" organizes this chapter in two ways. The first sense relates to the nature of experience, and what sets *an* experience apart from day-to-day routine, especially in teachers' capacities to integrate encounters with art works and classroom communities into meaningful interactions. To encourage reflection on these qualities, readers are invited to participate in an exercise, or etude, that involves examining their personal histories of especially vibrant moments with the arts in school settings, or places outside of school. The exercise also piques curiosity about the ways that teachers set up contexts to make these vibrant moments more likely. The second sense relates to music teachers' roles as "insiders," looking after their roles and responsibilities from a disciplinarian's stance, and how that stance widens when turned toward other subject matters in complementary interactions with music. To invite thinking about transformations from disciplinary to interdisciplinary mindsets, two additional etudes are suggested: one related to revisiting or reclaiming areas of study outside of music that inform and energize interdisciplinary work, and the other representing an arts-based overview of significant events in teachers' lives within music and other arts.

Etudes for Interdisciplinarians, Opus 1

Just as it is used in music as a short piece intended for practice, an etude is an opportunity to concentrate on a particular skill, technique, or in this case, an educational episode. The purpose of this first etude is to prompt artistic sensibilities and teaching insights stemming, in a phenomenological way, from one's own experience as the subject. I encourage the reader to respond to these etudes through writing, conversation, presentation, contemplation, or whatever medium leads to fruitful insights. In this first etude, moments of connectedness are chronicled.

- Think back on moments of artistic, intellectual, and personal connections to the arts in your own educational experience. Which instances stand out from the rest? Describe moments that served as a "moving force" in your elementary, secondary, or tertiary education.

- Were any of these episodes of crackling energy a result of making an intellectual, artistic, or personal connection to the areas of study you were engaged in at the time? Individuals refer to such moments of connectedness as the feeling of "things falling into place" or taking on larger significance as what was separated is suddenly integrated into what is already known. Can you recall the details? Where were you? What fell into place? Can you remember what had previously been separated that you were able to relate within a broader realm of understanding? How did that feel? What was the impact on the way you have thought about these topics or subject matters subsequently? Did the energy of these occasions last? Why do you think these moments stand apart in your recollection?
- If possible, consider the circumstances that led to these dynamic experiences. What conditions enabled these moments? If teachers were influential, in what ways did they set the stage for these distinctive experiences?

The Nature of *an* Experience

One of the central claims of arts education is that the arts intensify experience. The nature of experience in the arts infuses the personal histories of individuals with sounds, colors, texts, movement, and images. An artistic experience deepens and intensifies feeling, making encounters more vibrant, vivid, alive. The expressive dimensions of the arts, as their special province, opens special prospects for interdisciplinary work. The late Claire McCoy, building on ideas from Dewey's *Art as Experience*, captured this power with metaphorical grace[2]:

> Art, as a refinement and intensification of our human experience (Dewey, 1934), is a magnifying glass for the soul. A magnifying glass can be used to bring cloudy images into focus. It can also be used to focus sunlight with enough intensity that it can burn a hole in paper. The artist, through visual images, melodies, physical gestures, or poetic language, not only helps us clarify our thoughts about life experiences, but also helps us distill and intensify the feelings of joy, sorrow, wonder, or amusement we associate with those experiences. (Barrett, McCoy, & Veblen, 1997, p. 50)

Maxine Greene, in her visionary book *Releasing the Imagination*, reaches toward the arts as means to more vibrant conceptions of school life. Her use of italics in this next passage underscores how transformative the arts can be: "Participatory involvement with the many forms of art can enable us to *see* more in our experience, to *hear* more on normally unheard frequencies, to *become conscious* of what daily routines have obscured, what habit and convention have suppressed" (1995, p. 123). Through the arts, she calls persons "to awaken, to disclose the ordinarily unseen, unheard, and unexpected" (p. 28). Citing Dewey, she exhorts "people to plunge into subject matter in order to steep themselves in it, and this is probably more true of works of art than other subject matters" (p. 30). Linger for a moment to reflect on the ways that you have experienced such awakenings in your own experience, either in school or elsewhere, and the ways in turn that you responded to those moments. In what ways have the arts moved you to refine, distill, intensify, disclose, awaken?

PAUSE to access and view Jackson Pollock's *Autumn Rhythm* before continuing.

Curriculum scholar Patrick Slattery recalls such an experience during a field trip to the Metropolitan Museum of Art as a teenager. As he shuffled through the museum with his friends, he was arrested—in the sense of becoming transfixed—by Jackson Pollock's painting *Autumn Rhythm*. At the end of the tour, he asked to return to the painting as the class moved along, reflecting that:

> Hundreds of people must have come and gone while I spent an hour or more in the room. However, time stood still for me. I was not a painter; I had never formally studied art. I had never heard of Jackson Pollock, but I became the artist through his painting as his journey and my journey were united in a synthetical moment. When I reluctantly left the museum and caught up with my friends, I could not explain the mysterious events that occurred as I stood before *Autumn Rhythm*. (Slattery, 2013, p. 253)

What strikes me about Slattery's experience is the way this unexpected viewing of Pollock's painting engendered such a profound response at that moment in his youth. In a surprising way, he was not at all prepared for this encounter. Slattery had little basis for being drawn into Abstract

Expressionism, which many museum goers have found challenging. Nonetheless, he felt a pull to return to *Autumn Rhythm*, lingering and looking as "time stood still." This singular moment served as a fulcrum in Slattery's life. He went on to steep himself in Pollock's art, plunging into his paintings and building his awareness of the artist's life and influences. The potency of this first encounter fueled a lifelong quest for artistic experience.

"When conditions are just right or very close to it, the resultant transaction between self and surroundings constitutes *an* experience," writes Philip Jackson, in which "the experiencer changes by undergoing a transformation of the self" (1998, p. 5). Jackson examined Dewey's writings about the nature of experience and the nature of art, bringing them together.[3] As illustrated in Slattery's narrative, such a transformation earns the additional article that sets it apart as *an* experience.

PAUSE to access and view Marc Chagall's *America Windows*.

In thinking about the philosophical distinctions of aesthetics related to art and experience, I call up a complementary moment in my own adolescence that resembles Slattery's. On a family trip from my small farming community in Iowa to Chicago, I visited the Art Institute, the first breathtaking excursion of many. After passing through the entry, I was drawn through the first central corridor of medieval armor toward an intense blue glow in the distance, feeling a magnetic pull similar to a tractor beam. Standing in front of Marc Chagall's expansive *America Windows* of stained glass, I felt enveloped—nearly inhabited—by the rich, brilliant color. I recognized figures in Chagall's tribute to music, dance, literature, painting, and theater among the six panels, but beyond that, I knew little of Chagall's invitation by the city of Chicago to create the work in celebration of the US Bicentennial, or his gratitude for being able to create art without fear of persecution. I was unfamiliar with Chagall, his Jewish identity, his iconography, his struggles. But like Slattery, my lack of knowledge or exposure did not seem to matter as I was swept up in the radiant colors. I stood transfixed. I look back on that day as the start of a lifelong passion for art that has enriched my life in ways complementary to music. The word *numinous* comes to mind—what for some is described as an aesthetic experience in which individuals experience profundity, depth, expansiveness, deep reservoirs of feeling and meaning. How do our engagements with the arts trigger a sense of breath suspended, time slowed down, alert and vibrant engagement?

Educative and Miseducative Experience

These transformations may certainly take place in school settings, although as a teacher, I wonder how often I have had access as a witness to such turning points in students' minds and hearts. Occasionally, bright revelations and serendipitous discoveries burst forth, but of course, I look out for changes of thinking, perspective, and feeling that may not be quite as dramatic as well. What guidance applies to these subtler shades and hues of understanding?

Dewey, in his prolific writings and persistent inquiries, provides another telling distinction that can influence the very planning and design of classroom explorations toward these ends, particularly in the sense of continuity, the notion of an "experiential continuum" (1938, p. 28). He characterizes what makes an educational experience *educative* or *miseducative*. An educative experience does "something to prepare a person for later experience of a deeper and more expansive quality." In other words, it "takes up something from those [experiences] that have gone before and modifies in some way the quality of those [experiences] which come after" (p. 35). As teachers, we attend as best we can to the relationships of ideas that have been made meaningful through prior work, linking them through the present moment to make their educational value and use more apparent in the future—the "moving force" reappearing. Dewey also wrote about miseducative experiences, which have "the effect of arresting the growth of further experiences." In thinking about the miseducative, I call up instances that might have been enjoyable, but insubstantial, not likely to last beyond the moment. I can also regrettably recall encounters that dulled the senses, or that seemed so closed in their presentation as to turn persons away from inquiry and exploration. The trite and trivial sometime take center stage in classrooms, and surely this is miseducative, too. Miseducative experiences fail to invite students' engagement and curiosities with the immediate elements of the situation. They fail to ignite the senses or propel learning beyond the moment at hand.

Opus 1, Reprise

Before reading on, take a moment to return to the thoughts you generated in response to the first etude, and consider them in light of the concepts of experience in the deeply transformative sense as well as in the distinctions between an educative and a miseducative experience. If your first etude involved teachers, reflect on the ways that they influenced your educational pathways. In what ways might they have set up conditions for these moments as educative?

School Routines as Anaesthetic

Educators view schools as sites for awakening minds and hearts. They approach this honorable intention by providing the kinds of encounters students are less likely to come across in their daily routines outside of school, as well as constructing bridges between school and life outside its walls. The arts, of course, facilitate these moments of expressive impact. Regrettably, our idealized claims and images about the power of schooling to transform lives often fall short of these intentions for a wide variety of reasons. Greene cites Virginia Woolf's phrase "the cotton wool of daily life" to portray the kind of repetitive, mindless routines that often entrap students (and teachers, for that matter) in dreary, shapeless classrooms. The normative patterns of school—its predictable rhythms, structures, and prescribed roles—appear to work against feelingful engagement. Instead of vivifying experience, life in classrooms can become anaesthetic, dulling the senses instead.

Since the late 1990s, a body of work has focused on school as experienced by students, probing their perspectives, beliefs, criticisms, and interpretations of life in classrooms. Much of this work has concentrated on secondary school students rather than younger children, who tend to telegraph their feelings more directly. Pope (2001) shadowed five high school students nominated as highly successful by their teachers in her study of student engagement. She observed that although the "best and the brightest" (a term that begs for critique) appeared to participate during class with noticeable regularity and intensity, they also used the term "doing school" to confess that the busyness and industry they displayed on the surface was merely a façade to cover their general disillusionment with schooling. The quest for high grades as a portal to college admission eclipsed nearly all other motivations. Instead of pursuing knowledge widely and deeply, they rode the surface of the wave, doing what was necessary to "get an A" in hope of jumpstarting their pathways to future career success. In a related study, Pierce described students who navigated the "swirls of movement" in the hallway as they changed classes every 42 minutes throughout their day, but who maintained a neutral holding pattern during each class, waiting for the bell to ring (2005/2006). These portraits of disengagement are unsettling, as are the efforts students take to mask their curiosities and intentions.

In many instances, these portrayals of "doing school, going through the motions, waiting for the bell" do not align with many music teachers' personal accounts of school experience. Music teachers often look back on their own time as students as compelling enough to inspire career trajectories and potential teaching specializations. Many teachers attribute their own desires to teach to the inspiration of former teachers who made teaching and learning enjoyable and fulfilling, memorable and meaningful. These portrayals of student disengagement also do not mesh with many music teachers' impressions of their own students who see the music room as a haven, a site for socializing, a place to celebrate and express their identities.

Educationally Vital Experiences in School Settings

Music and the arts in general are often cited as antidotes to this bland portrait of life in schools as artistic forms of engagement draw students' minds, bodies, hands, and hearts into imaginative action. To build on the notion of educative experiences, a study of classrooms is in order, this one involving literature, and making the connection with integrative thinking clearer. Sam Intrator spent a school year observing students in a high school English classroom, looking for signs of their engagement, involvement, and intellectual awakenings. He was interested in the ways that the curriculum can be called aesthetic or anaesthetic, but also in the ways that curriculum can also be *monoaesthetic*, which he described as limiting "our perceptive faculties by focusing relentlessly on developing only narrow modes of knowing and representing the world" (2005, p. 176). He cited classrooms singularly focused on test preparation as examples of this monoaesthetic approach. Intrator's classification prompts further thinking on the ways that curricula in the arts, even music, can be monoaesthetic.

Intrator built on Dewey's notions of experience, coining his own phrase, "educationally vital experiences" or EVEs, which he also referred to as "spots of time that glow." He wrote about teachers who "have a vision in mind of their students engrossed in meaningful activity and the class surging along on the wings of intrinsic energy. These moments of transcendent possibility glow; they burn, they crackle, they hum with energy" (1999, p. 1). Although he found these moments to be rare, they contrasted sharply with instances in which students were caught up in the "inexorable chug of the routine" (2003, p. 4).

Mr. Quinn, the high school English teacher Intrator studied, exemplified practices that seemed to encourage these spots of time. In preparation for studying Steinbeck's *Cannery Row*, for example, he read a passage filled with Steinbeck's vivid descriptions of the novel's setting before inviting students to head to a nearby baseball field, spreading out in the grass to practice their powers of observation on the patch in front of them. This activity, an obvious deviation from the normal routine, delighted and captivated the students, exercising their descriptive powers. Intrator wove more sources into related investigations as the class met with a biologist whose work depended on observational clarity, studied historical photographs of the period taken by Dorothea Lange, and gathered other forms of representation. The students' journals and discussions reflected their sensory impressions, shifts of perception, and social interactions that enlivened their understandings of the novel and of the intersections of subject matters in complementary ways. Intrator's depiction of this classroom as "crackling with energy" is inspiring.

I am convinced that an educationally vibrant experience cannot be engineered by following a prescriptive formula. We can pay attention, however, to narratives of our own experiences and stay open to inspiration from others so that we can create classrooms more prone to these vibrant encounters. As I have asked music teachers to share what they have learned about vibrancy, some resonant themes have emerged. For many, the work itself "speaks," as teachers have incorporated captivating compositions, improvisations, paintings, poems, and plays into their classrooms with a receptive stance to what might be learned. Past teachers figure prominently, either through deliberate attention to the qualitative dimensions of classroom experience or through seemingly offhand comments about their personal interests that fired students' imagination. Open-ended projects are frequently mentioned, as the capacity to choose the project's content, shape, and direction enable students to pursue interests not typically studied in classrooms. Many teachers' autobiographical accounts address the special gloss of exposure to professional artists (composers, performers, theater companies, writers' workshops, poets, dancers, actors, directors, choreographers) as well as memorable visits to cultural institutions and community events (the concert hall, the museum, the ballet company, summer festivals, art fairs). Tours figure prominently, of course. Autobiographical pathways are another deep source of insight, through familial traditions, religious and spiritual practices, and the artistic and intellectual pursuits of parents and siblings. Especially germane to interdisciplinary thinking are those vibrant moments when meaning crosses over topics, subjects, or disciplines of interest that were previously dissociated. The feeling that comes when seemingly unrelated aspects of our knowledge become clear in relation to one another stands out as memorable embodiments of learning. Such moments leave indelible impressions. Through collecting these accounts and reflecting on their impact, abstract notions of experience materialize, take shape, and may even glow with vitality.

Teachers' Intentions in Crafting Experiences

Vibrant personal experiences leave a lasting residue. None of this can take place without enabling conditions, or what Dewey called "environing conditions" (1938, p. 40), the situations at hand in the milieu or context that ensure access and sustained growth. Teachers strive to set into place structures that will promote artistic exploration, such as multiple avenues for students to pursue in expanding their knowledge, and multiple forms of engagement. Jackson explains that an experience "takes place in the world itself, made up of our continuous interaction and participation with the objects, situations, and events that constitute our environment" (1995, p. 194). Teachers are well poised to enlarge the world of the classroom and school by employing curricular, material, social, and contemporary resources as contexts for learning.

Above all, teachers are primed to oversee students' development of understanding. With that understanding comes the stimulating prospect of witnessing the construction of deep and lasting meanings. Accordingly, teachers work toward development—the development of artistic sensibilities, the development of artistic values, the development of artistic thinking. This development is furthered through strong connections with particular works of art, from one work to another, and from works of art to varied forms of human experience and expression. As these circles of activity expand, so do the context, content, and scope of an interdisciplinary perspective.

The Pursuit of Disciplinary Depth in Music Teaching

The path that many music teachers travel from early years to their professional lives in classrooms, however, seems to work against this comprehensive perspective. Preparation to teach is first and foremost preparation to specialize in music, and often to specialize even further in certain sub-specialties we recognize as general music, choral, or instrumental music (divided even further into band and orchestra). Of course, each one of these types is a practice in itself, requiring knowledge, skills, and professional socialization. The varieties of types of music teaching and related practices, though, have expanded and continue to diversify as more teachers develop their capacities in areas of popular music, digital production, composition, and other compelling forms of professional energy. Music is central to these teaching identities, as it should be, but to move toward interdisciplinary stances requires some adjustment if music teachers as interdisciplinarians wish to claim integrity in their work.

In working with preservice teachers for several decades, I have observed a general path that conveys how music itself becomes increasingly specialized as persons become music teachers.[4] In early childhood, music is embedded in the overall fabric of development, centered in children's daily contexts of familial and familiar surroundings. Participation in music involves observation and imitation of peers and adults, and in exploring ideas through musical play. Full immersion in the "sonic surrounds" (Lum & Campbell, 2007) in elementary school, and recognition of children's attempts and expressions through singing, playing, moving, listening, and creating with sound, are often starting places for a musical identity throughout the lifespan. Some call this stage of embeddedness, immersion, and play "pre-disciplinary" (Gardner & Boix Mansilla, 1994).

In elementary school, though, music is rather quickly set apart as an entity of its own—one of the "specials." In most schools, music instruction is available for all children, scheduled one or several days per week. Children quickly learn that music making happens with a designated music teacher as the authoritative source of musical traditions, skills, and knowledge. They learn that sounds are grouped in patterns called melody, rhythm, harmony, texture, form. Occasionally, music seeps out from under the door of the specially designated music room into the hallways and gymnasiums when special events such as performances or concerts are celebrated.

For many, a landmark moment comes when it becomes possible to choose *more* music study through participation in instrumental lessons or ensembles of choir, band, orchestra. This is the gateway to music in the secondary school when music becomes an elective subject. One's musical participation becomes even more closely aligned with the medium of participation—as a singer, an oboist, a trumpeter, a cellist; or ensemble member—in choir, orchestra, band, jazz band. The social aspects of ensemble membership reinforce and strengthen these affiliations, as does involvement in youth symphonies and choirs, chamber music, private lessons, summer camps, festivals, competitions, and auditions. Students become even more focused as they study with applied instructors outside of schools, which further solidifies a performance identity. It is often at this secondary school stage that interested students decide that they will take up even more music in their college pursuits.

At the college/university level, the specialization in performing area and ensemble membership becomes even more pronounced as students are accepted for admission and into faculty studios as a piano major, a violinist, a guitarist, a jazz saxophone major. Close mentors as applied teachers, conductors, and other faculty encourage students to concentrate their efforts to attain sophisticated levels of technical facility and expression. Schools of music often telegraph this value toward specialization and depth more than they accommodate versatility and breadth. At the same time, music itself becomes more differentiated *within* programs, as students concurrently study music theory, music history, conducting, pedagogy, etc. For many, music study at the undergraduate or graduate level is so intense that it overshadows other engagements outside the academy.

Music teachers, then, enter into their first teaching positions well-schooled as disciplinary specialists. Music is often seen as a distinguished province within the school, with certain professional and community norms to uphold. Within the current challenges facing music education and arts education as a whole in these first decades of the twenty-first century, music teachers often find their teacherly responsibilities stretched even further by taking on the mantle of proponent, advocate, defender, and champion of their subject area. Pressures to increase test scores and improve academic achievement often displace general curricular commitments to music. This can trigger defensiveness and protective stances as music teachers strive to preserve valuable time for instruction in the overall program of the school. Music teachers, socialized as specialists while simultaneously upholding the musical life of the school, may feel pulled in too many directions. To alter one's conception of what it means to be a music teacher in an interdisciplinary direction may seem idealistic, even unwise. What is possible if music teachers seek to balance disciplinary depth and breadth?

Breadth as a Virtue

Breadth of knowledge is heralded as a virtue in most educational and social contexts. Individuals whose fields of knowledge are widespread and encompassing are acknowledged as Renaissance persons, with interests and abilities of such scope that they appeared extraordinarily positioned to draw connections across disparate fields and settings. A related term, *polymath*, has origins in the fifteenth century as well, referring to an accomplished and learned scholar with command of multiple areas of expertise. A term that is obsolete, but nonetheless interesting (if nearly impossible to claim), is an *omniscian*, defined in the *Oxford English Dictionary* as "a person who knows, *or professes to know*, everything" (italics added). Few individuals have such confidence or hubris as to claim the latter, but taken together, these terms represent idealized views of the educated person.

A closely related commitment to breadth falls under the umbrella of the liberal arts. The noted scholar of teaching Parker Palmer reminds readers that the term *liberal* derives from the Latin word *liber*, meaning "free." He explains the liberatory roots of a commitment to breadth:

> Knowledge of this sort is liberating not only because it steeps us in the wisdom of the past; it also accustoms us to ambiguity and paradox, preparing us to find our way into an unpredictable future. A liberal education helps us embrace diverse ideas without becoming paralyzed in thought or action. It teaches us how to claim our own voices in the midst of a clamorous crowd, staying engaged with the communal conversation of a democracy in ways that keep opening us to larger versions of truth. (2011, p. 84)

In my experience, the pull of specialization in our field is so strong that it is easy to forget the broad and comprehensive education music teachers have received alongside their musical upbringing. A generously conceived education allows individuals to develop knowledge, skills, understandings, and dispositions toward learning many disciplines, including the traditionally emphasized areas of English literacy and mathematics as well as science, history, geography, civics, languages, and the arts (music, visual art, theater, dance, and more rarely media arts, architecture, and design). These subject areas, when aligned with the aims Palmer describes, not only liberate the whole, they also become relevant to the aesthetic and artistic aims of arts education.

When music teachers are invited to re-engage these areas, they rediscover their relevance to their current classrooms. A few testify that their education has permitted these liberatory impulses to show in secondary schools when they elected courses that followed integrated models of curricular design, such as paired literature and history courses organized around a particular period, or broadly synoptic humanities courses that embrace a wide variety of social sciences, humanities, and the arts. Even if music teachers have not had access to such curricular fusions, they are drawn through their passions, curiosities, and social surroundings to branch out in their pursuit of subject areas beyond music as their primary discipline.

Lateral Knowledge

To represent the nexus of disciplinary depth and humanistic breadth, I investigated music teachers' *lateral knowledge* (Barrett, 2007), curious about the ways they stay close to the center or venture toward the edges of their knowledge landscapes. The teachers I interviewed were keen on using their eclectic backgrounds and interests, personal travel, coursework from undergraduate preparation, and participation in professional development opportunities to develop curricular ideas, although they cited various reasons for doing so. I assumed that each teacher would have characteristically personal profiles of favored subject matter areas, and in the small set of teachers I interviewed, this was the case.

Lateral knowledge stems from an amalgamation of a teacher's own experiences and the subject areas they find most easily related to music in meaningful ways, which often parallel the teacher's strengths. Lateral knowledge can be enhanced through formal educational experiences, informal experiences with the arts and other disciplines outside of school settings, and as a consequence of teaching within schools and learning more about the content, pedagogy, and initiatives of other disciplines. Side by side and across conference tables, teachers teach one another. Some schools foster this kind of exchange more openly than others, depending upon how collaboration is valued within the climate of the school.

The interdisciplinary knowledge base of music teachers is also strengthened through professional development initiatives that acknowledge teachers' broad interests, encourage them to refine their criteria for evaluating the quality of curricular initiatives, develop their craftsmanship, and engage them in collaborative efforts to work with other teachers on behalf of complementary curricular goals.

In the spirit of taking inventory of your lateral knowledge, the mingling of your specialized pathway as a music teacher with your general education, and the inclusion of your personal curiosities in your teaching, you are invited to participate in another etude. You may find that Figure 2.1 prompts your thinking about this exercise. I designed it to represent the "typical" areas of depth and breadth in undergraduate music teacher education without showing possible overlaps between. Imagine these intersections as you design your own image.

Etudes for Interdisciplinarians, Opus 2

Create a diagram of your lateral knowledge representing the depth of your musical preparation in tandem with the breadth of your knowledge across other subject areas and disciplines. For you, which areas "outside" of music are most closely related to music? How have you developed knowledge and expertise in other fields in ways that complement your musical understandings? Can you position these "other" areas to show which you gravitate toward in your

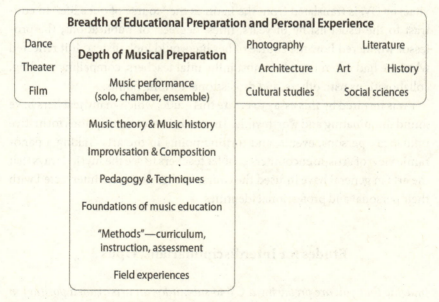

Figure 2.1 Music teachers' lateral knowledge

curricular work and which are seldom connected? You might also think about how students have revealed their interests and expertise and how those bright moments have moved a particular subject area closer to the center. Once you create your diagram, describe what you learned from the exercise with another teacher, or capture your insights in a journal entry.

To steer one's professional course both as a specialist and an interdisciplinarian may sound like an oxymoron, but when a teacher's far-ranging curiosity is developed and employed in making music education more holistic and comprehensive, these identities become symbiotic rather than separate. Recognizing the relevance of teachers' educational histories is the purpose of the next etude.

The Course of One's Life?

Years ago, I ran across a personal essay of a professor in one of those alumni magazines sent on behalf of one of my universities, the impact of which has stayed with me even though I can no longer locate the source. The professor began by musing on the frequent task of reviewing the résumés or CVs of other scholars and students, an activity usually prompted by hiring or recognizing someone's accomplishments. She explained that curriculum vitae, or CV, is translated from the Latin as the "course of one's life." In contrast to the usual listing of years, titles, degrees, or publications, the professor wondered how the course of her life would look instead if it reflected what she had taken from her most influential teachers, compelling reading, collaborations with others, and professional turning points.

I was inspired by this essay to create this etude, which many teachers have found illuminating and worthwhile. The etude invites descriptions formative influences, persons, events, and turning points in the arts. Taking a panoramic view of artistic encounters enables teachers to see the myriad ways that the arts in general have infused the course of their lives and intersected with their personal and professional identities.

Etudes for Interdisciplinarians, Opus 3

Imagine that you are preparing a CV to submit for an arts-related position in which you want to convey, in a condensed but clear form, ten key encounters, accomplishments, teachers, events, books/readings, works, or educational moments that have had the greatest impact on your life in the arts. Of the array of possibilities, which elements would make the list? Describe each in a brief annotation, concluding with a paragraph that highlights the significance of these ten elements in your personal and professional life.

When I have stepped back from my own educational path with music as a primary theme, I discovered that my complementary and enduring passions in art and poetry, with supporting reading in history, were fostered outside of school. I often regret that my electives in areas of the arts and humanities were all "double counted," effectively fulfilled by courses in music during my undergraduate program, so that I did not take advantage of more eclectic coursework. I do not regret, however, the transformative experiences I have sought out since that time, and eagerly look forward to more.

I have included etudes in this chapter to communicate vividly to readers that the landscape of one's experiences in music, related arts, and other disciplines has profound impact on inclinations toward and possibilities for an interdisciplinary perspective. Interdisciplinarity sits at the intersection of a music educator's specialized identity and their more eclectic, far-ranging interests and intellectual histories. Employed in the service of fostering students' abilities to make strong connections between music and other disciplines, realms of teachers' knowledge are continually in use and in flux. The work of an interdisciplinarian is enabled through lively curiosity, imagination, and open-mindedness.

Finally, in this chapter, to emphasize experience from the "inside out," I turn to Dewey once more. To "learn from experience," he says, "is to make a backward and forward connection between what we do to things and what we enjoy or suffer from things in consequence. Under such conditions, doing becomes a trying; an experiment with the world to find out what it is like; the undergoing becomes instruction—discovery of the connections of things" (1916, p. 140).

3
Multidimensionality as a Springboard for Connections
The Facets Model

Strolling through the exhibit hall at my state music educators' conference, I notice music teachers standing at bins packed with printed music, organized neatly with colorful labels that display the ensemble type, composer, and style period. The look on their faces is expectant, rapt, absorbed as they fan through the plastic tubs, pulling out scores for a closer look. At the close of one of the conference sessions, I watch general music teachers capturing the QR code on their phones for a presenter's handout listing hundreds of songs with creative instructional ideas. Later in the day, I pass by a line of teachers waiting for the doors of the grand hall to open for the honors concert. I overhear two choir directors rhapsodizing about the premiere of new choral works to be featured on the program. Their enthusiasm is palpable; their curiosity high. Clearly, the hunt is on for the latest piece to be published, acquired, studied, prepared, and brought into the lives of the students waiting somewhere in the realm of the near future.

Why Are Music Educators Worked Up over Works?

As the opening vignette suggests, music educators have long been fascinated by musical works—the repertoire that so often sits at the center of planning, performing, studying, and experiencing music. This fascination spreads far and wide, starting from the search for song literature at the heart of children's musical experience, recordings at the top of the playlist that pique students' interest inside and outside school, examples graded by difficulty level for the development of students' technical skills as they learn instruments, and the choral and instrumental works for large ensembles to be performed in concert cycles. Music teachers, as the opening vignette suggests, often serve

Seeking Connections. Janet Revell Barrett, Oxford University Press. © Oxford University Press 2023.
DOI: 10.1093/oso/9780197511275.003.0003

as curators of this repertoire. They weave tapestries of experience from the repertoires they select with care to bring into classroom life.

The musics at the center of music classrooms are not the sole province of teachers' decision-making, however. Consider, for example, the prevalence of soundtrack projects, in which students reveal their personal identities through their playlists. Think of the ways that students' improvisations, arrangements, and compositions enliven music rooms through creative activity. Listen to the productive buzz that rises up from classes in beatmaking, music production, and sound design as students mix and record original songs. To borrow a well-worn phrase from advertising, students exhibit their varied and expansive interests that make up the "fabric of [their] lives," woven from interactions of their own with many musical threads and often with one another.

Works—music sung, played, listened to, and created by those outside the classroom as well as in place and in the moment—figure prominently in the music curriculum. This prominence, however, is also the subject of a growing scholarly critique of music teachers' emphasis on repertoire. The critique raises questions about the curricular priorities of teachers in foregrounding certain musics over others. Scholars are busy probing the very origins and pathways of transmission for musical examples that have been obscured, thus also obscuring problematic histories and ideologies. Understanding the tensions in this debate is important to the main premise of this chapter, which will advocate for a focus on musical works in the curriculum while also provoking critical inquiry about those same works.

Why do some musics occupy more attention and hold more value in the curriculum than others? A central plank of the contemporary critique points to the ways that musical works are treated as aesthetic objects that privilege the persons, forms, and practices of Western European art music. In this view, the search for masterworks created by an elite pantheon of composers elevates their standing and status, placing them figuratively on curricular pedestals. Lively debates about enduring significance and musical quality often align with this prioritization of masterworks. Hess explains that this emphasis, which relegates other musical practices and styles to the margins, so dominates the curriculum that "Western music in music education acts as a colonizer" (2015, p. 336). By this, she means that what we commonly call classical music perpetuates a hierarchy that privileges some musics and tokenizes others. Alongside a Eurocentric body of works, scholars argue that analytical practices and means of learning music mirror this hegemonic pattern by relying on standard musical notation accompanied by a central focus on the musical elements used to analyze and understand common patterns and structures used in the music of the Baroque, Classical, Romantic, and Contemporary periods. An emphasis on "classical" repertoire—with its distinct forms of representation and organization—gives pride of place to works as objects, distancing their study and performance from the lived reality of the persons who create or experience the music. When this focus on works eclipses diverse cultural understandings and pushes other forms of musical expression to the side, the music curriculum narrows.

A related movement in this overall critique of the music curriculum attends to song literature and repertoires that are frequently taught, learned, performed, and studied but whose historical and contemporary meanings warrant critical scrutiny. Song collections assembled for elementary general music, for example, are an especially prominent forefront for these investigations. "Melody set to words constitutes much of the world's musical repertoire," writes ethnomusicologist Bonnie Wade (2009, p. 12), just as songs dominate elementary music. Teachers are urged to consider how these songs take hold in children's voices, minds, and bodies, and how their inclusion may be problematic.

A particular category of songs under scrutiny includes tunes whose origins in blackface minstrelsy have been lost or downplayed and whose lyrics have been scrubbed and sanitized for classroom use. Songs that have been taught to children for decades and included in song anthologies have been spotlighted through critical inquiry, exposing overtly racist roots. Song texts that have held pride of place in classrooms for decades, such as "Jimmy Crack Corn," "Jump Jim Joe," and countless others, are viewed as inacceptable when their insidious roots and intended denigration of persons are exposed. How can the seemingly hidden and pernicious associations of common songs be uncovered so that these problematic meanings can be confronted? The curricular impact of these efforts can be witnessed in conference presentations, podcasts, and articles aligned with this timely quest.

Others advocate downplaying the prominence of musical works with a renewed focus on musical practices instead, pointing out that an emphasis on practices more aptly corresponds to contemporary alignments with sociological matters. In music education at large, questions of musical identity, community, sociality, even social constructivism reflect this sociological turn. "Doing" music together with others, then, takes prominence over the "thing" itself—the musical work considered as an aesthetic object. Christopher Small captures this turn succinctly:

> The fundamental nature and meaning of music lie not in objects, not in musical works at all, but in action, in what people do. It is only by understanding what people do when they take part in a musical act that we can hope to understand its nature and the function it fulfills in human life. (1998, p. 8)

Scholars in music education and in music at large have raised these issues of curricular purpose and questions of emphasis with vigor, especially as individuals and institutions take up the aims of social justice seeking to uphold the dignity, diversity, and complex dimensions of those who engage in a wide variety of musical genres, traditions, and processes. Consider how ethnomusicologist Loren Kajikawa reflects the urgency of this work, here speaking directly to musicologists: "We can no longer tolerate a discipline that prioritizes aesthetic objects over the people who create, perform, and listen to them" (Kajikawa, 2019, p. 171).

How do music educators respond to this critique of musical works as the centerpieces of curriculum-making, which is, after all, so prevalent in elementary, secondary, and tertiary education? What responsibilities do music teachers bear in rebalancing curricular priorities and long-standing practices? Given the widespread inclusion of questionable examples in pedagogical materials, song collections, and repertoire lists, music educators need tools and resources for critical scrutiny of musical literature. These tools and resources may be particularly useful for those who support the relevance of classical music and especially the vibrancy of contemporary classical music alongside many other forms, traditions, and practices.

I take the stance that musical works can be used as touchstones, catalysts, cases, or prompts for experiencing music in ways that invite far-reaching explorations of cultures, histories, and realms of expression as well as deeply felt personal encounters with music from multiple vantage points and connections to lived experience. This stance moves away from a curricular focus on music as aesthetic objects by forwarding the human dimensions of musical repertoire *through* works. Keeping in mind the critique of Eurocentric exclusivity, though, I draw from examples that embrace these repertoires so commonly included in music classrooms while also advocating expansion beyond their scope to enlarge the possibilities for interdisciplinary relationships. Music teachers may find this works-as-catalysts approach valuable for prompting critical inquiry about the music at the heart of educative experience.

The Possibilities of Multidimensionality

One of the purposes of music education, and arts education as a whole, is to help students shift from *exposure* to *encounter* with this kaleidoscopic array of creative works in the world. Reflect for a moment on the musics that stream into our lives at any given moment, at any time of the day or night. A recent news release announced the mind-boggling figure that over 60,000 tracks are added each day to a popular streaming service, or over 22 million new tracks a year.[1] At a touch, we can search for familiar songs, create playlists, and share them with others. With a simple query, we have access to what seems like an ocean of unfamiliar possibilities. Much like the practice of channel surfing, we swim through this vast library, sampling snippets of sound, moving on, following the currents and sometimes treading in place for a while to take in a full track.

The educational surrounds of classrooms call us to pause and linger with specific works, in contrast to surface-level scanning and surfing. Students, celebrating the social bonds that music affords, share the musics that attract their attention and hold their fascination. Teachers select examples on the basis of their educative value, supporting their aims for learning. Often, a path of study settles in, at least for several days or weeks, resulting in a sustained focus on a manageable number of works to study, perform, inspire. This sustained focus on fewer works yields a number of musical and social advantages by providing a common frame of reference for students and teachers alike; fostering community around a work as the "social glue" of shared experience; creating an interpretive space for discovery, for meanings to unfold, for connections to be revealed; and triggering inquiry as students seek to know more, generate fresh questions, and push toward deeper realms of experience.

To sustain an encounter suggests engaging with musical works in a variety of ways over a range of instances, making it more likely that exposure turns into dynamic engagement. The notion of multidimensionality is crucial here—the intentional pursuit of different emphases or components of a work to deepen understanding and expression. By this point, the rationale for this aim should be clear, but just for good measure, I turn once again to Dewey: "Any experience, however trivial in its first appearance, is capable of assuming an indefinite richness of significance by extending its range of perceived connections" (Dewey, 1916/1944, p. 217).

In this chapter, a useful heuristic, the Facets Model, supports this multidimensional pursuit. Its value is both personal and pedagogical, as it invites students and teachers to inventory what is known and felt while also serving as a springboard for jumping into related avenues for inquiry in classroom settings. Think of this springboard as a vault into unexplored territory, a "deep dive" into realms of meaning, a triple twist in the air toward new directions. In this model, eight questions serve as strong yet flexible platforms for these moves.

The Facets Model often leads to the discovery of *intradisciplinary* relationships, or the connections that any particular musical work has to other musical works and genres (and of course, it can be used to explore intradisciplinary relationships in other realms of artistic expression as well). You may wonder what a multidimensional approach to a particular musical work has to do with *interdisciplinarity*, the relationship of music to other subject areas and ways of knowing. Although this might seem like an obvious conundrum, later chapters will illustrate how the model leads to closely related explorations with poetry, art, history, and other constructive realms for connection.

Introducing the Facets Model

Just as I will suggest later that origins can lead to insight, I briefly describe how the model came to be. In the mid-1990s, Claire McCoy and Kari Veblen and I began to develop ideas for *Sound Ways of Knowing: Music in the Interdisciplinary Curriculum* (1997). One evening after an initial planning meeting in which we circled around one another's ideas and failed to land on any shared meanings, we sat at my dining room table after dinner. We were bemoaning what passed at that time for integrated curriculum in collections of lesson plans for teachers, which were often organized on themes that bore only tangential associations to music through lyrics about recycling, the metric system, and other hot topics of the day. As we vented our frustrations, we fiddled with multisided dice that my then-young son Alex had strewn about the house (those of you who have played Dungeons and Dragons can call up these dodecahedrons in your mind's eye). Claire picked up a large blue one and put it on her hand, casually commenting that she wished the plastic toy would turn into a gorgeous sapphire with reflective planes and surfaces. Her playful wish triggered a provocative question: how do we come to know musical works with multiple planes and surfaces as well?

This question gave our conversation momentum. The three of us decided to test out possible answers based on a well-known piece, Copland's "Variations on Simple Gifts" from the ballet suite *Appalachian Spring*, grabbing legal pads to list everything we could possibly think of related to the music as we listened to a recording. We worked silently and separately before comparing notes to discover that some of the aspects of the work were common across all three lists; others were noted by just one or two. We listed the instruments we heard, noted how the theme is transformed in each of the variations, spoke about the distinct and evocative qualities of each one, and finally revealed our favorite moments and memories associated with the work. We knew we were on to something when this exercise generated more questions that we were able to answer in the most cursory way without consulting other sources, such as: What is the significance of the Shaker tune that inspired the variations? Did the beliefs and practices of the Shakers have anything to do with the song? Why did Copland decide to use the tune in the first place? What was the role of Martha Graham as the inspiration for the ballet? Why the curious title, *Appalachian Spring*, which doesn't have anything at all to do with the Shakers? What do the Shakers think about the popularity of Copland's orchestral work based on this melody? What explains the common observation that this music, like Copland's work overall, "sounds so American?" In that moment, Claire—with her characteristically poetic flair—looked down at the blue dodecahedron on the table and set us on a metaphorical path by observing, "A work of art is like a gem with many facets."

My coauthors and I engaged in the same process of "dimensionalizing" other works. Certain questions guided our inquiries with different examples. We decided to represent some of these questions in a visual model based on the gemstone metaphor, which became an organizing tool for the book (Barrett, McCoy, & Veblen, 1997) (Figure 3.1).

Over time, the Facets Model has been used as a strategy for curriculum planning in courses for undergraduate and graduate students, for elementary education majors and music education majors, and in workshops and presentations for teachers new to curriculum-making as well as seasoned

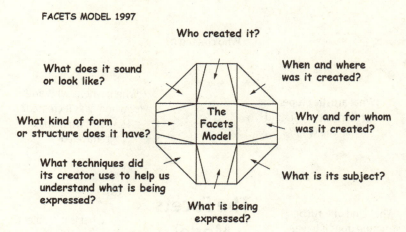

Figure 3.1 The Facets Model (1997)
From Barrett, McCoy, & Veblen (1997). Used by permission.

veterans. It has been cited in various books and used to guide collaborative projects, develop curricular materials, and in one instance, adopted by museum staff in North Dakota to create trunks of art materials that were sent to teachers in remote rural areas of the Great Plains. Several graduate students have used the model to write program notes and organize lecture recitals. Although its premises are fairly straightforward, its applications have been widespread in national and international settings.

In curriculum planning, teachers have found it useful to "walk around the facets" as they consider pathways, possibilities, and approaches. The questions posed by the model often give rise to articulating what is already known and what is yet to be discovered as multiple dimensions are explored. Pedagogical ideas often fire up as well. Familiar and unfamiliar works reveal their curricular possibilities as teachers study the time and place in which the work was created, the characteristic elements of the work and how these relate to one another, and the range of expressive meanings that the work conveys and evokes. The Facets Model is helpful in this sense as a heuristic, a "practical hub" (Eisner, 2002) for discussion and design, a rule of thumb that leads to flexible and fluent paths, rather than a game of Trivial Pursuit to gather up a set of facts.

In this chapter, an updated version of the Facets Model is introduced (Figure 3.2). The model is useful for exploring works of music, but also works in visual art, poetry, drama, dance, novels, and other forms. You can start

44 SEEKING CONNECTIONS

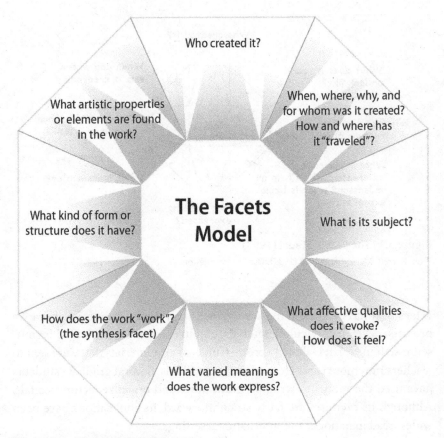

Figure 3.2 The Facets Model (2023)

from any point on the model, except perhaps the "synthesis facet," which illuminates and integrates multiple dimensions of a work after it has been explored from many sides.

An overview of this revised model follows. After introducing each of the comprehensive questions of the general model and their rationale for deepening experience, I show its application to a particular example, "Lift Every Voice and Sing," known as the Black national anthem. As with every specific work mentioned in this book, you are encouraged to find a recording of the song. Listen to it first to prompt what you already know; return to it repeatedly to enhance your thinking as you read on.

PAUSE to listen to any one of many available arrangements of "Lift Every Voice and Sing."

Context

Who created it and *when, where, why and for whom was it created?* Attention to context involves teaching music with the roots on. The origins of a work provide insight about the persons, their inspirations, and the social surrounds that influenced its creation. This origin story serves as a starting place for inquiry, but in contrast to static "composer reports" with tidy overviews of titles and dates, a fuller narrative traces the course of its reception through time and place as well. Consider the vast storehouse of musics you have studied and performed. As I contemplate my own decades of involvement in music, so many familiar pieces seem "free-floating" to me—oddly disconnected from their contextual roots that might influence how the music sounds, looks, or moves within me as a listener, performer, or teacher. It is almost as if much of my musical knowledge is ahistorical and placeless.

Occasionally, I have been drawn in by timelines in music history books to discover relationships with parallel events, intellectual movements, and political upheavals. These fascinating associations pique my curiosity in noting the alignment of artistic worlds with other events and achievements. However, if this pursuit of knowledge becomes uncoupled from the art works themselves, experiential insights can be lost. Think, for example, of upper elementary and middle school students dutifully consulting reference materials in print or online to produce composer reports filled with dates and names of works, sprinkled with a few colorful tidbits about their lives. What impact do these assignments have if separated from the experience of the music itself?

Context matters, and it matters more than its frequent relegation to "background knowledge," which implies that this knowledge is somehow incidental to experience. Increasingly, music educators recognize this importance, especially in light of our society's racial reckoning and pursuit of diversity, equity, and inclusion in our classrooms. Context and culture intermingle in the very DNA of music. The songs we sing, repertoire we perform, and even the musical expressions of composition and improvisation being created in classrooms at this very moment bear the influence of their surroundings and the persons expressing themselves. Think of this rich grounding as a "time and date" stamp. Without attention to context, music educators risk treating and teaching music as sonic artifacts shaken loose from their moorings.

Contextually savvy music educators seek to restore these contexts to musical examples that are frequently encountered in classrooms but whose connections to these points of origin have been lost. For example, think again to current efforts to uncover the historical roots of songs that have been included in elementary series textbooks and songs collections for decades—often sanitized by altering lyrics or by deleting versions—and whose underpinnings are implicated in blackface minstrelsy as a popular form of entertainment in the nineteenth century. Whether these roots subsequently serve as occasions for study depends on the circumstances of the classrooms, the teacher's aims, the students' interests, and the curricular matters at hand.

Tracing Contexts

How and where has it traveled? Music travels from voice to voice, hand to hand, heart to heart, movement to movement. Much can be learned by tracing how individuals and groups adopt music as their own, elevating a work by giving it symbolic meaning, or perhaps revising that meaning as cultural mores shift. In *Sound Ways of Knowing*, my coauthors and I also created an expanded facets model with a focus on culture and history. The idea stemmed from the premise that knowing about the origins of a work is beneficial, but so is following its movement as it is taken up and made familiar, adopted by strong associations, altered, or cast aside in its relation to individuals and groups. We advocated that the search involves several possible nodes of interest: "(a) the song at its point of origin, (b) the song's path of transmission and the multiple meanings it acquires on its journey, (c) the inclusion of the song in the repertoires of individuals and groups, and (d) the song's relationship to contemporary experience" (1997, p. 144). The importance of tracing paths has only gained traction in classrooms since that time.

Context, then, can become a criterion for curricular inclusion or exclusion if music teachers are knowledgeable about these processes of transmission and willing to embark on these trails. We can learn from musicologists and ethnomusicologists whose fields of study embrace the challenges and satisfactions of being on the hunt. When students take up these pathways, their searching becomes purposeful, driven by questions they are eager to pursue. When we go on a contextual exploration to find out more, understanding deepens in relation to so many other discoveries along the way.

These questions for tracing contexts were posed in the expanded facets model (p. 145):

- How and to whom has it been transmitted?
- Who performs, dances to, listens to, and values it?
- What is its function for individuals and groups?
- What does it mean to individuals and groups?
- How do differences in performance or interpretation change its meanings?
- How does it change through different interpretations or versions?

Supplement these questions with ones that lend an even more critical stance to this search:

- What meanings have been lost, erased, or obscured as it has traveled?
- What meanings may have strengthened?
- Who has altered these meanings and why?
- How does historical context influence our contemporary stance toward the work?
- How do contemporary issues and events cast new light on interpreting works from past eras?
- In what ways does your own lived experience play a role in the ways you respond to the work?

Through tracing, the meanings we associate with a work expand outward like the concentric rings of trees. What might seem initially straightforward in a work's origin story undergoes mutations and permutations of meaning as persons follow music's trajectory through social life. As any of these general questions become vivid when applied to specific examples, I turn to a familiar song as an illustration of contextual study.

"Lift Every Voice and Sing": Contexts

Performances of "Lift Every Voice and Sing" can be heard in many contexts—schools, churches, civic events, sporting events, and commemorations. Two brothers collaborated to create this song—James Weldon Johnson, who wrote the poem to celebrate the birthday of Abraham Lincoln, and J. Rosamond

Johnson, who set the poem to music, and planned to have it sung by 500 children at a school assembly on February 12, 1900, Lincoln's birthday. At that time, James Weldon was serving as the principal of the Stanton School in Jacksonville, Florida; Rosamond was the music teacher at a neighboring school. They dedicated the performance to Booker T. Washington, founder of the Tuskegee Institute. Scholar Imani Perry marks the significance of this moment:

> The song proved to be, both and soon thereafter, much bigger than an ode to any one leader or icon. It was a lament and encomium to the story and struggle of black people. The Johnsons at once wrote black history and wrote black people into the traditions of formal Western music with their noble song. (2018, p. 7)

The brothers had grown up in Jacksonville, returning there after pursuing college degrees, the only educational path available after their eighth-grade graduation, the highest level of education afforded to them in Jacksonville's segregated school system. A known orator, James Weldon had recently passed his bar exam to practice law. His literary talents were prodigious, his poetic voice powerful. Rosamond, who had studied music at the New England Conservatory before returning to Jacksonville, created a musical setting that reflects the formal musical traditions he had studied at the conservatory. The song was quickly taken up by children and adults in many settings. Later musing on the rapid spread of "Lift Every Voice and Sing" throughout the Black community, James Weldon acknowledged, "we wrote better than we knew" (1933, p. 166).

The song's trajectory throughout the twentieth and twenty-first centuries speaks to the meanings it has held for individuals and groups, and its significance in Black communal life. Here is a brief sample of its prevalence through a century and more:

- Performances of "Lift Every Voice and Sing" grew through the early part of the twentieth century as it was reproduced in newsletters and pasted into the covers of hymnals. It quickly became part of the social fabric of Black life when sung at the opening or closing of school events, meetings of civic associations, and church services.
- In 1920, it was named as the official song of the National Association for the Advancement of Colored People (NAACP), the same year that

James Weldon Johnson was also named the executive secretary of the association.
- As various political movements sprang up during the Harlem Renaissance, the song was heralded in artistic circles of African American modernism.
- The poem was woven into speeches given by Martin Luther King Jr. shortly before his assassination in 1968.
- In response to Colin Kaepernick's decision to take a knee during the playing of the "Star-Spangled Banner" at football games, and in recognition of the Black Lives Matter movement, the National Football League decided to open games during the 2021–2022 season with the "Star-Spangled Banner" followed by "Lift Every Voice and Sing."
- In the aftermath of George Floyd's killing in 2020, oboist Titus Underwood and twelve orchestral musicians from across the United States produced a video for "every protester, every freedom fighter, everyone who needs to be lifted up, and to honor George Floyd, Breonna Taylor, Ahmaud Arbery and the numerous others whose lives have been stolen by police violence."[2]
- Representative James Clyburn of South Carolina introduced a bill early in 2021 to make the song the US national hymn.

These bullet points mark but a few inflection points when "Lift Every Voice and Sing" was adopted, taken up, and made significant in the lives of individuals and groups. Its significance echoes well over a century through the moments in its reception history sampled here.

Properties

What artistic properties or elements are found in the work? We encounter music at every turn, and perhaps without registering, respond to the very properties of sound that constitute that music. For example, recall watching young children move rhythmically with joy and abandon whenever songs enter their environment. Their spontaneous reactions remind us of the visceral ways that bodies and minds spring into action when music is "in the house," sharing commonalities with the vast storehouses of musics we carry with us. We perceive the distinctive combinations of properties that allow us to welcome that special song, that recognizable piano piece, that particular octavo for choir. The properties of a particular work are the building blocks of recognition and memory. As a result of education, both formal and informal, we label and categorize these properties as ways of heightening perception and attending to the relational power of parts to wholes—the way a particular quality corresponds to another.

Music education has long prioritized a curricular emphasis on musical elements, with their familiar categories of melody, rhythm, harmony, texture, timbre, form, etc. As students develop more-nuanced ways of perceiving and naming these elements, their capacity for creating, responding, and performing music expands. Like any system, however, the ways that music education (and music theory at large) has developed and instilled these systems signifies more than just sonic characteristics. The system used widely in many classrooms reflects certain ways of perceiving and responding to music that most closely align with Western European frameworks.

When I introduce new pieces to college students by playing recordings, for example, I often ask a broad and rather nebulous question as a pedagogical experiment for teasing out these patterns—*What do you notice?* Many times, students' responses fall right into line with this system as an analytical framework as they begin by cataloguing the meter, mode, tempo, and other salient aspects of the music. Eventually, other responses emerge having to do with personal associations, the expressive feel of the music, and occasionally, insights related to the origins of the piece if it is fairly familiar, or comparisons with other pieces if it isn't. This phenomenon of inventorying the elements as the first move is not surprising since many music teachers have been carefully taught to approach new works with an analytical framework in mind, most often through music theory classes steeped in the academic traditions of European art music. However, we can readily see the validity of approaching these properties in other ways.

Awareness of these properties heightens perception, and I can draw a parallel from my late-in-life study of art. When a knowledgeable art historian or critic speaks about a painting or sculpture by drawing attention to the visual properties of the work, their talk often gives me new ways of seeing. What I might have previously glossed over becomes a way to look at painting and sculpture with greater intent. My general curiosity about artists' marks, for example, becomes more specific, as do my questions—are those lines descriptive of a representational object? Are they expressional? Do they lead my eyes in certain directions? When I play with lines in my own recreational painting, I draw on these properties to try out new ideas. I realize in addition how learning about these properties becomes infused in my perception of the works of others as well as my own creative art-making. Testing out these ideas in an art form that stretches my horizons leads me to reflect on this curricular emphasis on musical properties and its usefulness.

When this foregrounding of the elements become so prominent in curricula and classrooms that it overshadows other valuable ways of knowing, however, we take pause to consider alternatives. Rose and Countryman (2013) critique the field's attention to musical elements as a "dominant culture framework, an unquestioned Eurocentric way of thinking about music, emerging from a position of privilege and power" (p. 48). They point out that its widespread use positions musics that do not "fit" as outside the canon, a hegemonic process of "othering." Rose and Countryman call for music teachers to question how the elements serve as prominent frameworks for the curriculum, especially if they eclipse, overshadow, or discount students' ways of knowing. They suggest that teachers first engage students in describing music's properties and relationships of sound in ways that make sense to them, thus opening up space for constructive insight.

It stands to reason that if our classrooms embrace more styles and genres of musics across multiple traditions, and if more music teachers rebalance their approaches to foster more student input, while resisting tendencies to lead with the musical elements, new vistas for musical understanding may open up. So how might we respond to the question, *What artistic properties or elements are found in the work?* Consider leaning into the ways that students respond, react, and name their ways of interacting with music, using common elements as general and flexible guides when that framework makes sense. Insights may also be gained from drawing on systems of organizing music by its social functions and practices (Wade, 2009), its qualities related to particular styles and genres, such as hip-hop (Rose, 1994), or its musical vocabularies derived from oral traditions (Hill, 2018).

Forms

What kind of form or structure does it have? Early on in my teaching career, I spent considerable time drilling melodic and rhythmic patterns with children to build their notational skills, which I remember as effective for that purpose. Later, during graduate study, I rethought this commitment, though, wondering why I had devoted so much time to music-related, but not truly very musical pursuits. After some soul-searching, I realized that my priorities were somewhat misguided in this first decade of my teaching. What was missing was vital—more attention to the experience of music as part of a whole entity or gestalt—with beginnings, middles, and ends; openings and closures. Looking back, I felt as if I had devoted too much time to stretching exercises before dancing without the pleasures of the dance itself.

The forms of music—the larger patterns of organization that brings coherence to our listening, performing, and creating—are crucial, just as the forms of other arts are important. In music, we take a journey *over time* with a work of interest. The temporal aspects of that journey are satisfying, especially as we sense the ebb and flow of the music in more expansive swaths of sound. The temporal aspects of music (along with poetry read aloud, dance, theater) are part of its delights. The forms of painting, sculpture, and architecture work differently in that their spatial qualities suggest this coherence.

A related idea has to do with specific *forms*, or particular maps for structuring the journey. In music education, we learn to recognize these forms—from the simplest musical idea followed by a contrasting one—what we label as "A B," to complex forms that have their historical precedents in eras and specific genres, such as sonata-allegro form, twelve-bar blues, symphonic marches. Musicologist Tom Turino makes a distinction between the forms that are fixed by the conventions of Eurocentric traditions—with expectations of repetition and contrast, balance, and large-scale structures—which he calls *closed* forms, and the more fluid forms of participatory musics that are "open ended . . . repeated for as long as the participants and situation requires" and often with "'feathered' beginnings and endings" (2008, pp. 37–38).

The composer Libby Larsen also takes the view that forms are fluid, ready to shift as cultures change. She observes: "I believe that a culture will evolve the sonic forms and instruments that it needs in order to represent life through sound and music."[3] I recall, for example, hearing Larsen describe how she became fascinated by the structure of television programs in typical thirty-minute situation comedy segments, punctuated every few minutes by advertising. She wondered how this familiar form from broadcasting might be transposed into a musical work. Hearing her speak about other forms that might be explored and invented helped me think beyond the large structures typically taught in music classrooms. Part of the joy of discovery when encountering works of art involves our openness to fixed and fluid forms, moving into the ebb and flow of repeated ideas that provide stability as well as unexpected turns that trigger delight and surprise.

"Lift Every Voice and Sing": Properties and Forms

Composer J. Rosamond Johnson drew on his formal training in music at the New England Conservatory while setting his brother's poem to music, and thus "Lift Every Voice and Sing" exemplifies these formal traditions. Perry relates these attributes to Black formalism, of which the Johnson brothers were a part, the "ritual practices with embedded norms, codes of conduct, and routine, dignified ways of doing and being" that served as "an articulation and expression of grace and identity that existed in refuge from the violence of white supremacy" (2018, pp. 7–8).

Johnson's use of the building blocks from his study at a music conservatory can be found in his setting of his brother's poem. The very rhythm of the first three notes followed by longer durations over the rolling compound duple meter feel sets singers on a path strengthened by the repetition of the figure through the opening phrases. When we reach "sing a song full of the faith that the dark past has taught us," the durations reverse—long before short. The melding of text and tune is felt in text painting as we reach for perfect fourths on "let our rejoicing rise" and "facing the rising sun." Johnson's use of the contrasting phrases—starting with "sing a song"—bring tonal ambiguity once the sixth is flatted, making the very act of performing the melody more complex and expressive. The fermata suspends the forward motion of the march and the singer together, before the last phrase "marches on."

Subject Matter

What is its subject? Although answering this question may seem straightforward, thinking about the subject matter of a music work, or any art work for that matter, is surprisingly complex. The way we think about this dimension has particular implications for interdisciplinary work, since subject matter often serves as a starting place for curriculum. Pause for a moment to recall instances when you may have been asked to contribute music for a particular event focused on a theme, or to coordinate curricular units with other teachers centered on a certain topic. You may have welcomed these requests when they complemented your educational goals or been frustrated when the requests felt at odds with your values and aims.

The very title of a work can seem descriptively fixed or ambiguously fluid. For example, consider what I often think of the "songs about" problem, starting from concrete nouns (songs about dinosaurs, songs about the ecosystem) to more abstract concepts (songs of commemoration, songs of protest, songs of freedom, etc.). At one end of the spectrum, the concrete nature of the noun pinpoints and names a topical category; at the other end, the abstract nature that is more thematic gives considerably more room to roam and interpret what commemoration or protest or freedom might mean in certain contexts, both past and present.

A title often instills confidence in saying that the subject matter is about particular ideas, objects, events, and feelings. That confidence, however, gives rise to several puzzles. Can a title be trusted? What if the title of a piece is just a convenient placeholder for its creator? Must a title evoke particular responses when students listen to or perform a work? Must every work have a title to carry meaning? Think of the many sonatas or symphonies or other forms that have simply been numbered or thousands of paintings marked "Untitled." Must a work point to an idea "outside" the work, often called "extramusical," as if it exists in a separate plane of existence from the sound itself? I recall a moment in Leonard Bernstein's Young Persons' Concerts when he remarked that Mussorgsky's "Great Gate of Kiev" could evoke images of the mighty Mississippi river, if Mussorgsky had chosen that title instead. I have watched with delight as clever music teachers have shown their students an array of titles in multiple choice fashion when introducing a new work to provoke students' curiosity and debate about the evocative power of a title.

The notion of a composer's intent poses even more fascinating puzzles for inquiry. Although sometimes this phrase points to the fidelity of a performer's realization of a musical score ("did we faithfully follow the composer's intent by bringing the notes on the page alive?"), consider, too, how intent works when a composer/songwriter explicitly sets out to depict an image, scene, or event in musical terms. In what ways does (and even can) the subject matter of the musical work depict, represent, or convey these ideas? In what ways and according to what compositional decisions made by the composers, songwriters, and improvisers who imagined these notions embedded in the music? Music teachers may engage students in questioning and wondering about these depictions as they gauge their fit and shape.

Program notes written by the composer or available interviews with composers often provide even more clues for this puzzle work, a seemingly limitless universe of possibility. These notes often have multiple purposes, guiding interpretation for the performer or providing helpful road maps for listeners. I often consult these notes hoping to learn more about the composer's inspirations for the piece, whether speaking to their intent in shaping particular musical dimensions, or pointing to ideas beyond those dimensions. Katz and Gardner (2012) interviewed "new music" composers to suggest that some rely on the "within-domain" strategies, involving the creative possibilities afforded by manipulating musical materials themselves; others rely on "beyond-domain" processes, "influenced mostly by conceptual frameworks such as metaphors and associations from outside of the discipline of music" (p. 107). And of course, many composers fuse and meld and intertwine these distinctions.

When "outside" inspirations reach even further, though, to depict, describe, or represent something other than musical material itself, we think of *program music*. Often, this term is applied to instrumental music so that the full weight of the description or depiction rests on sound rather than texts-in-sound. Music teachers draw on this notion when they introduce "music that tells a story." Exploring the capacities of music to represent ideas from other realms of experience is a fruitful exercise for considering how music might perform this representational feat, and how other arts convey subject ideas as well in their distinctive ways and through various media. As you think of music you have performed, studied, or created, can you name the germ of an idea that fueled its creation? How does this knowledge influence understanding or interpretation of the piece? When have you come close to depiction, and if so, how?

Song literature, of course, in its melding of text and tune, deserves especially rapt attention. Songwriters and composers fuse layers of meaning as they evoke feeling and convey realms of human experience. Whether setting an already composed poem to music, or creating both elements at the same time, the ways that text and tune weave together draws us in. The question of "aboutness" seems more straightforward here, but still not fixed as if we could possibly home in on "the right answer." Texts are remarkably open to interpretation and multiple points of view, offering rich potential for discussion. Probing multiple meanings of a text, and the ways that the musical setting enhances those meanings, is recognized by choral music educators in particular as a fruitful interdisciplinary zone. The pedagogical artistry involved in helping singers interpret songs and large works calls choral music educators to be strong poets as well as strong musicians.

"Lift Every Voice and Sing": Subject Matter

Songs—whether sung by individuals, small groups, or large choirs—most often carry subject matter through texts conjoined with the realization of those texts in musical settings. For "Lift Every Voice," we attend to the original poem composed by James Weldon Johnson, its vocabulary, its phrasing, its evocative capacity. Each verse seems to take on a distinctive tone and expressive character, inviting singers to bring out nuances of meaning and expression. Perry writes: "the three stanzas have often been described as praise, lament, and a prayer" (p. 19). Take a moment to study the lyrics before you read on:

Lift Every Voice and Sing

Lift every voice and sing,
Till earth and heaven ring,
Ring with the harmonies of Liberty;
Let our rejoicing rise
High as the list'ning skies,
Let it resound loud as the rolling sea.
Sing a song full of the faith that the dark past has taught us;
Sing a song full of the hope that the present has brought us;
Facing the rising sun of our new day begun,
Let us march on till victory is won.

Stony the road we trod,
Bitter the chast'ning rod,
Felt in the days when hope unborn had died;
Yet with a steady beat,
Have not our weary feet
Come to the place for which our fathers sighed?
We have come over a way that with tears has been watered.
We have come, treading our path through the blood of the slaughtered,
Out from the gloomy past,

Till now we stand at last
Where the white gleam of our bright star is cast.

God of our weary years,
God of our silent tears,
Thou who hast brought us thus far on the way;
Thou who hast by Thy might,
Led us into the light,
Keep us forever in the path, we pray.
Lest our feet stray from the places, our God, where we met Thee,
Lest our hearts, drunk with the wine of the world, we forget Thee;
Shadowed beneath Thy hand,
May we forever stand,
True to our God,
True to our native land.

James Weldon Johnson
Set to music by John Rosamond Johnson

Lift every voice and sing, Till earth and heaven ring. The opening verse invites the singer to join with others in a celebration of hope and faith. Poet Molly Peacock suggests that imagery is one of the three primary systems of a poem, representing the "visual art of the poem" (1999, p. 21).[4] Tracing the strong nouns in this first verse confirms the luminosity and expansiveness of Johnson's emphasis: "voice, earth, heaven, harmonies, liberty, skies, sea, faith, hope, present, sun, day, victory." These strong nouns sit in full view of Johnson's acknowledgment of the "dark past."

Stony the road we trod, bitter the chastening rod. The phrases in the second verse tell a story of struggle, again palpable through gathering up the key phrases and images: "hope unborn . . . weary feet . . . place which our fathers sighed . . . way that with tears has been watered . . . blood of the slaughtered . . . gloomy past." Although James Weldon Johnson does not refer to the lamentable history of slavery by name, he viscerally portrays its despicable hold on those who suffered through enslavement. Again, as a pivot, the text lifts toward the "white gleam of our bright star" in the last phrase.

God of our weary years, God of our silent tears. . . . This verse is often approached as a prayer of supplication, performed with hushed reverence and gravity. Its lyrics reflect what Perry call "a ritual bridge between the political and spiritual dimensions of Black social life that were so often deeply connected" (2018, p. 47). A point of resilient arrival is mirrored in the voices of singers as they land on the promise, "may we forever stand," as a declaration of strength and hope for the imagined future.

Affective Dimensions

What affective qualities does it evoke? How does it feel? How often have you posed or heard others pose the question, "How does this music make you feel?" In many years of teaching and observing others teach, I have noticed that responses to this question rarely surprise me. Often, the question falls flat or elicits brief replies of a "happy, sad, mad, glad" nature. For years, I tried following this question with: "And what in the music makes you feel that way?" which sometimes opened up more interesting windows on students' responses. Trying to understand the complexities of talking about the affective qualities of music—the way it moves in and through us—I realized that looking at students' faces and bodies involved in music often conveyed so much more than they could describe verbally. Yet in spite of the complexities involved in what are often thought of as subjective and idiosyncratic matters, this aspect of music's expressive power compels us to address this remarkable capacity for engendering feeling.

Cognitive psychologists have studied how various musical cues are associated with various emotions—the ways that certain sounds and combination of elements correlate with happiness, sadness, anger, fear, and tenderness, for example (Juslin, 2009). An early example is the work of Kate Hevner, who conducted psychological experiments in the 1930s and 1940s. She arranged sets of adjectives in a circle to prompt participants' responses to various musical examples, such as Debussy's "Reflections on the Water" or Mendelssohn's "Scherzo" from *Midsummer Night's Dream* (1936, updated by Schubert, 2003). Curious about this use of verbal labels, I wondered if this strategy might be useful to teachers, so I developed my own version of Hevner's adjective circle to test out (Figure 3.3).

Playing with this notion of words to convey the evocative feel of music opened up another set of conundrums. Are there advantages in using adjectives to describe these qualities? Drawbacks? Students in my classes and workshops quickly come to realize its limitations as a piece of music rarely

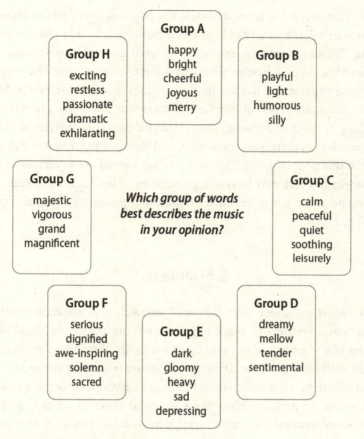

Figure 3.3 Hevner's adjective circle
Adapted from Schubert (2003)

stays put. Capturing the dynamic journey a person undergoes while listening, for instance, requires moving around and between the various locations. The path often ventures completely outside the diagram when the adjectives, and any verbal descriptions of emotion, for that matter, prove inadequate in capturing forms of feeling. Concentrating on this realm, we come to discover firsthand that "emotion and feeling are not identical. Feeling takes emotion further" (Reimer, 2003, p. 72).

These playful exercises also took our explorations into the realm of the ineffable—that which cannot be expressed in words, as well as the marvelously subjective realms of individual responses that vary from person to person, and from one encounter to the next. To use an analogy from painting,

I know that only a few tubes of watercolor pigment—red, yellow, blue—can produce an infinite variety of hues when combined. So it is with the hues of feeling. The philosopher Suzanne Langer comes to mind as someone who captured the visceral, fleeting nature of subjective experience. She explained that these experiences usually have no names to reach for except for the broad categorical labels of emotion or metaphor to convey the relation of one thing or another. At some point, words fail us, as the experience of an art work resides in subtle nuances, shades, and blends. Langer writes metaphorically of this phenomenon: "The ways we are moved are as various as lights in a forest; and they may intersect, sometimes without canceling each other, take shape and dissolve, conflict, explode into passion, or be transfigured" (1957, p. 22).

Meanings

What varied meanings does the work express? This question challenges students and teachers to think beyond the more putatively literal subject matters of a work to the ways that persons assign their own significance to certain works in their lives. These meanings are frequently enrobed in individual experience, the associations that fuse a certain song or piece to a time, place, event, or person. Often, these personal associations call up details, feelings, and visceral resonance in our minds and bodies whenever we hear these examples.

Meanings ascribed to music by groups can also be traced. For example, consider how some songs have been adopted by political groups, religious traditions, or various movements as anthems—songs whose identities become affiliated with social movements or trends, for example. These affiliative meanings may also shift over time, providing opportunities to search for and recognize those shifts.

Musicologists have undertaken reception histories of works, asking how these social meanings adhere, affix, and transform in different spheres. Samson writes about the "afterlife" of a musical example, its path of transmission after its initial creation: "In its afterlife a work threads its way through many different social and cultural formations, attaching itself to them in different ways, adapting its own appearance and in the process changing theirs. The work remains at least notionally the same object— at any rate it is the product of a singular creative act—but its manner of occupying the social landscape changes constantly" (2001, p. 1). Pay attention to the dynamic nature of this passage, recognizing that the work not only is changed through these pathways, but also changes the landscape of social life in turn. The permeability of music is at play here. Influence flows in multiple directions.

"Lift Every Voice and Sing": Affect and Meanings

How does one access something as private, personal, and subjective, but also shared, communal, and historical as the feelings evoked while singing, playing, or listening to "Lift Every Voice and Sing"? Given its prominence in communities for over a century, what might be said that does not reduce its expressive power to superficiality or trite slogans?

To celebrate the centennial of the song's genesis, civil rights leader Julian Bond and collaborator Sondra Kathryn Wilson invited 100 prominent individuals to write short essays to honor their recollections of learning, hearing, or performing it with others (Bond & Wilson, 2000). The resulting anthology contains testimonies of the expressive qualities that took hold in the writers' minds and hearts, their individual narratives, and the panorama of meanings it has inspired. Together, these essays convey a bright tapestry of experience with the song.

The poet, actor, scholar Maya Angelou describes how the song was woven into a morning ritual of her primary school experience in Stamps, Georgia, starting with recitation of the Preamble to the US Constitution, followed by the singing of the "Star-Spangled Banner," and closing with "Lift Every Voice and Sing." Like many schoolchildren, she recalls that the song had little impact for her beyond the way it marked the daily opening of class. During her eighth grade graduation, however, she experienced a seismic shift of meaning. A White donor speaking at the ceremony touted his contributions to local schools highlighting newly acquired equipment for science labs at the White school while pointing to improvements in the playing fields at the school Black students attended. His address underscored inequities in the very ambitions and future visions that the students held for themselves. Angelou recalled how her eighth grade peer scheduled to speak next unexpectedly started singing the song after the guest speaker's remarks, and in that luminous moment, what had become routine gave way to insight. Angelou realized that she had "never heard the words, despite the thousands of times

I had sung them. Never thought they had anything to do with me....The depths had been icy and dark, but now a bright sun spoke to our souls" (in Bond & Wilson, 2000, p. 11).

Perry cites cultural critic Benedict Anderson's concept of *unisonance* to describe the feeling of belonging to larger purposes when singing together in a collective group: "a way of feeling in one's body, resonating through one's breath and flesh, membership in a community bigger than simply those in the room" (in Perry, 2018, p. 39). Perhaps this embodied moment of occupying one's place in relation to matters beyond the immediate moment expresses what Angelou felt as one of these souls standing in that spot at that time with others, illuminated by the lyrics as they conveyed their connective power.

The history educator Sam Wineburg makes a distinction between *lived memory* and *learned memory* (2001, p. 234), marking how events may be experienced more directly in our own lifetimes and personal histories, in contrast with learning about those events in the lives of others through more distanced means. I think about this distinction as I read the accounts in Bond and Wilson's collection. As a White, cisgender woman who grew up in the Midwest, I have no recollection of hearing "Lift Every Voice and Sing" until well into my forties, no doubt as a result of the times, places, racial, and cultural surrounds of my life's path. I have only learned memory of this important marker of musical and cultural history, which is admittedly much less direct and evocative than the narrative accounts of the song's impact in early school experience, families, and community settings I have read or heard about. I am only able to access what I know from the life experiences of others, their lived memories. As they become available to me in whatever form, these accounts, then, become even more poignant and powerful as I read or hear them. Learning from the lived experience of others transforms these witnessed meanings into an educative moment, as it might be paralleled in other classroom settings. Through a multidimensional approach, tempered with humility, empathic understanding becomes possible.

Synthesis

How does the work "work?" Once you have devoted your attention to deepening your understanding of its inspirations, origins, and paths of transmission, its distinctive properties and the ways these elements come together in an artistic whole, the various ways that its subject matters, meanings, and affective qualities infuse your experience of the work, what can possibly be left to consider? The question at hand moves toward a synthesis, but again, not in the sense of knowing everything there is to know, feeling everything there is to feel. In dynamic fashion, stepping back to contemplate an artistic work in a holistic way invites students and teachers to move from consideration of its dimensions to integrate and interrelate them. In this dynamic space, attention is drawn to overlapping insights—how the time and place influence the artistic languages, conventions, and practices; how the affective qualities bring the subject matter to life; how the ways that individuals and groups have embraced, adopted, and adapted its meanings attest to the expressive complexities and evocative power of art works.

When students and teachers move from introduction to inquiry to reflection to valuing, these aspects of synthesis develop over time as encounters with the work are repeated and sustained. At the heart of educative experience, this multidimensional journey of "walking around the facets" opens up vistas for breadth, depth, and meaning (Figure 3.4).

"Lift Every Voice and Sing": Synthesis

At some point, we confront the challenge of conveying how engagement with various dimensions of a work coheres, resulting in a whole that is bigger than a sum of the individual dimensions. This is the challenge for "Lift Every Voice and Sing." Although putting these complexities into words is bound to inadequately capture the depth of understanding that accrues as a result of sustained encounters, I take it up in a compact sentence, knowing there is certainly more than words can say: *The intersection of text and tune written for a school assembly transformed into an enduring reminder of the journey toward justice and the resilience of those on the journey.*

The historical trajectory of this song is told in compelling synthesis by the scholar Imani Perry, who gathered stories, interviews, historical documents, and scholarly accounts in *May We Forever Stand: A History of the Black National Anthem* (2018). She traces the song from James and Rosamond Johnson's school assembly in 1900 through four generations of African American life in the United States. Reading her richly textured commentary confirms the song's significance in educational settings, religious communities, civic associations, and larger political movements.

64   SEEKING CONNECTIONS

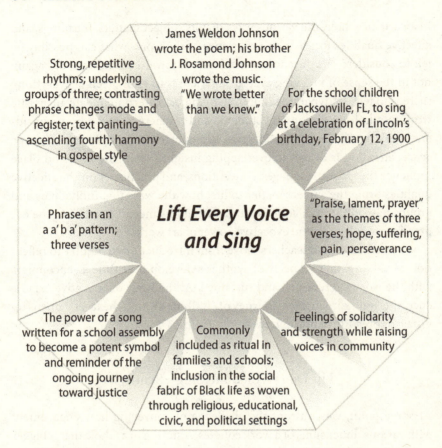

Figure 3.4 Facets Model: *Lift Every Voice and Sing*

Perry's preface speaks to a synthetic view informed by her personal identity:

> Every moment and movement bleeds with the ink of a previous era. This truth emerged dramatically as I researched the history of "Lift Every Voice and Sing." It was the epic anthem embraced by black institutions as well as black and multiracial social movements. . . . Even as it was embraced by widely divergent political actors, some aspects of its meaning were and are resilient. It tells the singer to see herself or himself as emerging magnificently through struggle. It nurtures an identity rooted in community. It is a song that moves regionally and internationally, yet holds fast to a sense of particular belonging. It has remarkable longevity due to both its beauty and

its vision. Perhaps most important, it was and is the song of a people, *my* people. (p. xiv, italics in original)

As students and teachers pass from superficial acquaintance to consider a plurality of meanings, the hope is that experience is transformed. In the case of "Lift Every Voice and Sing," these meanings may emerge and resonate with students whether you are singing the song with J. Rosamond Johnson's harmonization in hymn-like fashion, reading one of several children's books based on the song, exploring gospel style along with Kirk Franklin, singing Roland Carter's arrangement in a choir, playing jazz in the style of Preservation Hall Jazz Band, learning Lettie B. Alston's variations for piano, viewing Beyoncé's performance at Coachella, or preparing to perform Omar Thomas's "Of Our New Day Begun" for wind ensemble. Even the numerous versions and variations of "Lift Every Voice" speak to the enormous potential for discovery, inquiry, and depth.

An Experiential View

Although the Facets Model is often used by music teachers as a heuristic strategy to guide planning, the benefit of multidimensionality lies in its potential to personalize and deepen experience. A heuristic acts as a general rule of thumb to guide action and reflection, appraising the value of pondering each and every dimension before stepping back to ask, "So what does this mean?" For teachers, new pedagogical avenues may appear—aspects of study worth pursuing, or even gaps that yield tantalizing open questions. Finally, imagine the sides of the facets diagram folding up and overlapping, reminding us that the components of the music itself and the trajectory of our experiences with them form wholes (what Dewey meant by "consummatory experience").

Stemming from these sorts of representations, music teachers will be encouraged to involve students in similar exercises so that they begin to see the multidimensional nature of music more comprehensively, with its concomitant fascinations and avenues for personal experience. These "Experiential Facets" come from the inside out, moving the inquirer to the center of the action, and inviting individualized realms of knowledge, feeling, curiosity, and expression to the surface so that they can be celebrated and shared with others (Figure 3.5). This experiential representation provides a

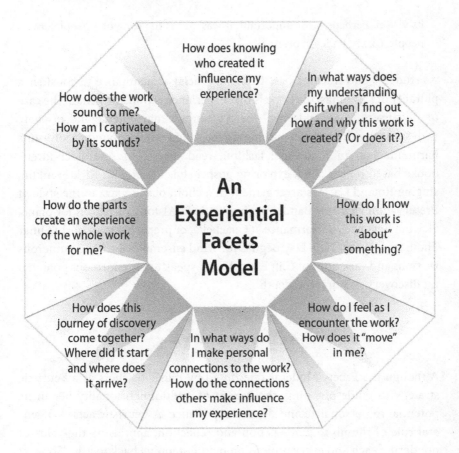

Figure 3.5 Experiential Facets

springboard for connections with many fluid dimensions of a musical work and toward meaningful encounters.

Stretching Exercise

Use the questions from the Experiential Facets, or better yet, your own questions, choose a work that intrigues you. Immerse yourself in the work, following your curiosities to explore its facets in multidimensional ways. Where might this exercise lead?

4
The Musics of Our Time

In which we begin in an unexpected place . . . the Garden of Cosmic Speculation.

> PAUSE. *Before you launch into this chapter, search for images of the "Garden of Cosmic Speculation" and take a moment to wander through the photographs or videos you find.*

When you think of gardens, what comes to mind? You most likely would not jump from this simple question to ponder the origins of the universe, the principles of physics that govern matter and space, or the discoveries of biological science that help us to understand diverse forms of life, I would imagine. Charles Jencks made this leap, however. As an architectural theorist, critic, designer, and scholar of postmodernism, Jencks was "inspired by the science of complexity" to create a garden in Scotland as a microcosm of the universe, in which the forms and shapes draw on quantum mechanics, the underpinnings of nature, and cosmological themes as aesthetic sources. He was fascinated by recent discoveries and developments in contemporary science, observing that for most persons, though, these fascinating realms lie outside of everyday experience. With plentiful resources of imagination and eclecticism, Jencks launched forth to bring these worlds together, integrating science and landscape architecture.

The resulting garden, open only once a year to the general public, reflects Jencks's prodigious curiosity, which is echoed in turn by visitors' wonder and delight. Bridges, landforms, fences, sculpture, gates, water, land, sky, curves, angles, spirals, undulations—these elements heighten the senses at every turn. Jencks makes his challenge to visitors clear: "A garden should present a . . . puzzle to be fathomed, some things very clear and others veiled" (2003, p. 25). Even when familiarity comes from video tours rather than firsthand experience, mediated strolls through its imaginative structures open up vistas for thinking about cosmological matters in living form. For example, a stroll might introduce visitors to:

68   SEEKING CONNECTIONS

- the Black Hole Terrace, inspired by Einsteinian physics, a series of Astroturf tiles and aluminum that give the impression that the very ground will be swallowed up, as if "the warp of real gravity pulls one downward toward the vanishing point, just as it would inside a black hole" (2003, p. 170);
- the Jumping Bridge, a sinuous curve of red appearing and then disappearing, which "jumps across two streams and burrows into the ground with fractal, or self-similar shapes" (p. 139);
- the Willowtwist, entered through a winding path under a canopy made of one long piece of aluminum that bends and loops in a circle overhead;
- and a Universe Cascade, a waterfall and staircase that rises up from the pond below in overlapping courses. Jencks imagined "cosmic history as a flaring fan, or trumpet" with "breaks in symmetry" that "map . . . the evolution of the universe" (p. 189).

Jencks's garden is a triumph of the imagination arrayed in a glorious profusion of lakes and landforms, plantings, buildings, and sculpture spread over thirty acres. Like nature, the garden evolved over time from its creation in the late 1980s until Jencks's death in 2019. During that period, he continued to add more structures and elements. Although I have not yet visited this garden, photos and videos help me imagine what it would be like to experience walking through these verdant acres punctuated by the unexpected; relishing the slowing of time, the delight of discovery, the heightening of senses in seeing how natural elements combine playfully with designed forms.

What could this garden possibly have to do with music? I recall attending a performance of the Chicago Sinfonietta that featured a piece titled *The Garden of Cosmic Speculation* accompanied by photographs of Jencks's garden displayed on large scrims behind the orchestra. Caught up in the juxtaposition of photographs with the dynamic progression of movements in Michael Gandolfi's piece, I was intrigued to find out more about the garden and the music composed in its honor. I learned how Gandolfi stumbled upon an article about this extraordinary garden while working out on his treadmill in the United States. Serendipitously, theoretical physics was one of Gandolfi's major hobbies. He was so captivated by what he read that he traveled from his home in Boston to Scotland to visit the garden. His visit subsequently inspired him to compose several movements to evoke structures in the garden. Gandolfi's composition, in its first iteration, was premiered by the Atlanta Symphony Orchestra in 2004.

Like the universe and the garden, though, Gandolfi's musical work expanded over time, beginning with four movements in 2004 and moving through various additions to arrive (at least for the time) at twenty movements by 2017.[1] Gandolfi suggests, "It is intent that any arrangement of movements, in any order, may be selected for a given performance" (liner notes). After all, visitors to the garden likely take different paths; these options for wandering through the music parallel those idiosyncratic journeys.

> PAUSE. *If you can locate recordings, listen to the ways that Gandolfi realized Jencks's imaginative structures in sound. Listen for quotations from a chronological survey of Western music from Gregorian chant to fragments from Palestrina, Bach, Berlioz, Stravinsky, Miles Davis, to Steve Reich as you metaphorically climb the stairs of the Universe Cascade. Just as fractals form the scarlet-red Jumping Bridge that emerges and then disappears, percussive energy propels the syncopated repetition of the main motive in Gandolfi's corresponding movement. Juxtapose the Willowtwist's spiraling melodic shapes as they rise and fall over a dancing rhythmic ground with the image of shapely aluminum ribbons floating like Möbius strips above the walkway.*

Clearly, the garden and Gandolfi's music are connected in many ways—primary among them multiple bridges of inspiration moving across intellectually expansive theories of cosmology and physics; historical trajectories of past discoveries informing the present; creative bridges of shaping materials (earth, metals, sounds) into forms; and even an aesthetic of transformation. Jencks writes: "Gardens, like cities, are whispering games in which the key is to pass on meaning even as it changes. They may reach momentary equilibrium, but should never be pickled. Respect is shown by continuing and transforming the plots" (Jencks, 2003, p. 13).

Although it may be unlikely for music teachers or students to travel to Scotland to visit the Garden of Cosmic Speculation firsthand, or for a school orchestra to have the musical resources to perform Gandolfi's challenging movements, this artistic pairing opens up the main territory of interest—how the richly variegated music of our time offers avenues for educative experience, and how cultivating an exploratory stance toward artistic innovation can infuse music classrooms with creative vibrancy. Our metaphorical stroll through the garden builds on the notion of multiplicity while introducing themes to be developed in this chapter, which include expansiveness of the search for educative materials, openness to artistic experience, and deep wellsprings of curiosity as a foundation for curriculum.

Imagining a Lifelong Musical Profile

I am surprised and delighted at the end of each year when one of my preferred music streaming services sends me a compilation of the songs and instrumental pieces I have listened to during the previous calendar year, marvelously wrapped in a tidy package for my consideration. Reviewing this compilation gives way to surprise as I recall particular examples associated with important events, fleeting fascinations, teaching episodes, research projects, and other roles that accompanied earlier moments during the prior year. This personal overview can only capture the music I listened to on that particular platform, of course, and while impressive, it still stops short of the full array of musics I encountered, performed, enjoyed, and taught in everyday life. Nonetheless, it offers a fascinating vista wrapped up in what is oddly called habits of "consumption."

Etude: A Lifelong Musical Profile

Imagine a lifelong musical profile. Imagine if you had access to an application that could trace and track a lifetime of musical involvement in the way these streaming services work. What would you notice in stepping back to reflect on this enormous library? Would certain repertoires and styles appear as touchstones, zones of familiarity worth returning to time after time? Might you find turning points in the musics that captured your attention? Periods of expansion? Periods of distillation? How would your lifelong musical profile reflect influences of your family, friends, teachers, community, travel, life experiences? What would you learn from your role as a teacher about encounters with music in school settings that have made a lasting musical imprint on your life? Before proceeding, take the time to capture your thoughts as you ponder these questions. You may find it helpful to represent your answers in a visual diagram that will trigger your reflective thinking. Share your insights with others.

Especially germane to this chapter is what this fanciful exercise might reveal about the times when your musical understandings have been enriched and expanded by moving across the permeable membranes of music as a subject area and then moving back. Which particular instances in your personal portfolio show these dynamic intersections of music with other realms of knowing? Can you identify several "Garden of Cosmic Speculation" moments when you found yourself on an unexpected path outside of music, inspiring you to bring together what you previously thought were separate interests? When I have led similar thought experiments with teachers, I am often surprised by the difficulties they share as they try to recall these intersectional moments in school settings. Their struggles sometimes elicit provocative critiques on the insularity of their music classes. Some teachers, however, tell compelling stories of integrated projects and pursuits that stood out at the time while also leaving a lasting trace in their educational history. Thinking about these bright moments fuels their desire to adopt an interdisciplinary stance for the benefit of their own students.

From Omnivore to Interdisciplinarian

Sociologists who study how race, class, and gender (among other forces) influence patterns of cultural identity would be interested in examining a set of lifelong musical profiles such as the one you generated for this thought experiment. They might be curious to identify tendencies of taste and musical preference that align with a person's membership in various social strata, for example, such as what might be classified as "highbrow, middlebrow, or lowbrow" tastes, as fraught with peril as those categories certainly are. You might also imagine how this research is complicated by the exploding universe of possible musical classifications, and the fluid nature of a teacher's personal identity (Akkerman & Meijer, 2011). Yet you probably noticed some patterns in your own riverbed of experience, reflecting shifts that align with the eddies and flow of your life's course.

A concept arising from this sociological stream of inquiry is the notion of a "cultural omnivore," a person who exhibits an openness to appreciate anything (Peterson & Kern, 1996). In a gustatory sense, omnivores seek energy from multiple sources, both plant and animal. One of the purposes of this chapter is to encourage an omnivorous approach to exploring musics that can serve as the centerpiece of educative experience in classrooms. Omnivorousness can serve as a prelude to interdisciplinarity. This relationship can be traced through several assertions: the more eclectic a teacher's musical engagements, the more likely it is that those engagements will lead to potential sources for interdisciplinary curriculum work. The more expansive the search becomes, the more likely that teachers' musical searches will overlap with students' musical interests. The more fluid the search, the more likely that boundaries will be crossed rather than patrolled.

Musical categories are similarly fluid, despite attempts to classify and categorize genres in well-defined taxonomies. I am reminded of a remarkable graphic of super genres, sibling genres, and subgenres with the fascinating title "Musicmap: The Genealogy and History of Popular Music Genres from Origin till Present (1970–2016)," developed by Kwintin Crauwels,[2] which displays a visual taxonomy of musical classifications. I also think of the Music Genome Project, an initiative to label musical examples with nearly 500 attributes that allow sorting and searching as the driving force for personalized playlist recommendations.[3] Technological advances such as these have given rise to what Stephen Tepper calls the "curatorial *me*," an emerging capacity to become "connoisseurs and mavens, seeking out new experiences, learning about them, and sharing knowledge with friends" (2008, p. 367). Tepper's "me" readily morphs into a curatorial "we" as persons begin to identify themselves with groups of musicians and listeners that cluster into genre categories, and as teachers think about the social surrounds that influence the musics to be shared in classroom settings.

Although the algorithmic procedures that create these sophisticated blueprints of musical preferences belong to the realm of programmers and data scientists, these developments also point to problems teachers face in grappling with the complexities of labeling musical genres. The impulse to sort artists, songs, and works into the bins and buckets of various genres quickly runs into categorical walls that constrain free movement across styles and types. Just as we understand students' identities as a complex blend of intersecting affiliations and characteristics, so it is with musical types. The complexity compounds if teachers think they can easily identify students with the musics that make up their daily life worlds—labeling them by the musics they perform and enjoy. Students' musical worlds are fluid and multiple, too.

Enabled by the permeability of disciplines, you are encouraged to move back and forth in an omnivorous search for musical works that may foster curricular connections. You might think this chapter's title a bit too ambitious—"the music of our time." The diverse, living, dynamic musical practices of the present encompass both teachers' musical worlds and students' musical worlds, as broad and eclectic as those worlds may be. They may be affiliated with well-known genres, such as what we think of as "school music," composed for children and young persons in familiar ensemble settings, or be drawn from the panoply of genres whose reach extends far beyond school walls. Even naming these genres immediately runs the risk of leaving out important musical traditions and styles. As I offer a list of superordinate categories, I am confident that you will notice omissions to add to this lineup: Bluegrass, Blues, Classical, Country, Dance, EDM, Folk, Gospel, Hip-Hop, House, Jazz, Latin, Metal, Opera, Pop, Rap, Reggae, Reggaeton, Rock, R&B, Soul, and "World" categories. Within those deep pools lie infinite possibilities for the intermingling and continuous overlapping of new relationships in sound. And, as one might guess, new relationships between sound worlds and related worlds of experience.

Trailing an Omnivore

Who comes to mind when you think of the phrase "citizen of the world," or someone who exhibits an omnivorous curiosity and presence in multiple circles? Rhiannon Giddens, whose musical paths cross historical and international boundaries, rises to the top of my list.

Her biography speaks to her lifelong engagement in multiple musical traditions, and to her collaborations as a singer and versatile instrumentalist with bluegrass, folk music, opera, and classical performers, just to name a few. Her ensembles, including the Carolina Chocolate Drops and Our Native Daughters, bring songs of oppressed voices into the clear, vibrant light. Recognized for her powerful performances by a Grammy Award, a MacArthur Fellowship, and the Steve Martin Prize for Excellence in Banjo and Bluegrass, among other recognitions, she is sought after for her catalytic leadership in arts organizations, including being named as the Artistic Director of Silkroad. The announcement of her appointment speaks to her professional standing as well as her boundary-crossing sensibilities: "For 20 years Silkroad has embodied radical cultural collaboration, both modeling and teaching the importance of connection across difference. Giddens' incredible mastery at excavating the music of America's past, knowledge of history and diverse cultures, and ability to bring people together from all walks of life, make her perfectly suited for the Artistic Director position."[4]

Stretching Exercise: Searching for Omnivores

Identify a cultural/musical omnivore such as Rhiannon Giddens. Trace the roots and branches of their musical engagements, as well as their broad passions and curiosities. Gather up recordings, podcasts, transcripts of interviews, and other materials to gain a sense of the person's artistic wandering and development.

- Set out on a listening tour to explore some of the fascinating paths they have traveled. Look for intersections of opportunity, collaboration, and interest that pique your interest further.
- Imagine interviewing this person, or if you are fortunate to know a musical/cultural omnivore personally, plan to conduct such an interview to find out more about the extensive breadth of their engagements and experiences.
- What can be learned from this exercise? What lessons might be drawn to infuse the music curriculum with such bright vision?

When I thought of someone who moves fluidly in contemporary music circles and who thrives on forming partnerships with artists across multiple styles and media, Melissa Ngan came immediately to mind. The projects she has fostered and facilitated as a chamber musician, artistic director, teaching artist, and visionary leader exemplify many possibilities for creative collaboration and artistic expression.

Profile of a Boundary Crosser: Melissa Ngan

Melissa Ngan is on a mission to bring twenty-first century music to audiences, classrooms, and communities. As founder of the chamber group Fifth House Ensemble (5HE), Melissa, a professional flutist, created a vibrant group of instrumentalists who redefine what it means to play chamber music. The mission statement for the 5HE captures this expansive ambition, promising that the group: "taps the collaborative spirit of chamber music to create engaging performances and interactive educational programs, forging meaningful partnerships with unexpected venues, artists of other disciplines, educational institutions, and audiences of every type."[5] Their performances have been praised for their keen musicianship and inventive flair. In her current role as president and CEO of the American Composers Orchestra, Melissa has taken on the ambitious aim of "reshaping American orchestral space through its repertoire," as she works with composers to explore new sonic landscapes and realms of expression.

I first met Melissa when we collaborated on a project sponsored by the Ravinia Festival to bring their artistic resources to schools in the Chicago area. Our goal was to create vibrant educational experiences for schoolchildren by first introducing their teachers to orchestral works such as Holst's *Planets* and Mussorgsky's *Pictures at an Exhibition*. We collaborated on workshops intended to inspire the pedagogical creativity of teachers enrolled in the program, and in turn, enliven school visits that enabled the children to hear the works performed by the orchestra at Ravinia's beautiful grounds adjacent to Lake Michigan. I saw firsthand how Melissa and her 5HE cohorts animated the project with their signature mix of playfulness and passion.

Melissa describes herself as an "endlessly curious person, obsessed with growth." Drawing on her upbringing in a family of Brazilian, Cambodian, Chinese, and Vietnamese heritage, she learned early on, as a self-described "cultural chameleon," to savor the unexpected serendipity that diverse persons bring to the table. Driven by her enthusiasm and collaborative savvy, she has built on those early lessons to become recognized as a visionary catalyst for innovative programs and practices.

A small sample of these creative projects shows these boundary-breaking tendencies across disciplines. 5HE partnered with video game composer Austin Wintory to produce *Journey LIVE*, the first ever performance version of Wintory's Grammy-nominated score featuring musicians responding to game players in real time as they made their way through dunes, caves, and mountains in a parable of life's trajectories.

PAUSE to access the soundtrack or video clips of Wintory's *Journey*.

A partnership with a graphic novelist, Ezra Claytan Daniels, resulted in *Black Violet*, a three-part concert series featuring the story of a black cat living during the black plague in seventeenth-century London. As audience members were swept up in the story and Daniels's darkly compelling images, 5HE played movements of chamber works that they curated with Daniels to amplify the narrative arc. In an artistic exploration of the water cycle, *Rivers Empyrean*, the ensemble worked with conservation groups in Chicago as well as First Nations groups to challenge anthropocentric views of humans as taking advantage of nature rather than honoring it. The collaborative performance featured new compositions, including a piece by Shawn Okpebholo that imagines water as a musical instrument, and the title work, *Rivers Empyrean,* created by Patrick O'Malley with data from Friends of the Chicago River.

Inspired by a David Attenborough film on the wonders of the natural world, Melissa holds "musical biodiversity" as a central value in her work that engages music creators across styles and genres. She looks for opportunities to move beyond and through fixed labels and categories, seeking to reintegrate music-making into the human experience in ways that transcend language. Process-based connections—how something works, what questions it explores, to find the "glue that holds it together even when it might not appear that way on the surface"—energize her. As Melissa forms partnerships, she strives to "create open space to prototype, to experiment," which invites more risk-taking. During the pandemic, for example, when the American Composers Orchestra faced the dilemma of holding simultaneous performance in digital spaces, she produced *New Canons*, a project featuring works by Ray Lustig and Trevor New that engaged a live orchestra, multiple string quartets, and soloists performing live on network in real time, using latency as an artistic element rather than a technical problem to be overcome.

When we talked about the infinite range of possibilities for the dynamic nature of new music to step over the threshold of school music programs, Melissa offered several doors that music educators might open. "Consider chamber music," she advised, which provides so much flexibility in instrumentation and size. "Focus on creation, not just replication." She spoke compellingly of the need to engage students in composition and improvisation to provide a well-rounded educational experience. *Unchained Melodies,* by 5HE's artistic director and composer Dan Visconti, is a musical work composed of improvisatory games for young performers that fosters their abilities to "listen to one another in new ways," simultaneously building community and creativity. In our conversation, Melissa encouraged teachers to branch out through commissions and residencies: "Establish a composition program, and establish relationships with living composers." She speaks of the excitement that attends learning to perform a work that has been created through close collaboration in the settings where it was generated. Melissa also recommends working with pieces that are not traditionally notated, reflecting on the ways that these opportunities fuel creative thinking. One of her influences has been the work of the groundbreaking composer Pauline

Oliveros, whose Deep Listening works explore the intersections between community, creativity, and consciousness. In her interview, Melissa spoke of using other instruments besides her flute as the gateway toward transcending her own classical music training and gaining courage in improvisation. As she described the notion of "experience design," in which all elements of a performance are designed to engage the audience before, during, and after the event, I thought of parallels to the design of educational experiences in their vibrancy, generativity, and lasting impact.

Melissa believes that "creative acts can transform the world." In her passionate advocacy for the importance of nurturing the practice of creativity through sound-making and play, and through the expertise she has developed as a connector of communities across artistic forms of communication, she embodies the vibrant dispositions of an interdisciplinarian.

Inspiration from the "Cutting Edge"

Like Melissa, who stands at the nexus of twenty-first-century creativity and contemporary music, I draw curricular energy from contemporary performer/composers and their exploratory tendencies, which often capitalize on music's connections with other realms. Recall the insights of Claire Chase, the founder of ICE quoted in the first chapter, whose creative vision invites, and perhaps even depends upon, integrative mindsets. What can be learned from these contemporary voices? What ideas might infuse their energy into curriculum-making?

Accordingly, I have introduced teachers to Caroline Shaw's *Partita for 8 Voices*, a choral work whose movements are titled for Baroque dances (Allemande, Sarabande, Courante, Passacaglia) reimagined in new sonic guises.

PAUSE to access "Allemande" from Caroline Shaw's *Partita for 8 Voices*.

In performance with Roomful of Teeth, a "vocal band dedicated to reimagining the expressive potential of the human voice,"[6] Shaw and her fellow singers employ extended vocal techniques in an interlocking assemblage of sighs, speech, timbres, and harmonies.[7] One source of inspiration for the work was an exhibition of wall drawings by artist Sol LeWitt. In one particular drawing, 305, LeWitt describes the "location of one hundred random specific points"[8] to be used by drafters as they map out the lines, arcs, and junctures of the visual problem space. Shaw opens the "Allemande" with excerpts from this text. Widely recognized for her creative vision (she received the Pulitzer Prize for *Partita* in 2013), Shaw's work is at once familiar through the way she relies on the most intimate of instruments—the human voice—while stretching toward surprise and astonishment in its capabilities. *Partita* stretches our expectations, as well, and as a result our listening becomes more supple. When I had the privilege of hearing this work performed live by Roomful of Teeth, I felt as if my entire body had been lifted up, released into flight, and then set down again.

What sonic canvases open space for students who want to play with new palettes of vocal sound? How might exploring imaginative works like Shaw's *Partita* lead to discoveries, that in the words of the text, show us that "far and near are all around?"

Another exploration involved Mason Bates's *Alternative Energy* symphony, each movement set in a different sonic and temporal landscape. The composer's program notes offer a glance at the way the work invites listeners to travel through time and space:

> *Alternative Energy* is an "energy symphony" spanning four movements and hundreds of years. Beginning in a rustic Midwestern junkyard in the late 19th Century, the piece travels through ever greater and more powerful forces of energy—a present-day particle collider, a futuristic Chinese nuclear plant—until it reaches a future Icelandic rainforest, where humanity's last inhabitants seek a return to a simpler way of life. (Bates, 2014)

I introduce the second movement, "Chicago, 2012," which for my students, feels close to home, albeit in unexpected ways.

> PAUSE to access the second movement of Mason Bates *Alternative Energy*, "Chicago, 2012."

Before revealing the title, composer, or program notes, we listen several times, building up a wall of sticky notes with questions, observations, curiosities. Stepping back from our wonderments, we prepare for the "reveal," finding out that Bates traveled to the Fermi National Accelerator Laboratory, or FermiLab for short, in Batavia, Illinois (not far from where some of the teachers live and work) to record the sound of a particle accelerator firing

THE MUSICS OF OUR TIME 79

up. Bates intersperses these nearly otherworldly sounds with orchestral instruments in a driving mix that feels alternately foreboding and playful. Later, our collection of sticky notes comes in handy when looking at the work from a multidimensional perspective (Figure 4.1).

What experiments might start with the juxtaposition of recorded and acoustic sounds? What stories, sampled from the past and the imagined future, might inspire students' thinking? Again, this work fires up curricular possibilities, hoping they collide in unexpected and illuminating ways.

Contemporary classical music, twenty-first century composition, "new music"—whatever the label, these works of our time sit alongside the panoramic output of other genres and styles. Just as it is nearly impossible to capture these musics with any one categorical label, it makes sense to resist generalizing about "our time" with broad brushes. Critic Alex Ross says that

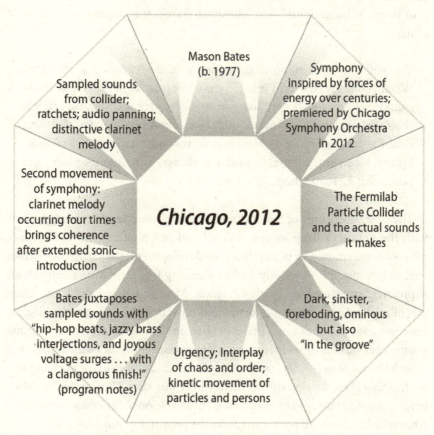

Figure 4.1 Facets Model: Mason Bates, *Chicago 2012*

twenty-first-century composition is "sometimes intent on embracing everything, sometimes longing to be lost to the world" (2007, p. 542). I see great promise in pursuing understanding of particular works to gain access to this rich body of art. The dynamic nature of their creation, unexpected sonic dimensions, and visceral relationship to contemporary fields and current issues call out for curricular exploration. In pursuit of avenues for making this exploration more likely, we turn again to multidimensionality and our search for educative starting points.

Works with a "High IQ"

Philosophical writings in music education often address key questions for teachers to keep in mind when constructing curricula, such as "What music is of value? Who decides?" Randall Allsup frames this inquiry as a matter of ethics:

> The philosophy of responsible choosing is the philosophy of ethics. Whether one uses the term "ethics" or not, the practice of arriving at a well-considered decision is part and parcel of everyday teaching. Yet, simple choices about matters of music curricula do not become *ethical* choices until the educator grapples in a personal way with notions like tradition, history, biography, culture, context and change, as well as the values and beliefs that surround them. (2010, p. 215)

The very concept of multidimensionality encourages entanglement with the notions Allsup names. As explored in Chapter 3, when multifaceted works seem rich in possibilities for development, they lend themselves well to interdisciplinary study while extending from the work's contextual, expressive, structural, or synthetic facets. Moving beyond the sonic analysis of musical properties and forms, and especially delving into the origins, transmission, and meanings that have become affixed to works for various purposes at various times in history, uncovers aspects of social meanings that must be brought to light as teachers weigh the educative value of studying and performing these works with students of various ages. Now more than ever before, music teachers are embracing these responsibilities for examining what may have seemed previously to be the province of musicologists.

Alongside the works of "new music" described in this chapter, many others spring to attention as especially viable candidates for classroom exploration. As a form of shorthand, I have come to think of these works as having a "high IQ," but unlike the acronym for intelligence quotient, this repurposed acronym stands for a high Interdisciplinary Quotient. A work with a high IQ brims with potential for curricular connections. You may have already developed such candidates or have a "wish list" just waiting for the right opportunity to stretch your curricular imagination. The principle of permeability can be useful for addressing how music influences the subject areas adjacent to and overlapping with the music, and to grapple with the ways this other realm similarly influences music. Just as music educators have expressed frustrations when music is used in superficial ways in curricular efforts that claim to be interdisciplinary, music educators pay attention to the characteristic ways that poetry, art, history, or culture are approached as disciplines in their own rights.

Although capacity for connections has rarely been named as a key criterion in the selection of musical examples, searching for works with a high IQ makes this dimension a high priority. The search also accommodates students' voices in shaping the curriculum, reflecting of the kind of give-and-take in its creation that Ayers describes so well: "Curriculum, then, is a dialogical process in which everyone participates actively as equals—a turbulent, raucous, unpredictable, noisy, and participatory affair, expression and knowledge emerging from the continual interactions of reflection and activity" (Ayers, 2019, p. 41). How might students' musical choices be integrated into classroom experience, and how might those choices reflect students' broad interests beyond music specifically? What budding expertise can they bring to bear? What might emerge from the unpredictable but exciting interactions of musical worlds, subject matters, persons, places, and ideas?

If you wish to expand your storehouse of works with a high IQ, consider the two categories of stretching exercises below, which first "go wide" to invite expeditions into unexplored repertoires and sources, and then "deep" to foster multidimensional understanding of the works you audition for curricular development. Any of these ideas could easily be revised to engage students' responses rather than teachers'. How do these strategies stretch your horizons for interdisciplinary work in the music classroom?

Stretching Exercises for Going Wide

Soundtracks as starting points. Student soundtrack assignments have become a popular tool for music teachers who wish to inventory the musical worlds of their students. I was delighted to find a project of this sort with historical roots. A fascinating example of this sonic inventory of identity can be found in a broadcast turned podcast from the British Broadcasting System (BBC). In 1947, a weekly radio program was introduced with a relatively simple premise in which a host interviews invited guests, called "castaways," about the top eight pieces of music they would absolutely want to have with them if marooned on a desert island. During the pandemic, the BBC broadened the scope of this program by sponsoring a contest inviting listeners to post their picks on social media, asking them to list their top eight pieces; add a book and a luxury; incorporate the hashtag #DesertIslandDiscsChallenge; and invite eight friends to join the fun.

- A connection-infused version of the Desert Island Disc challenge might involve listing your top eight pieces that are *connection-rich*, complementing your already solid understanding of related disciplines or *connection-building*, stretching your imagination beyond what you already know.
- If you identify a missed opportunity, or musical work or genre you have taught without sufficiently emphasizing its relational attributes to history, culture, art, poetry, literature, dance, or other possibilities, take the time to note what might have been addressed. Recognizing missed opportunities can lead to stronger commitments in the future, so see these underdeveloped instances as opportunities rather than failures.
- As a fascinating variant, you may want to pair up with another music teacher to interview one another about your lists, playing excerpts, and discussing their significance in your curriculum. Listening to the BBC podcast might inspire this exchange.

Eclectic Week. If your musical involvements during a particular week could be tracked on a daily basis the way that fitness trackers work, your weekly reports would no doubt reflect the activities, genres, and patterns that make up your quotidian sonic landscape. This landscape may already reflect an omnivorous stance, but if you need to branch out, be intentional and strategic. The purpose of this stretching exercise is to plan such adventures, and especially those that might feature music in tandem with related subject areas.

- Search for opportunities in your community that fall outside of your usual roster of activities—diverse musics in community settings, lecture-recitals, invited talks in the arts and humanities that might touch on musical topics, public library events, multi-arts performances or exhibitions.
- Include available opportunities for digital exploration as well. During the pandemic, many arts organizations made their resources more widely accessible in digital form. Browse the rich and remarkable resources posted by museums, performing arts organizations, and other available sites.
- Consult digital sources for print material. For example, search for instances of "music" being mentioned in the professional literature of history, social studies, art, literature, theater, dance education journals. Do any of those sources use a works-based approach in making connections from outside the field of music education?
- Ask friends whose eclectic tastes lead them to roam in circles other than yours to meet for a sharing session over coffee or a meal.

Stretching Exercises for Going Deep

The purpose of this exercise is to deepen your understanding of a musical work with a high IQ that may be a prime candidate for meaningful connections. These suggestions can be thought of as vehicles for "transporting" a person from standing outside a work to feeling as if you inhabit the work from the inside. Again, add more strategies you find useful in getting to know a new work well.

- Search for a musical work that you have recently taught, studied, or performed that deserves further exploration. What music has recently caught your ear? What have you yearned to follow in more depth? What intrigues you? In the spirit of this chapter, follow the intrigue to map out some initial connections in related subject areas, historical eras, or cultural practices.

- If you have the time and inclination to audition several possibilities, keep track of the way that you sort and sift through a range of choices. Which dimensions make a difference as you settle on a particular work?

Soak it up and take it in. Use the power of repetition to bring the work closer to your understanding. Use the power of variation to encounter it from multiple angles and perspectives. Here are some suggestions to guide this process, but feel free to invent your own:

- Make good use of *repeat play*. Listen to the example if you can locate a recording, play it or sing it when traveling about or performing everyday chores.
- Doodle as you listen. Try mapping out the rise and fall of the melody, the textures, the ebb and flow of the rhythm with a large piece of paper and colored pens or pencils.
- Jot down evocative words, snippets of text, or feelingful qualities that come to mind.
- Move as you listen—tap, gesture, move through space. Notice when the qualities of your movement begin to mirror the qualities of sound.
- Visualize someone else moving to the music—a dancer, an ice skater, a child, a conductor.
- Let your imagination roam freely to evoke a scene, a location, an animation, or an event that evocatively depicts the music.
- Saturate yourself with this music, but also follow the trail if the music leads you outward to other paths. See where they lead.

Build your knowledge of the work by informing your appreciation of it. After you reach a point where you have internalized the music, move out on a search to learn more. I have noted how quickly the urge surfaces to search for information online. I recommend trying to resist this urge to reach for a search engine until you have the chance to trust your own ways of knowing first and foremost. When the time comes, however....

- Read up on the work. Consult friends, colleagues, experts. Reach out to whatever resources you can locate.
- Discover what you can about the circumstances of its germination and creation. What can you find out about the person(s) who created it?

What can you find out about how the work has been adopted, embraced, celebrated, critiqued by others?
- Listen to several different versions of the example, if they can be found. What does this parallel listening tell you?
- If your work sits within a tradition that is usually notated, search for a copy of a score. Follow it.
- If this exploration of the work leads you outward to other closely related works, topics, disciplines, or ideas, follow those paths to see where they lead.

Represent the dimensions you have discovered through this exploration of the work.

- On a large piece of paper, write the title of the work in the center. Radiating outward from the title like rays of the sun, draw and label all of the dimensions you have identified through this exploration. If you wish, play with a different metaphor—fronds of a plant, tentacles of a cephalopod, branches of a tree, etc.
- Use mind-mapping software to show the dimensions of the work and avenues for exploration.

Reflect on the exercise.

- What did you discover about the musical example that you did not know before you started?
- Which aspects of the work were deepened or strengthened through this exploration?
- How far afield did this exploration take you? In what ways did new possibilities rise up? Did you find yourself in new territory as you followed your curiosities?
- Examine your visual representation of the dimensions. Can you group any dimensions into categories? Do any dimensions stand alone?
- Would you say that your understanding of this work has deepened? In what ways is this work more meaningful to you?
- Do any immediate possibilities for your classroom spring to mind? What paths of exploration might students travel?

5
The Foundations of an Interdisciplinary Pedagogy

Spontaneity and synchronicity lead to luminous moments in our classrooms. When a student reveals an unprompted yet meaningful connection they have just made, we stop to savor what has just been revealed. When some topic or subject in the classroom appears quite suddenly to parallel something outside the classroom, we linger for a moment to celebrate this remarkable alignment. Serendipitous moments such as these often stand out from the usual flow. Time may seem suspended. Stop for a moment to revisit the last time you witnessed such serendipitous happenings in your own classroom—the popping up and lining up of new meanings. If these bright moments cannot be engineered in advance or prescribed, how can teachers create circumstances to make them more likely?

Believing in the power of the arts to transform lives, teachers draw on their own experiences with powerful works, artists, and media to design thoughtful classroom encounters for their students. They shape these encounters artfully and intentionally. How this shaping enables students' growth, and how classroom encounters enliven students' educational experience, is of primary concern. Greene challenges teachers to move beyond routines and prescriptions to counter apathy and passivity, intensifying their efforts to rouse imagination. "It is my conviction," she writes, "that informed engagements with the several arts is the most likely mode of releasing our students' (or any person's) imaginative capacity and giving it play. However, this will not, cannot, happen automatically or 'naturally'" (1995, p. 125). As an advocate for multiplicity, for awakening, for resisting forces that reduce education to training, Greene's vision of classrooms alive with students' resonant voices calls teachers to scrutinize their pedagogical practices.

Pedagogy reveals teachers' beliefs in action. Music educators have developed powerful modes of instruction by taking initiative, exercising creativity, and collaborating with others. A notable example of these constructive dispositions is on display at every professional conference as teachers stand up in front of peers to present promising strategies for working with students. Many of these techniques and approaches have been developed over time before being refined and extended by new generations. They deserve our attention. At the same time, they reveal what kinds of music-making teachers consider worthy. Consider the inherited practices that you have integrated into your daily teaching. Of the various pedagogical branches of music teachers' knowledge, how would you evaluate your capacity in teaching students to perform, to compose, to improvise, to analyze music, to make connections?

Music educators have cultivated many areas of pedagogical strength. Musical performance is a prime example. As a field, music education has developed a sophisticated and complex system of curricular options, instructional approaches, and assessment strategies for teaching students to sing and play instruments in lesson settings while also teaching them to perform in small and large ensembles, including choir, band, and orchestra, as well as jazz and musical theater. This system is prominent, and in many classrooms, accompanied by a parallel progression of techniques for reading standard music notation.

Many teachers and scholars have turned their energies toward the development, expansion, and refinement of other pedagogical avenues for music teaching and learning. Since I began teaching in the 1970s, I have witnessed an impressive burgeoning of approaches for teaching improvisation, both genre-specific such as jazz and more eclectic forms such as free improvisation. Composition pedagogy has developed by leaps and bounds, as have approaches for guiding digital creation. These initiatives broaden the curriculum toward more comprehensive ideals. Music teachers can turn to instructional materials, research studies, and professional development seminars to guide processes of performing and creating in ways that bring more breadth and variety to classrooms.

A Portrait of Pedagogical Initiative: Miles Comiskey

A particularly promising avenue for pedagogical breadth comes from those who are developing courses and curricula through their own ingenuity, typically "outside" the aegis of their undergraduate preparation or professional development. These music teachers are creating new practices and promising offerings by exercising agency and resourcefulness. One such example of pedagogical creativity can be seen in the work of Miles Comiskey, who inherited a music appreciation class when he stepped into a teaching position in an urban magnet high school nine years ago. He quickly learned that the main musical focus and instructional character of this course had not been updated for decades. Convinced that the school administration was far more interested in increasing student engagement and enrollment than maintaining the historical focus of the high school general music class, Miles set about reinventing options. He describes himself as a "horizontally oriented music teacher," explaining that he draws from eclectic skills in guitar, music production, voice, drums, and violin, far-ranging musical interests, and experience in the audiovisual industry as resources to guide students as they explore their own curiosities. Over time, Miles has created a roster of specialized opportunities that appeal more directly to students' musical interests, among them sound engineering, hip-hop, music theory, and an advanced music production class.

Miles has crafted a pedagogy of mutuality in which students work on musics they love as he helps them in turn to "hear their music in new ways," drawing from his musical breadth to find intersections of process, trace the influences of various musicians and genres, and teach flexible musical techniques. Sometimes his students lead the explorations with their favorite tracks; sometimes Miles leads with his. His goal is that students make music that feels like an expression of self and of their musical worlds; accordingly, he views his role as providing them with musical concepts, strategies, and techniques to facilitate their intentions.

The intellectually vibrant atmosphere of the high school in which Miles teaches invites relational thinking. Students rely on their hip-hop sensibilities as they interpret texts, relate concepts from physics courses as they explore recording technologies and acoustics, and draw on social studies and history classes as they discuss critical events and political themes in the musics they study and create. Students enrolled in film design, animation, and art bring their skills and curiosities to projects involving music videos and album cover design. Miles welcomes the range of choices students have in their elective courses, takes inspiration from their passions and curiosities, and appreciates the flexibility his particular school context affords him to shape educative experiences with purpose and flexibility.

Setting the Stage

Creating environments for students' creativity, connectedness, and critical thinking depends on music teachers' visions and commitments to these values. In my view, the field has much to learn from the fluid and responsive approaches of music teachers such as Miles Comiskey alongside imaginative curricular variations to support students' varied interests. Much can be learned from embedding these values and dispositions in general music and ensemble offerings that are more prevalent and historically grounded in school settings.

I am convinced, however, that most music educators lack an articulated, well-conceived pedagogy to teach for connections, and that teacher education programs rarely address this important aspect. What frameworks help to explain what might be needed in the development of this capacity for understanding? In what ways might a more keenly articulated interdisciplinary pedagogy have an impact on students' relational thinking? Which practices lend more readily to integrated ways of thinking? What do we expect from a pedagogy that is supportive of interdisciplinary thinking in the arts in complementary ways to music? I have been searching for decades for theoretical or practical guidance along these lines with limited results.

Principles and general heuristics provide discussion points for a more integrated approach. I turn to the writings of Jerome Bruner to consider a pedagogy of mutuality, which is particularly germane to support aims of relational thinking. In contrast to prominent models of curriculum planning and interaction with students, I address the notion of soft planning as a more flexible approach. As an illustration of soft planning, I describe a collaborative curriculum project involving partnerships with music students and contemporary composers sponsored by the American Composers Forum. A multifaceted curriculum design for one of the works in the project, Michael Colgrass's *Old Churches*, places the ideas in a musical context. Finally, I offer guidelines for choosing works with potential for relational thinking, setting up interpretive zones for exploration of multidimensional aspects, and grouping works in proximity to prompt connections.

Seeking a Pedagogy of Mutuality

For interdisciplinary approaches in the arts, a theory of instruction should be especially congruent with the experiential nature of the arts. Most keenly, an interdisciplinary theory should account for relational thinking, the negotiation of multiple meanings through interpretation, and examination of the strength of these connections. Professional discourse about theories of instruction is riddled with dichotomous pairs such as teacher-centered or student-centered classrooms, emphasis on transmission of knowledge or construction of meaning, traditional or progressive approaches, and discipline-specific or interdisciplinary contexts. Analysis of the dichotomies often underscores fundamental differences between seemingly irreconcilable positions or viewpoints.

Jerome Bruner, whose ideas have influenced educational psychology, curriculum theory, and philosophy, disrupts this dialogue in *The Culture of Education* (1996). Bruner speaks about a *pedagogy of mutuality* that bridges many of these common polarities by addressing how the thinking of both teachers and students is subject to mutual modification in classrooms as each works on the other. He portrays educational environments as powerful spaces for situating the individual within culture, thus linking social realities to negotiated meanings found in lively, thought-provoking classrooms. Productive instructional territory lies at the nexus between the object of study and the individual. "A culture . . . is constantly in process of being created and recreated as it is interpreted and renegotiated by its members," Bruner asserted (1982, p. 838). In his negotiatory or transactional view of education, language is the primary mediator of the socially constructed process of creating meaning. Thinking from an interdisciplinary perspective, multiple forms of representation take their place alongside language as avenues for meaning.

Bruner describes how theories of mind, what he terms *folk pedagogies*, influence the way teachers design lessons, select materials, sequence content, and make decisions. If left unexamined, these folk pedagogies can constrain or delimit the kinds of educative experiences students may have. This concept led me to wonder what folk pedagogies are prominent in music classrooms that claim to teach for connections.

Bruner categorizes four prominent models of mind that function correspondingly as models of pedagogy (1996, pp. 53–63). The first casts children as imitative learners and teachers as skilled models. In an apprentice/master relationship, the teacher demonstrates disciplinary "know-how"; by observing these skills, students perform and produce with increasing mastery. Thinking about Bruner's characterization led me to consider how music teachers model their relational ways of thinking for the students in their charge. Many times this modeling is of musical skills. How often, though, do teachers "think out loud" to exhibit their ways of making sense of the world? How do they model their perceptual processes and curiosities when encountering an unfamiliar art form or work, for instance? The way teachers demonstrate habits of listening, looking, observing, and focusing on elements or dimensions of an art work can convey artistic openness. In contrast, teachers can also model a quick rush to judgment or superficial grazing. Although imitation of teachers' ways of thinking is no substitute for students' capacity to think on their own, the ways that teachers think, and the ways that more complex thinking is made available to students, encourages me to view this model in more generous ways.

The second model operates on the notion that the teacher presents facts, rules, and principles to be remembered and applied; the role of the student is to acquire and reproduce this knowledge. The teacher's transmission of propositional knowledge relies on the successful acquisition of facts and principles by students through passive receipt rather than formation. Here, I think about multidimensionality, and in particular, the contextual knowledge that situates a particular artistic work in its time and place. Knowing that a song, painting, or poem has been created by a particular person or group in certain contextual surrounds of time and place informs understanding of that work, as does understanding how subsequent persons have passed a work from hand to hand, or voice to voice. Reducing the teaching/learning encounter to transmission and restatement of these details, though, fails in many ways. The point of these contextual underpinnings is not to turn the classroom into a game of Trivial Pursuit. It is rather how propositional knowledge becomes useful in the ways we respond to, interpret, re-create, or transform a work. Paulo Freire's words come to mind: "to know how to teach is to create possibilities for the construction and production of knowledge rather than to be engaged simply in a game of transferring knowledge" (1998, p. 49).

Bruner's third model views students as capable thinkers who develop understanding through discourse, collaboration, and negotiation with more knowledgeable adults and peers. In this view, the principle of mutuality can be seen most vividly, as the "teacher is concerned with understanding what the child thinks and how she arrives at what she believes" (1996, p. 56). Intersubjectivity, or understanding of others' minds, is formed through this process. Particularly in the arts, I think back to Greene's vision of releasing capacities and "giving [them] play." It is perhaps in the classroom interchange of interpretations, responses, and formative understandings that the notion of mutuality is most explicit. "Such a pedagogy of mutuality presumes that all human minds are capable of holding beliefs and ideas which, through discussion and interaction, can be moved toward some shared frame of reference" (p. 56). In classroom communities founded on inquiry, on respect for multiple points of view, and on the search for rich interpretations of art works and their meanings, this mutuality takes precedence.

The last model is based on a view of students as knowledgeable agents who reconcile the knowledge they have formed with the cultural knowledge of the past. In this manner, understanding is tempered by situating it in culture, time, and place. This last pedagogical distinction made by Bruner reminds me of Randall Allsup's concept of the "living tradition," in which knowledge of the past "remains vital only when it embodies some kind of mutuality between preservation and innovation" (2016, p. 80). Bruner's notion speaks to the aims of relational knowledge as well, especially as connections are placed in longer trajectories of artistic ideas and values, their resonance to the present kept in view.

In school contexts, these various models of mind are observed to varying degrees in different settings. "Real schooling, of course, is never confined to one model of the learner or one model of teacher," cautions Bruner (1996, p. 63). Each of these models of mind contributes insights to an interdisciplinary pedagogy; upon reflection, we see how teachers' beliefs about students' minds implicate their approaches to providing a richly connected environment.

The Challenges of Shifting Pedagogies

Pedagogy and curriculum are inextricably linked. How we teach and what we teach are usually areas for teachers' decision-making that align with their educational philosophies, rooted in deeply held beliefs and values. The complexity of teaching often throws these beliefs and values into question, though, in classroom contexts filled with uncertainty and competing demands. Consider for a moment how stabilizing it may feel in the early years of teaching to rely on curricular materials and sources for ideas. Consider how disconcerting it can be to enact these plans to discover that they "don't work." To be asked to take on a more elastic approach to planning and interaction may seem a tall order, but that shift seems necessary if greater mutuality is sought. Teachers accustomed to feeling in charge and in control of their choices may find a more fluid and flexible approach to pedagogy unfamiliar, uncomfortable, or even risky.

In a study of teachers' views of unpredictable interactions and events in the classroom, Howard and his colleagues found that educational goals to enable students' risk-taking necessarily depended upon teachers' willingness to model risk-taking as well. They observed: "Pedagogy comes with all the inherent risks and emergent sensitivity to the needs of young people that defy the certitude of teaching methods and educational theories and is an inherently risky way of being in the world' (2018, p. 8). Recalling the previous discussion of music teachers' specialist identities, this riskiness might mean redefining primary roles and habits of curricular planning especially. Well-established routines may fall apart; familiar strategies may come unhinged in the pursuit of valid alternatives.

Seeking Flexibility in Planning and Instruction

Interdisciplinary instruction requires a reconceptualization of planning and preparation. Predominant models of curriculum planning are often prescriptive and linear. They begin with the assumption that the teacher will define in advance what students should know and be able to do, and from that premise, to work backward from those articulated goals of instruction. Next the teacher chooses materials and activities, arranging them in a sequence to be followed to realize the planned educational experience. In some teacher education programs, for instance, preservice teachers are encouraged to slice their lesson or rehearsal plans into segments of time, and to anticipate the approximate time spent on each step of their written plans. In implementing the plan, the impression is often conveyed that a successful plan adheres closely to these predetermined segments and should not veer off course (I am reminded of this dilemma every time a student teacher apologizes that they did not "complete the lesson plan"). Although these assumptions may make sense at first glance, they run counter to important beliefs that undergird interdisciplinary instruction. They make it very difficult to work toward a pedagogy of mutuality.

As Eisner reminds us, the educational system embraces a form of technical rationality that prizes efficiency, alignment, and predictability. "Efficiency is largely a virtue for the tasks we don't like to do. . . . What we enjoy the most we linger over. A school system designed with an overriding commitment to efficiency may produce outcomes that have little enduring quality" (2002, p. xiii). In a classroom that prizes connections, one might find a more generous incorporation of students' prior knowledge alongside an ongoing expansion of teacher learning. One might also notice shifts in the design and aims of the educational encounter that occur along the way, even if those shifts require ignoring the clock. In place of closed and prescriptive ideas about planning, interdisciplinarians lean toward more open and responsive models, what I am calling *soft planning*. Using the word *soft* might suggest an approach in which "anything goes," or for which an easy sketch of a few ideas is sufficient. In contrast, I have found that soft planning requires more extensive thinking, akin to composing a "plan with variations."

Another assumption of curricular planning is *linearity*, or that the instructional pathway from introduction to ending proceeds through a series of steps that can be followed sequentially. This assumption flies in the face of more sophisticated models that convey the learning process, and thus curricular planning, as cyclical and recursive. The curriculum scholar Herbert Kliebard writes: "Modern teachers are continually urged to state specifically what it is that must be learned and then to charge straight up the hill—to resolutely pursue achievement of the designated objective." Building on Dewey, he suggests that "an indirect approach—winding paths, so to speak—may ultimately be far more effective in getting up the hill" (2006, p. 117). Kliebard's acknowledgment that learning is seldom as neat and orderly than it is made out to be runs counter to what many teachers are taught. More aptly, learning happens in fits and starts, even doubling back to prior ideas for added depth of understanding.

In place of a stepwise progression, perhaps a more useful metaphor for interdisciplinary planning is a branched tree, with various limbs to pursue of various degrees, sometimes returning to the foundational trunk before branching off in new directions. The paradox of interdisciplinary curriculum planning lies in the tension between defining the territory to be explored in advance, balanced with the need to expand or delimit the territory responsively while en route. A journey too tightly planned in advance may hinder the progress of understanding along the way; a journey too loosely imagined may not provide for deep and lasting understanding.

> PAUSE for a moment to reflect on your awareness of your teachers' pedagogies in your educational history. PAUSE to reflect on your attempts to change the ways you plan, teach, and assess, thinking about the way those shifts felt risky or comfortable. PAUSE to revisit your history of prescriptive and linear planning, recalling moments when you broke free of these constraints and what you learned as a result.

Heuristics as General Guides for Interdisciplinarians

Heuristics, or "rules of thumb," are in order in place of a fixed set of rules or procedures, which would be antithetical to an interdisciplinary perspective. An interdisciplinary pedagogy should elicit relational thinking, give rise to multiple meanings through interpretation, and capture students' insights to guide future work. Such a pedagogy should provide strategies and approaches to foster richly connected encounters with music and the other arts, guided by Eisner's eloquent promises that the arts

> refine our senses so that our ability to experience the world is made more complex and subtle; . . . promote the use of our imaginative capacities so that we can envision what we cannot actually see, taste, touch, hear, and smell; and . . . provide models through which we can experience the world in new ways. (2002, p. 19)

Eisner also admonishes that "good curricular materials emancipate and educate teachers" (1990, p. 65), a principle that guides the search for informative examples. An interdisciplinary perspective should free teachers and students to learn rather than constricting learning.

The key ideas to be explored in the remainder of this chapter include:

- The notion of *soft planning*, which enables interdisciplinarians to move responsively between and among topics, works, or questions of interest in the classroom;
- The selection of works with *a high interdisciplinary quotient*, leading fluidly to the study of closely related works, art forms, and eras;
- Instructional principles that support meaningful connections, including propinquity and juxtaposition, to create *interpretive zones* in music classrooms;
- Expanding repertoires of *questioning techniques* as pivots to draw attention to relations between works, art forms, and content areas;
- General principles that underpin a music curriculum rich with opportunities for relational thinking.

Subsequent chapters will develop strategies for cross-arts inquiry, including *triptychs*, a form of aesthetic puzzle, and offer guidance in assessing the strength of connections that students form while engaged in richly connected classrooms.

An Example of Soft Planning

I was fortunate to participate in a project sponsored by the American Composers Forum, BandQuest, which involves engaging contemporary composers in writing for school ensembles and creating new repertoire that incorporates the musical ideas of students.[1] Through partnerships, composers work with music teachers and their students in the schools, creating new works for band in partnership with the school ensemble. Imagine playing through "rough drafts" of a composition in progress and interacting with the composer as the piece takes shape.

An advisory board for the project, initially called New Band Horizons during its early years, was further interested in commissioning pieces that would have rich musical content as well as related curricular implications. They commissioned composers who were keen to break free of the rather formulaic pieces often written for middle level band. In the grant proposal for the project, the advisory committee wrote:

> Building upon young people's innate receptiveness to the new, [the project] will harness the energies of living composers to enliven music teaching in the schools, connecting students with some of the central figures in contemporary music, and dissolving the prevalent image of the "composer" as a remote, bewigged creature. (American Composers Forum, Vision, 1997, p. 1)

The composers were encouraged to incorporate extramusical associations suggested by the students as integral thematic material, again supported by the aims described in the proposal:

> A distinctive and unprecedented feature of New Band Horizons is to reflect the conviction . . . that music thrives in proportion to its integration with other human pursuits and with everyday life. Accordingly, we seek to initiate a broad spectrum of curriculum-wide links between music and other disciplines, hoping thereby to overcome the artificial barriers that have historically isolated music from other school activities. (American Composers Forum, "The Product," 1997, p. 1)

After the compositions were finalized, a small team of curriculum planners set out to design related curricular materials to accompany the scores and parts. I assisted with this phase of the work, thrilled with the collegial playfulness of the process. The curricular materials were made available to teachers in the form of a CD-ROM, which allowed for a more recursive and cyclical approach to planning. This format also enabled flexibility in following paths of interest as teachers and ensembles explored the multidimensional aspects of each work. I regret that these materials are no longer available as CD-ROMs, as the hardware to play them has become obsolete.[2] However, I describe this project as a metaphorical illustration of a flexible approach.

A dashboard was selected as the navigational metaphor for these curricular materials (see Figure 5.1).

Think of curriculum planning as a road trip. A particular destination, or aim-in-view, sets intentional planning in motion. Preparation for the journey involves gathering whatever may be needed along the way, resembling the way that teachers assemble curricular resources and materials they anticipate students will need. Although the destination beckons, so do inviting paths along the way. Some of these related excursions are anticipated beforehand; others tempt us as they appear en route. Passengers, after all, will certainly have their own ideas about exploring the attractive possibilities that branch off in appealing directions. In the spirit of mutuality, these unexpected discoveries are welcomed.

The curriculum planners for BandQuest incorporated these ideas into the dashboard, inviting teachers and students to explore the work, the process

Figure 5.1 BandQuest dashboard, *Old Churches*
American Composers Forum. Used by permission.

the composer took to create the piece, and resources to assist the teacher in preparing the work for performance, as well as teaching musical concepts and closely related ideas in and through the work. To illustrate the flexible approach, I will describe the curriculum for one of the works, *Old Churches*, by the composer Michael Colgrass (2002).

> PAUSE to listen to a recording of *Old Churches* by Michael Colgrass, making note of what you notice as you listen.

Imagine, for example, informing yourself about the piece to decide whether to perform it with your ensemble. The four buttons in the middle of the dashboard linked to resources for the teacher, including an analysis of the work—its instrumentation, form, technical challenges, and other elements; suggested teaching strategies for the special compositional techniques Colgrass used; and exercises resembling "warm-ups" that teachers might use to introduce particular rhythmic or melodic figures in the piece. For example, the score calls for aluminum kitchen bowls of various sizes, aleatoric "murmuring," and overlapping entrances of melodic figures as cued by the conductor. Other resources included a guide teachers could use to invite students in creating their own program notes for the work rather than relying on notes supplied by the publisher.

The ten buttons on the right-hand side of the dashboard invited flexible exploration by teachers and students. They linked to Colgrass's biography as well as video of the composer being interviewed by the middle school students at Winona Drive Middle School with whom he collaborated. "How do you come up with your ideas? What kind of composer do you call yourself?" the students asked. Colgrass, whose approach embraced many styles and genres, answered their questions by describing his collaborations with various artists and ensembles, and unpacking his inspirations for *Old Churches*.[3] As a jazz drummer and percussionist, Colgrass wove unexpected timbral choices into his piece. Committed to writing for young ensembles and teaching composition, he hoped the project would fuel students' interests in learning to compose. Colgrass spoke of the challenges he encountered while writing for middle-level band, intending to create a "simple, enduring, expressive work."[4] Another choice linked to listening guides written for students so that they could follow the various sections, motives, and features of the piece while listening in ways other than looking at their scores.

Colgrass incorporated graphic notation in the score of *Old Churches*, inviting performers to create murmuring sounds with their wind instruments, or ethereal sounds with percussion. These techniques establish the evocative and contemplative mood that intertwines with melodies resembling Gregorian chant. Another set of options on the dashboard invited students to investigate graphic notation on their own—imagining new sounds and inventing their own systems to represent the sounds. In this way, one of the BandQuest's central aims was fostered—to encourage compositional activity prompted by students' close encounters with living composers.

A set of options on the dashboard encouraged a panoramic array of closely related investigations, what I considered as the interdisciplinary branches. A timeline of Gregorian chant gave rise to questions about the ways that music evolved in these historical traditions from neumes to the present. The timeline described how free organum must have sounded in the large cathedrals and abbeys, providing sound clips and samples of scores. Another option chronicled the development of written notation, the challenges of "freezing" sounds on paper, with examples from lute notation, tablature for guitarists, shape notes, lead sheets in jazz, microtonality, Harry Partch and his use of non-Western systems, John Cage's use of chance, and electronically mediated forms. Students could investigate how each of these invented systems, much like Colgrass's graphic notation, captured some aspects of sound and not others. Students were invited to speculate on "What's next? What can you come up with?," which connected back to the section on inventing your own notation. Colgrass sensed students' enthusiasm for writing music with new representations in his work with the Winona Drive students, forming a "composition team" to create their own pieces using a mix of graphic and conventional notation.[5]

Since *Old Churches* evoked the feeling of being in a sacred space, another path considered how music is experienced in sacred spaces in both the built environment (cathedrals, synagogues, temples), as well as the natural environment. This branch led students to ask how acoustical space, architecture, and religious traditions influence the way persons respond to music in different expansive contexts.

Each of the works in this curricular phase of the project (Libby Larsen's *Hambone*, Chen Yi's *Spring Festival*, Tom Duffy's *A+: A "Precise" Prelude and an "Excellent" March*) was composed in collaboration with school groups, relying on the imaginative planning of music teachers and project leaders to develop the instructional resources. An additional example deserves mention here to show the breadth of the initiative, *Grandmother Song* by Brent Michael Davids (2002). His piece, a tribute both to his own grandmother and Grandmother Earth, was derived from his musical traditions as a member of the Stockbridge Munsee nation. A distinctive feature of this work is the use of vocables, which either band members can sing or a choir can perform. Davids also invents musical instruments, including a crystal flute, so part of the exploratory dimensions of the curriculum enabled students to consider how the science of sound influences timbre and instrument design. The vast and varied traditions of Native American music were represented in another area of the CD-ROM, where students could hear examples and read about indigenous musics of the Northeastern Woodlands, Plains, Southwest, Northwest Coast, and other areas of North America. This curriculum was rich in cultural traditions, the physics of sound and instrument design, historical contexts, and other areas of inquiry.

Lessons to Consider from the BandQuest Approach

As an example of soft planning, the design of the BandQuest project served many simultaneous curricular goals. Certainly, music teachers can (and do) acquire scores, teach the parts, prepare the music carefully through focused rehearsal, and present a polished, expressive performance of any of the works in the series (after all, this mirrors the process followed by professional ensembles). My participation in the project, however, heightened my sense of what is missed when this most efficient and highly linear route is privileged over other paths. For me, the lessons from this project have lasted far longer than the creation of the technologically limited CD-ROM format. Although BandQuest is by no means the only model of fluid curricular planning, its design enabled more flexibility and compelling inquiries than many models do. Certain strategic moves that guided its development can easily be borrowed, adapted, and artistically shaped for other initiatives.

The musical content at the center of the project was thoughtfully designed to focus on the work while branching outward from it. The curriculum team worked to provide options that would inform as well as free teachers and students to roam in multiple directions. These curricular materials were used by teachers in their planning as well as during instruction. Teachers also made the materials available to students outside rehearsals. For example, students were welcomed to explore the CD-ROMs in practice rooms

FOUNDATIONS OF AN INTERDISCIPLINARY PEDAGOGY   101

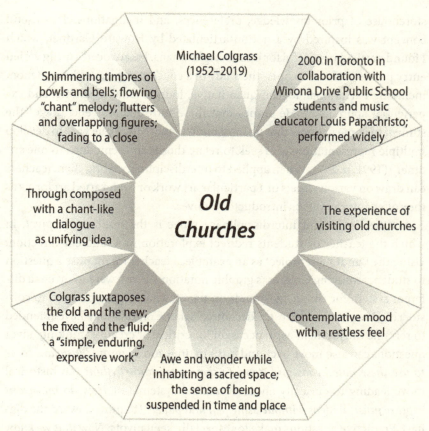

Figure 5.2 Facets Model: Michael Colgrass, *Old Churches*

as they pursued their own questions, and as their curiosities arose. As you might imagine, the Facets Model was used to explore the multidimensional nature of each work and its related areas of connection, such as this example of Colgrass's *Old Churches* (Figure 5.2).

Multiple Entry Points, Pivots, and Culminating Activities

In place of suggesting only one first step in an instructional sequence, the project provided *multiple entry points*, supported by the multidimensional view of the musical work. Providing several introductory moves acknowledges that students may begin an investigation of new work(s), media, or eras from different initial positions, depending upon their storehouse of prior knowledge, preferences, and inclinations. This useful concept was inspired by a notion articulated by Howard Gardner, which I found particularly useful for interdisciplinarians. He advocates using varied entry points or doors to open the study of a concept, topic, or phenomenon, including narrational, logical-quantitative, foundational, aesthetic, and experiential approaches. He argues that these introductions encourage "the student to come to know that phenomenon in more than one way, to develop multiple representations and seek to relate those representations to one another" (1991, p. 247). When applied to interdisciplinary work, then, teachers can draw on various facets of a particular art work or even varied art forms as they offer entry points as introductory moves.

Another important interdisciplinary move is the notion of a *pivot*, in which the teacher or students redirect exploration in a different direction. Using the BandQuest project as an example, a teacher might pose a question to students studying Colgrass's graphic notation, "If you were to invent a different system for capturing sounds on paper, what might you need to consider?" This pivot shifts from "decoding" what Colgrass may have intended to reframe the moment as an occasion for critical or creative thinking. Pivot questions can also move back and forth in time, too. *How did musicians come to use these note heads and stems to show pitch and rhythm?* (an historical move leading to curiosity about notational systems) or *How do musicians capture musical ideas without using pen and paper?* (to move toward the digital). Predictive questions make for especially keen pivots: *Now that we know Colgrass's early history as a percussionist as well as an inventor of graphic notation, what do you predict the score for this piece might look like before we take the music out of your folders?*

An especially synthetic dimension of soft planning that comes into play through the open-ended design of *culminating activities* that offer choices for student demonstration of meaningful connections. Culminating events prompt students to make their relational learning public and communal. Often, the products of study and exploration linger in memory longer than moments of process; they punctuate life in schools and stand out from the daily progression. Like a musical work, curriculum planning often strives for coherence from imaginative introductions, artistic shifts from one movement to the next, and the synthetic satisfactions of articulating and representing new relationships through a culminating demonstration, exhibition, performance, paper, presentation, podcast, or new work.

Responsive and flexible approaches to planning are essential to interdisciplinary curricula. They require teachers to "do their homework" in advance by choosing works and themes that can stand up to multifaceted study and that can be sustained. They invite students to branch out as well. Within the overall music curriculum and depending upon the level and type of course, these multifaceted works take their place alongside other works chosen for other purposes.

Repertoire That Leads to Interdisciplinarity: Works with a "High IQ"

Music educators take special care in selecting repertoire—the body of works to be performed, studied, and valued. Scholars have debated the core repertoire, or canon, to be held up at the center of the curriculum; this debate is ongoing, lively, and often tinged with passion. Repertoire often connotes musical works that have been created by others and that are intended to be performed or listened to in the context of the music classroom, but this is a relatively static stance given the ever-evolving expansion of musical styles and types. Greene speaks to a more expansive vision: "the canon, once defined by a certain number of men in time past, must always be skeptically conceived and kept open so that we no longer ignore the new and different as they appear" (1995, p. 136). Not only does this openness draw our attention to music at the edges of the familiar but it also encompasses emerging expressions—particularly the musics that students and teachers improvise and compose as they exercise their creative thinking in the classroom.

Consider criteria often used in choosing repertoire. Reimer identifies these qualities of musical works to guide selection: (a) craftsmanship, the "expertness by which the materials of art are molded into expressiveness"; (b) sensitivity, "the depth and quantity of feeling captured in the dynamic form of the work"; (c) imagination, "the vividness of an art object and its performance"; an (d) authenticity, the "genuineness of the artist's interaction with his materials in which the control by the artist includes a giving way to the demands of the material" (1991, pp. 332–336). The Comprehensive Musicianship through Performance (CMP) project cites these characteristics of well-written music: "form, design, unpredictability, depth, consistency, orchestration/voicing, text, transcendence" (O'Toole, 2003, pp. 103–104). As you will note, among these criteria for selection are few considerations of connectability (although nearly any one of these elements could be used for that purpose). The standards for judgment most often refer to the qualities of the work itself, rather than potential of the work to lead to meaningful relations outside of the work, except perhaps for CMP's focus on transcendence, which encourages a more expansive view.

To play with the widely used acronym for "intelligence quotient," I refer to works that are especially well situated for interdisciplinary connections as those that have a "high IQ." Judging a musical possibility as one that has a high interdisciplinary quotient implies that it lends itself to multiple avenues for panoramic study and lesson ideas. This criterion implies that musical aims for interacting with a work can complement aims that support students' relational thinking, that encourage them to approach music in terms of its permeable streams of influence. Music teachers have asked whether any piece can be developed for its interdisciplinary potential, a valid query for certain. I hold, however, that some works call out for a multidimensional treatment, and lend themselves well to interdisciplinary study extending from the work's contextual, expressive, structural, or synthetic facets. Of course, these principles hold for art works in forms other than music as well.

Stretching Exercise: Works with a High IQ

Develop a list of five or ten works that show promise for educationally vibrant curricular experiences and that, in your view, qualify as "works with a high IQ." Music teachers who have taken on this exercise have sometimes returned to works they have taught in the past but have failed to explore with their students in multidimensional ways (in other words, "missed opportunities"). For each work, list key avenues for exploration both musically and in closely related subject areas (the questions posed by the Facets Model may help you to take a multidimensional approach). Contemplate meaningful aims for each of the works, and if desired, share your list with another teacher to discuss the kinds of growth such a project might inspire.

Creating Interpretive Zones for Interdisciplinary Work

A primary responsibility of educators is that they not only be aware of the general principle of the shaping of actual experience by environing conditions, but that they also recognize in the concrete what surroundings are conducive to having experiences that lead to growth. Above all, they should know how to utilize the surroundings, physical and social, that exist so as to extract from them all that they have to contribute to building up experiences that are worthwhile. (Dewey, 1938, p. 40)

Imagine, as Dewey envisions in this passage, especially conducive surroundings that elicit vibrant ideas from students, particularly in terms of the social interactions that promote growth. To uphold this idea, teachers concern themselves with identifying concrete conditions that form the nexus for educative experience. As I stop to envision such classrooms, I call to mind students engaged in lively debates about the similarities and differences among the arts. I listen for students grappling with philosophical questions such as: What makes music distinctly expressive? How does visual art take us in places that music cannot? How is poetry indispensable to an individual's life in the contemporary moment? I suspect that schools need to provide more spaces for students to develop strong affiliations with the arts and gain confidence in interpreting their kaleidoscopic meanings. I want to visit schools in which artistic valuing is woven through multiple classrooms and embedded in school culture. I also want to eavesdrop on professional development seminars in which teachers are thinking through aesthetic questions and sharing strategies for guiding students through puzzles of meaning like these and more.

The interdisciplinarian knows how to create an instructional environment—an interpretive zone—in which multiple perspectives are invited and explored. In contrast with moments that come to a halt upon their arrival at commonly accepted or "fixed" meanings, the interdisciplinarian strives to establish a territory of openness, a safe space for tentative ideas to grow toward shape and definition.

Orchestrating room for interpretive work runs counter to many pedagogical maxims about efficient pace, tight sequencing of lessons, and relentless "hands-on" activity. It requires slowing down; staying in the moment; tolerating hesitation, ambiguity, confusion; following, rather than leading, students' flights of thought; and most vital, seeking "minds-on" engagement of contemplation, comparison, reflection, association, and playfulness. Soft planning enables this fluidity. An interpretive zone enables students to respond, create, and pursue new associations prompted by the study of related works and ideas. Analysis and discussion are central to this interpretive work, but creative responses invite more varied modes of expression beyond the verbal in generative fashion.

I am perplexed by tendencies in music education to reduce processes of interpretation to figuring out the "composer's/performers' intent," and supporting students' and teachers' ideas by referring to the use of common elements in the piece. These objectives, which seem to narrow possibilities rather than expand them, often show up in standards documents at the state or national level. I have followed responses from art educators (under the shared umbrella of core arts standards), who offer a different perspective that seems friendlier to interdisciplinary aims.

Art educator Terry Barrett writes extensively about the processes of interpretation that engage students with historical and contemporary art. He outlines more flexible principles for teaching interpretation to children, adolescents, and adults. Barrett recommends these principles to guide teachers' thinking in place of more prescriptive methods, steps, or stages that oversimplify (or calcify, I might add) what can be learned or experienced from encountering art works. Barrett describes the process in simple yet generous terms, "To interpret a work of art is to respond to it." He acknowledges idiosyncratic and social conditions at play: "Interpreting art is an endeavor that is both individual and personal, and communal and shared." Especially helpful in countering narrower approaches to interpretation is Barrett's guiding statement: "Artworks attract multiple interpretations and it is not a goal of interpretation to arrive at single, grand, unified, composite interpretations" (T. Barrett, 2000, p. 6).

Finally, I cite Parsons's quote that connects interpretation to integration as part of students' sense-making in the context of experience. "Integration occurs when students make sense for themselves of their varied learning and experiences, when they pull these together to make one view of their world and their place in it. It takes place in their minds or not at all" (Parsons, 2004, p. 776). When students file out the door, having spent time in a creatively fertile zone, we hold to the prospect that their growth has been enabled through encountering *multiple* views of the world and through strengthening their interpretive sensibilities.

The Principle of Juxtaposition

If bright moments cannot be engineered nor prescribed, then what is a teacher to do? Given my love of words, I reply, "propinquity invites serendipity."

Placing works in the neighborhood of one another—next door—is an artistic move for making connections more likely. Students' curiosities are piqued when they encounter unexpected pairings or groupings of art works. This notion stimulates instructional creativity.

The artistic process of choosing, assembling, grouping, and sequencing works is central to concert programming, museum exhibit design, poetry anthologies, and many other instances in which works within the same art form are meant to be experienced together. Commonalities and distinctions arise in our awareness as listeners, viewers, or readers as we encounter diverse works side by side. The principle of juxtaposition has at its base an inherent faith in transfer of knowledge. This transfer, or connectedness in the case of interdisciplinarity, is less likely when potentially illuminating elements are kept isolated or left up to chance. As Bruner notes, "Subject matters have to be demonstrably within reach of each other to improve each other. There isn't infinite transfer" (2006, p. 146). The same goes for juxtaposition in integrated forms of curriculum.

The arts are especially fruitful in this regard, since teachers and students can put works or examples together in many ways—by historical era, by place of origin or reception history, by topic or theme, by artists or schools of artists, by issue or theme. Similarly, teachers can foster sound connections through artful juxtaposition of works. When known relationships among works are identified by teachers as starting points, it seems a natural extension of planning to bring them to students in imaginative groupings. From that introduction, students can identify known relationships and explore new ones.

In the chapter that follows, many of these heuristics of interdisciplinary planning—soft planning, works with a high IQ, interpretive zones, entry points, pivots, culminating events, and creative juxtaposition—will take shape through experiences that search for connections in imaginative groupings of works across various art forms.

6
Triptych Play

Mention *triptychs* to a music educator and William Schuman's *New England Triptych*, Puccini's trio of one-act operas, or Eric Whitacre's *Ghost Train Triptych* may come to mind. Mention triptychs to a literature teacher, and well-known trilogies may spring to attention—*Lord of the Rings*, *The Hunger Games*, or Toni Morrison's novels *Beloved*, *Jazz*, and *Paradise*, for example. Tripytchs—sets of three related works in an artistic medium—can also be found in film, dance, and photography. Most often, triptychs are associated with visual art, referring to paintings with three panels or sections. In the eras of the Middle Ages and Renaissance, artists typically portrayed religious subjects for altarpieces mounted on wooden panels, with the center panel larger and higher than the surrounding panels and the entire work hinged together so the piece could be quickly closed and moved from place to place. Triptychs also include paintings of any subject matter presented in three related panels or canvases, such as Hieronymus Bosch's *The Garden of Earthly Delights*, Monet's *Water Lilies*, or Francis Bacon's *Three Studies of Lucien Freud*. Whatever the form or medium, artists strive to make the relationships among the movements, novels, or panels of the triptych evident to the listener, reader, or viewer to enhance the overall experience. Interacting with triptychs invites us to relate the parts to the whole, grappling with the aesthetic question of whether the whole is greater than the sum of the parts.

This chapter features explorations of triptychs using different art forms as starting points for curriculum while illustrating different overarching themes for possible integration. Instead of three related works *within* an art form, however, the focus is on creating groupings of three works *across* art forms. Music, visual art, and poetry are called upon to create these trios, although the ideas in this chapter can easily be transferred to artistic groupings across other art forms as well. The triptychs described here draw attention to what is shared across the arts while also building understanding that art, music, and poetry work in distinctive ways.

Juxtaposing multiple arts beckons as an especially imaginative, infinitely adaptable, and compellingly playful design for interdisciplinary instruction. Possible groupings may arise from original designs of artists/creators or as juxtaposed by artists/teachers to form a cohesive whole. Think of any form in which creators draw from multiple sources to create something new—collage, found art, parody, flower arrangement. Creating a new arrangement is an exercise of interpretation. Making a "set" stretches one's abilities to identify and form new connections.

Forming a triptych exercises powers of curation in bringing elements together in purposeful ways. Long associated with museum personnel who select art works to be included in an exhibition, the term *curation* has been applied to similar processes in many different settings, such as interior design, landscape architecture, fashion, even closet organization. Artist/entrepreneurs have created entire careers by culling and prioritizing the objects in our environment. When scanning works for a triptych, teachers serve as curators by selecting, arranging, juxtaposing, and emphasizing relationships through intentional placement and design for educational purposes. Many of the pedagogical elements of soft planning, interpretive zones, and creative response explored in the previous chapter align with this flexible strategy as well. Students already curate aspects of their lives as resources in forming identity; these curricular moves amplify those tendencies.

The Triptych Strategy

The idea for the triptych strategy came to me while browsing in a bookstore. I was drawn to Jan Greenberg's book *Heart to Heart: New Poems Inspired by 20th Century American Art* (2001). Greenberg chose forty-four different works of American art ranging from painting, sculpture, photography, and installation art for her project. Building upon her childhood experiences in which she was encouraged by her mother to write down ideas for poems as she visited art museums, Greenberg sent photos of these works to contemporary American poets, asking them to select an art work and write a poem in conversation with the work. Her compelling collection presents readers with the resulting diptychs as poems and paintings are paired.

As I stood in the bookstore, delighted by the juxtaposition of the beautifully reproduced images and their parallel poems in multiple forms and styles, I had a strong sense that something was missing. I felt that a natural complement to the pairing of visual art and poetry would be music, half expecting to see a CD glued to the end sheet of the book. I immediately started wondering which compositions would complete a "set" of three. Thus, the idea for interdisciplinary triptychs sprang up—a carefully chosen set of three works consisting of a musical composition, whether already composed or created for the occasion; a painting, photograph, or sculpture; and a poem. A review of *Heart by Heart* in *Publishers Weekly* took me in yet another fruitful direction: "editor Jan Greenberg puts ekphrasor and ekphrasee in happy proximity."[1] What do ekphrasor and ekphrasee mean, I wonder? My trusty *Oxford English Dictionary* defines *ekphrasis* as: "a literary device in which a painting, sculpture, or other work of visual art is described in detail" (OED Online). In a larger sense, ekphrasis refers to the process of crossing over from one artistic realm to another, a process that has fueled creative expression for centuries. I reasoned that the bridge of representation the ekphrasor carefully describes—in whatever artistic medium—invites the perceiver, the ekphrasee, to walk across.

The triptych strategy lends itself to curricular invention using various organizing schemes that bring coherence to groupings, while still preserving flexibility for discovery. Some of these schemes might include: (a) a common theme across all three art works (such as portraits in sound, image, and text; groundbreaking leaps from tradition; metamorphosis as a generative theme); (b) related elements and forms across all three art works (such as repetition and contrast, theme and variations, harmony, balance); (c) a common time or place of origin (three works from the Harlem Renaissance, Elizabethan England, the civil rights movement); or (d) expressive characteristics shared among the three works (bold exuberance, playfulness, reverence, awe). Most likely, multiple intersections may be identified, named, probed, and appreciated as they come to light.

From the universe of possibilities, I provide several examples that were inspired by Greenberg's book that in turn, may inspire your triptych play. I underscore the importance of responding to the invitation to PAUSE embedded throughout—either to access art works, poetry, and music, or to generate your own interpretations of the works. Following these examples, I describe an exhibition conceived as a constellation of interdisciplinary ideas presented by music educators at a professional conference as they applied this triptych strategy to their own classrooms.

"Painting Itself a Self"—Creating a Triptych through Curation by Starting from a Painting

At the moment of writing, the lifelong output of artist Jasper Johns is being celebrated in the art world through an especially unusual double retrospective exhibition, *Mind/Mirror*. Two museums—the Philadelphia Museum of Art and the Whitney Museum of American Art—are displaying the collected works of this groundbreaking painter (b. 1930) across decades of his life. Among the many subject matters occupying his attention, Johns was drawn in the 1950s and 1960s to common figures such as flags, targets, numerals, and letters. He was driven to "take things the mind already knows" (Lanchner, 2009, p. 19) as images, which he transformed in ways that arrest the viewer's attention.

Many persons familiar with Johns's oeuvre call to mind his flag paintings in particular. Starting in the 1950s, he began to explore using the US flag with its iconic stars and stripes, transforming the thing itself, held as a revered symbol of national identity, into a two-dimensional representation.

PAUSE to access images of Jasper Johns's flag paintings before continuing.

Johns superimposed multiple flags on top of one another (*Three Flags*, 1958), used thick encaustic in monochromatic ivory while retaining the shadowy outline of stars and stripes (*White Flag*, 1955), and in one instance, painted the flag in black, green, and orange (*Flags*, 1965). This variation invites the viewer to stare at the unusual colors before moving their gaze to a dot below, causing the color receptors in their eyes to create an afterimage in red, white, and blue.

As might be imagined, Johns's use of the flag as subject matter created controversy as some found his work shocking, unpatriotic, disrespectful. Although Johns dismissed these nationalistic associations, his flag series, put in the context of the time, calls for discussion and reflection. The Whitney retrospective offers this commentary on the flags: "Created when the United States was in the throes of the Cold War, the civil rights movement, and the

112 SEEKING CONNECTIONS

Vietnam War, they conjure contradictory attitudes toward a divided nation, ranging from hope and jubilance to pessimism and despair."[2]

Another well-worn image that intrigued Johns was inspired by a gift from a friend. Artist Robert Rauschenberg gave him several mimeographed copies a map of the United States and North America, with states and provinces outlined. Johns transferred the outlines to an enormous canvas, choosing bold colors to create a textural, overpainted panorama from border to border[3] (Figure 6.1). Composer John Cage, another friend, witnessed Johns at work, saying that after he transferred the outline,

> With a change of tempo he began painting quickly, all at once as it were, here and there with the same brush, changing brushes and colors, and working everywhere at the same time rather than starting at one point, finishing it and going on to another. . . . I asked how many processes he was involved in. He concentrated to reply and speaking sincerely said: It is all one process. (Cage, 1967, p. 76)

Linger with the painting before moving on.[4] Consider how this *Map* differs from maps usually displayed in classrooms.

Johns upsets typical cartographic conventions by using blue for landforms rather than bodies of water, by obscuring borders of the political map, and by stenciling names and abbreviations in irregular fashion. Paint drips and erupts across the continental United States as well as parts of Canada and Mexico. Large in scale (the original is 6′6″ by 10′3⅛″), reproductions of this exuberant painting sometimes find their way to principals' offices or school hallways. (One of my treasured pedagogical "tools" is a poster of the same size as the original. When I unroll it, teachers gasp in delight.)

> PAUSE. Before reading on, stop to imagine that you have been invited to write a poem based on Jasper Johns's *Map*. Respond to this pivot question: What would you want this poem to capture about the painting? Jot down a few words or phrases that come to mind.

An Ekphrastic Turn

The relationship of poetry to painting is strong and historical. Poetry's generative spirit is well suited to triptych play and to the educative aims we seek

Figure 6.1 Jasper Johns, *Map*
© 2022 Jasper Johns / Licensed by VAGA at Artists Rights Society (ARS), NY

here. As Parini notes, "The poet is a maker (*poetry* itself is derived from *poiein*, the Greek word meaning 'to make'), shaping words, creating a pattern of experience on the page" (2008, p. 113).

After a career teaching economics at the college level, J. Patrick Lewis turned his primary attention to poetry, writing numerous books of poetry for children. He was recognized by the Poetry Foundation as national Children's Poet Laureate from 2011 to 2013. At Jan Greenberg's invitation, he chose Johns's *Map* as the inspiration for a poem of the same name. Read Lewis's poem at least twice—both silently and aloud.

>**Map**
>J. Patrick Lewis
>
>>Brash canvas,
>>Bleeding borders,
>>Kindled calm,
>>This is oxymoronicamerica,
>>Forged out of iron and lace
>>By people strapping and raw,
>>Who wrestled and pinned history
>>To the map.
>>
>>Happy as a circus boy,
>>Spirited as an outlaw,
>>Rough as a gandy dancer,
>>This continent of tinted steel
>>Spread an easel of colors
>>On fifty pieces of scissored history—
>>And painted itself a self.

PAUSE to notice Lewis's ekphrastic response to Johns's painting before you read on. Which aspects of the painting does he represent in poetic form? What ideas does he play with?

Crossing the bridge from one art form to another, the poet interprets the painting. Analyzing the poem provides a window to his interpretive moves. Lewis pays attention to the contradictions that arise while viewing Johns's picture in phrases such as "bleeding borders" and "kindled calm." He notes how the people of America (notwithstanding Canada and Mexico, of course, since he speaks to "fifty pieces of scissored history") defined the rugged and contentious borders of states as they "wrestled and pinned" these distinctions to the map.

Lewis coins a neologism, *oxymoronicamerica*, to convey the spirited and often absurd juxtapositions that capture our attention when the past and present collide, just as the colors overlap. After a chain of similes, Lewis nods to the constructed nature of the painting itself and to the subject matter of the painting. He seems to suggest that just as we construct our boundaries, we construct our history. Even though we slice territory into tidier parcels, the national spirit cannot be bound or contained. What other bridges do you see between Jasper Johns's *Map* and J. Patrick Lewis's poem of the same name? How many dimensions cross over and what is the strength of their shared commonality? How do they speak to some shared ideas while showing how painting and poetry "work" in their distinctive ways? You may find the Facets Models for each helpful as you explore these connections (Figures 6.2 and 6.3).

Becoming Curators: Opportunities for Engagement

Having been introduced to the diptych of painting and poem, one inspired by the other, a lively aesthetic puzzle presents itself, just as I imagined when I stood in the bookstore. Which musical works complement and counterbalance the other two? Can you identify multiple possibilities to audition? What criteria you will use for selecting the work that best fits the relationships you find intriguing or meaningful? Along how many dimensions can you find connections that will help you to choose the musical work and explain your reasons for choosing it?

To share the insights that come from triptych play, invite students to curate a musical performance or exhibition in which these musical works will sit alongside the other two examples in this triptych. For example, students might present their "solutions" to the aesthetic puzzle by creating a presentation that represents the connections they discover, answering questions from others to convey what they learn. As an illustration, here are two musical works that music teachers have explored as triptych "solutions," each quite distinctive in style and emphasis. Treat these as suggestions for your own groupings (be sure to PAUSE as you access recordings).

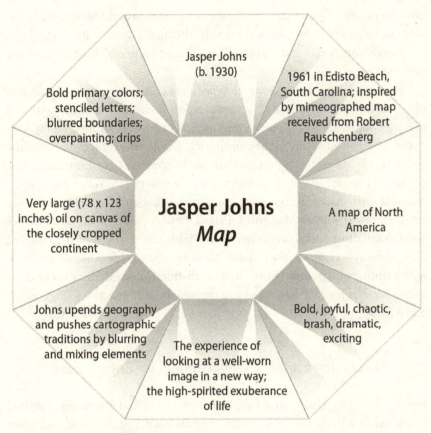

Figure 6.2 Facets Model: Jasper Johns, *Map*

Aaron Copland's "Hoedown" from his 1942 ballet, *Rodeo*, bursts forth with bold orchestral color—exuberant, brash, kinetic, much like Johns's *Map*. Just as Johns took a familiar image as inspiration, Copland incorporated folk tunes, "Bonyparte's Retreat" and "Miss McLeod's Reel," as he transformed existing material into something new. Both appear at first as familiar and accessible, but yield more nuance once you begin to notice the way their particular elements create a vibrant artistic whole.

Jimi Hendrix's performance of the *Star-Spangled Banner* at Woodstock, New York, on August 18, 1969, is held by many as iconic. In pyrotechnic fashion, Hendrix imitates the sounds of war with his guitar, a visceral expression of antiwar protest. His musical commentary provoked strong reactions, just as Johns's flags did earlier in that era. The artistic theme of transformation applies here as well, with inescapable political overtones. Musicologist Mark Clague, for example, names this moment as an enduring "exemplar of music's political potency."[5]

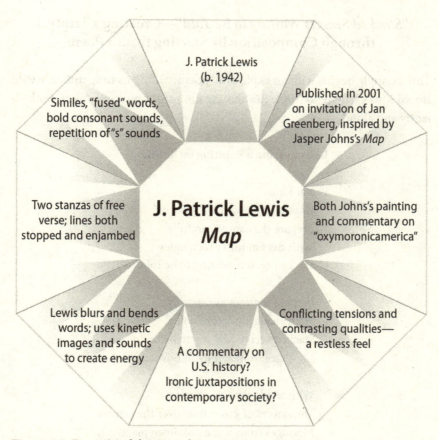

Figure 6.3 Facets Model: J. Patrick Lewis, *Map*

Studying these triptychs in close juxtaposition can extend and challenge what students know. With soft planning in mind, students can set forth on a multidimensional journey with each work, and in turn, establish an interpretive zone in their midst. Opportunities for growth may emerge by practicing curation. Consider exploring questions such as these as they arise from this triptych (and remember that "artists" here refers to poets, composers, songwriters, painters, novelists, and others who create):

- What possibilities arise when artists start with "what the mind already knows?"
- How do artists convey paradoxes, oxymorons, or opposing tensions in images, texts, and sound? How does holding paradoxical ideas in mind simultaneously influence the way you respond to such works?
- How do paintings, poems, and musical compositions offer distinctive forms of expression?

"Stacked Secrets Waiting to Be Told"—Creating a Triptych through Composition by Starting from a Poem

This example begins with an ekphrastic poem, calling us to spend time with Bobbi Katz's tribute to Mark Rothko. Again, read it multiple times, both silently and aloud.

Lessons from a Painting by Rothko

Bobbi Katz
> How would you paint a poem?
> Prepare the canvas carefully
> With tiers of misty rectangles
> Stacked secrets waiting to be told.
>
> Prepare the canvas carefully
> With shallow pools of color
> Stacked secrets waiting to be told
> Messages from some unknown place
>
> With shallow pools of color
> Thin layers of gauze float over the canvas
> Messages from some unknown place
> Where soft shapes expand above a glow.
>
> Thin layers of gauze float over the canvas
> With tiers of misty rectangles
> Where soft shapes expand above a glow.
> How would you paint a poem?

PAUSE to trace the repetitions of the phrases in this poem and to linger in its shimmering imagery. Can you find a pattern? Music teachers reading this poem have sometimes color-coded the lines as a helpful strategy. Note how the repetitions "land" in unexpected places. Read the poem aloud to notice how the repetitions sound. Try reading aloud in a manner that seems to evoke the shimmering, gauzy feeling of the poem.

Bobbi Katz created a tribute to the painter Mark Rothko by employing a distinctive poetic form, the pantoum.

The pantoum is a Malayan form from the fifteenth century, and has its roots in Chinese and Persian poetry. . . . [It] is written in quatrains. The second and fourth line of each stanza become the first and third of the next. Usually, too, the first line becomes the last line, and then the third line of the poem gets put into the very last stanza as the second line. (Addonizio & Laux, 1997, p. 163)

In addition to the repetition following the form of the pantoum, Katz makes the subtle phrases even more transparent by choosing sounds that slide and elide from line to line. Although these repetitions do not fall in a predictable pattern, hearing the same line repeated again later creates momentum, drawing the listener/reader forward. She seems to offer a recipe for creating a poem that mirrors her responses to Rothko's paintings, associated with the "color-field" school in which painters applied thin layers of paint to canvas, almost like staining (see Figure 6.4).

Figure 6.4 Mark Rothko, *Untitled 1953/1954*
© 1998 Kate Rothko Prizel & Christopher Rothko / Artists Rights Society (ARS), New York

Rothko's paintings have distinctive form and a remarkable luminescent quality. Those who have been privileged to view actual paintings rather than reproductions are drawn into their translucency, the shimmer that makes it seem as if the colors and shapes are in motion. The word "spiritual" is often evoked by those who spend time with the paintings. "Hung in a room, a painting by [Rothko] immediately affects everything in the room. His canvases have a curious way of transforming the people standing before him," observed artist Elaine de Kooning (as cited in Gabriel, 2018, p. 596).

Musicians often know Rothko on the basis of his fruitful collaborative relationship with composer Morton Feldman, who composed a piece for the opening of the Rothko Chapel in Houston, Texas, in 1971. To commemorate the fiftieth anniversary of that opening, composer Tyshawn Sorey recently premiered a new site-specific work in the Chapel, "Monochromatic Light (Afterlife)," showing his reverence for silence and sound in a double tribute to Rothko and Feldman.[6]

Christopher Rothko, Mark Rothko's son, wrote eighteen essays on his father's work, compiled in *Mark Rothko: From the Inside Out* (2015). After spending time with Katz's poem, one chapter in particular leapt out to me, entitled "Stacked." Christopher[7] begins the chapter by admitting he was tempted to sum up his thoughts in one sentence: "NEVER EVER USE THE FORBIDDEN WORD" (p. 112, upper case and italics in original). He argues that calling the rectangles "stacked" compromises Rothko's aesthetic intent, which might be better conveyed by the term *floating*. Christopher's description speaks to the heart of Rothko's expressive impact on the viewer:

> The rectangles that appear to hang weightlessly are filled with their own sense of motion, most often expanding outward, at times falling inward, but always in dynamic interplay with the periphery of the painting. Stacked rectangles could have no such motion. They would be contained, married to their place in the pile. I will add that stacking is something you *do* to rectangles. Float is something the rectangles do on their own. (2015, p. 117)

Consider how the multidimensional character of Rothko's painting and Katz's poetic tribute to his work open up multiple avenues for interpretation and creation (see their Facets Models, Figures 6.5 and 6.6).

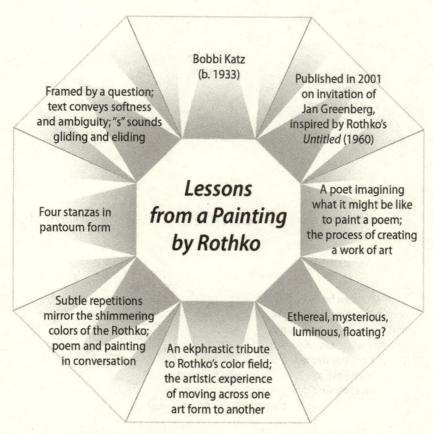

Figure 6.5 Facets Model: Bobbi Katz, *Lessons from a Painting by Rothko*

Composing to Create a Triptych: Opportunities for Engagement

- Use whatever musical resources are available to create eight phrases that can be arranged in the form of the pantoum: a b c d / b e d f / e g f h / g c h a.
- As you compose, strive for the expressive character of floating (taking cues from Christopher Rothko's essay and Mark Rothko's painting) and/or the evocative word choices of Bobbi Katz.
- Stage a performance of the composition with a reading of the poem, and the viewing of Rothko's paintings.
- Reflect on what is learned, felt, experienced through this creative exercise.

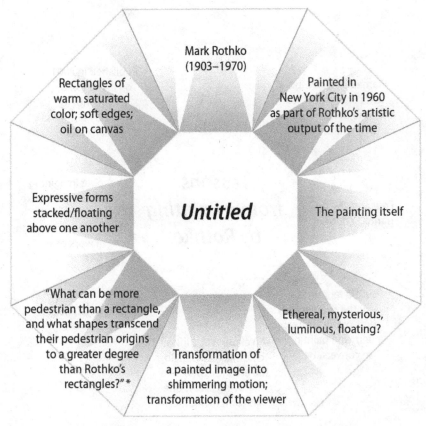

Figure 6.6 Facets Model: Mark Rothko, *Untitled 1953/1954*
* from C. Rothko, 2015, p. 116

- Consider these questions:
    o What difference does it make in your compositional process if you see Rothko's rectangles as stacked or floating?
    o How does composing in a given form provide both structure and freedom? How does that feel?
    o What are the challenges and satisfactions of conveying the expressive mood or character of Rothko's paintings or Katz's poem?

"Immense, Intense Self"—Starting from Music to Create Poetic Portraits

PAUSE to listen at least twice to Philip Glass's *A Musical Portrait of Chuck Close: Movement I.* Familiarize yourself with the music on your first listening. During the second listening, either draw what you hear or imagine drawing the musical figures. Repeat, as you wish.

How can piano music, absent any text, serve as a portrait of a person? As I listen, I note characteristic figures—the oscillating opening thirds punctuated by a minor chord in syncopated restlessness, followed by smooth ascending scales under a similarly insistent chordal figure, an arpeggio-like exclamation mark. Later, the upper voice cascades up and down. At one point, I draw large X's on paper as the scales cross in both voices—meeting in the middle before reversing course to move apart. Over rumbling figures toward the end, more punctuation marks drop in again in the higher voice, becoming more muted toward the end. (As a pianist, I stop to think how devilishly difficult this piece would be to play, grateful for the prowess of Bruce Levingston, the pianist who commissioned this piece from Glass, and who also performs it.)

Philip Glass composed a piece consisting of two movements in tribute to his lifelong friend, the artist Chuck Close. Known for what others often refer to as minimalism (a label Glass dismisses), Glass's iconoclastic style is recognizable in his use of shapely patterns, repetitive figures, and oscillating chords. His artistic output includes film scores, operas, orchestral and chamber works, and collaborations with dancers, filmmakers, playwrights, and contemporary ensembles such as Bang on a Can. Subject matter is a key source propelling Glass's creativity, as he explains that the "subject inspires and dictates the direction of any new music" (cited in Crowe & Watkins, 2008, p. 6). In his memoir, he addresses the power of visual imagery as an especially potent and synaesthetic source of inspiration in his compositional process:

> I've had dreams where I dreamed music and saw it as having width, length, breadth, color: a visual object. Once I was having a dream about a piece of music, and I came to a modulation, and what I saw was a door on a hinge. It was a perfect image of modulation.... What I did in the dream was to create a shorthand to represent the modulation by seeing it visually. (Glass, 2015, pp. 383–384)

Glass first met the artist Chuck Close in the late 1960s, the start of a lifelong friendship between two artistic mavericks. Close took a photograph of Glass in 1969, which he used as the subject for over 100 explorations of Glass's face in various media, including familiar watercolor, acrylic, and oil paints, but also stamp pad, tapestry, and lithograph. Glass described Close's process, noting how he elaborated on the images very quickly, sometimes painting with dots, sometimes with fingerprints, and even using wads of white and gray paper.... He told me once that the reason he liked the image was because of my hair.... [I had] a very wild, oceanlike head of hair. (Glass, 2015, p. 246)

Figure 6.7, a portrait of Philip Glass in fingerprint, is one of this series.

> PAUSE to examine this portrait. Access multiple versions of Chuck Close's portraits of Philip Glass, or his compelling portraits of persons from many walks of life. Search for images of his painting process at close range to see how he approaches faces through building up small units of color or pigment to create the artistic whole. If you have the opportunity to see his works in person, move back and forth to experience the effect of the parts melding into the whole.

Close is known for large-scale portraits, which he calls "heads." Surrounded by Abstract Expressionists in his early years, who were turning away from representative images, Close took a distinct turn by exploring portraiture, initially in a style called photorealism. In 1988, he suffered a spinal aneurysm, which might have left him unable to paint. Instead, Close reinvented the way he interacted with canvases by suspending them from pulleys so that they could be lowered and raised mechanically, enabling him to move his wheelchair directly up to the surface. The "bricks," as Close sometimes calls them, are laid out in grids, their colors coalescing from a distance into what he thinks of as equivalent to a "musical chord."

Glass describes Close's paintings as consisting of "modules that are put together and shaded with different values.... And I've used that idea with modular music also." He speaks to larger themes shared in their work, "creating art out of an exhaustive and detailed process, so that the entirety of the work is a reflection of the integrity of the process."[8] Close describes the first movement of Glass's portrait in terms of what they were exploring in their artistry at the time:

> The first movement is . . . like what Phil did when I first painted him ... severe, reductive.... At that time, I was making things that were full

Figure 6.7 Chuck Close, *Phil (Fingerprint)*
Digital image © Whitney Museum of American Art / Licensed by Scala / Art Resource, NY

of self-imposed limitations—just diagonal lines in a grid—in the same way that Phil was limiting himself to seven notes played on a crummy electronic organ. (cited in Comita, 2007)

Both artists were exploring, what can be done creatively when pushing against limitations. In 2007, the American Ballet Theatre took this pairing into a new realm by staging a ballet to Glass's composition while displaying images of Close's art.[9]

PAUSE to reflect on a pivot question: How would you draw from your interactions with the music of Philip Glass and the art of Chuck Close to create a poem to highlight their connections? What units of meaning would you create using words in place of sounds and images? What compositional influences might you borrow from their emphasis on process?

Creating Portraits in Poetic Forms: Opportunities for Engagement

The author Jan Greenberg took up this challenge. In the form of a diamante, an unrhymed poem of seven lines, Greenberg pays tribute to Chuck Close. The shape of the poem, like concrete poems, mirrors a diamond ("diamante" is Italian for diamond). You can easily imagine this shape mirroring the lozenge-like "bricks" of color favored by Close. She describes his "curlicues" and the synthetic moment when the bricks coalesce into a wall-filling image of the artist.

Diamante for Chuck
Jan Greenberg

Ovals
Luminous, Hot
Popping, Pulsing, Swirling
Curlicues of Color, A Kaleidoscope
Blurring, Blending, Focusing
Immense, Intense
Self

Greenberg's poem reminds me of "biopoems" in which students create portraits of classmates using similar short phrases arranged in a distinctive shape. With the lasting friendship of Philip Glass and Chuck Close as themes, and drawing from their signature use of "units" of color or sound, invite students to create. Possibilities include creating an autobiographical diamante, interviewing a peer to create a portrait, conducting searches to inform a portrait of someone famous, and perhaps grouping all together to contemplate how the collective whole is greater than the sum of the parts.

Students might also explore painting and composition "in the style of" Close and Glass.

Consider these questions:

- Why do artists impose limitations on their work to fuel their creative inspiration?
- How do artists overcome personal hardships to find new means of personal expression?
- What responsibility do creators carry as they represent someone's image, character, or identity in an artistic medium?

"You Can Paint the World You See"—Following the Path of Cross-Arts Inspirations

In her autobiography, the iconic painter Georgia O'Keeffe recounted hearing music pouring from the art studio of one of her mentors, Alon Bement, at Columbia University. At that time, art instruction was based on learning to paint by copying from the masters, a practice that Bement disdained. Instead, he encouraged students' originality, an idea in line with the more progressive educational philosophies emerging at the time. In his classroom, students drew while listening to music, which O'Keeffe said, "gave me an idea that I was very interested to follow later—the idea that music could be translated into something for the eye" (O'Keeffe, 1976, p. 14). O'Keeffe is frequently associated with other modernist painters in the early decades of the twentieth century who were also captivated by the notion that art could break free from representation by emulating music. Like Joseph Stella, Arthur Dove, Marsden Hartley, and Piet Mondrian, O'Keeffe experimented with translating the abstraction of musical sound into visual form.

During this same period, O'Keeffe read Wassily Kandinsky's *Concerning the Spiritual in Art*, which no doubt intensified her interests in exploring this relationship. Kandinsky's musical metaphor, widely quoted, describes the effect of color to evoke spiritual power:

Color is a power which directly influences the soul. Color is the keyboard, the eyes are the hammers, the soul is the piano with many strings. The artist is the hand which plays, touching one key or another, to cause vibrations in the soul. (Kandinsky, 1914/1977, p. 25)

Kandinsky's observation that "the arts are encroaching upon one another, and from a proper use of this encroachment will rise the art that is truly monumental" offered a challenge to which O'Keeffe responded (p. 20). She painted *Blue and Green Music* and *Pink and Blue I* and *II*, some of the first oil paintings in her career, using sinuous shapes and conversations of color.

Just as O'Keeffe played within the creative space of this "encroachment," many composers have created works for all kinds of performers and ensembles stimulated by O'Keeffe's paintings, both from her musically invoked paintings of the early years and from the large body of exuberant florals and luminescent scenes from the desert Southwest that characterize her life's work. What compels composers and songwriters to pay musical tributes to O'Keeffe? Composers' notes provide a window on these fertile pairings:[10]

Libby Larsen composed *Black Birds, Red Hills: A Portrait of Six Paintings of Georgia O'Keeffe* for viola, clarinet, and piano.

PAUSE to locate a recording of Larsen's *Black Birds, Red Hills*.

Larsen explores the "V shape of the hills outside O'Keeffe's window" in two movements, as well as the rocks and birds as metaphors for the passing of time.[11] She describes O'Keeffe's style "as lines that never go from point to point but flow infinitely" [as] "lines and sounds often come out of infinity only to return" (Larsen, as cited in Scott, 2010, p. 79).

Kevin Puts drew on O'Keeffe's writings by using her correspondence with photographer, mentor, and husband Alfred Stieglitz over their years of physical separation (O'Keeffe in New Mexico, Stieglitz in New York) for his orchestral song cycle, "The Brightness of Light." The piece was composed for the soprano Renée Fleming, singing excerpts from the letters as O'Keeffe, with baritone Rodney Gilfrey singing as Stieglitz. Puts was captivated by their nearly poetic exchanges, the title taken from a quote of O'Keeffe's that catalyzed the project: "My first memory is of the brightness of light, light all around."[12]

Flights of Compositional Inspiration: Opportunities for Engagement

PAUSE to view Georgia O'Keeffe's *Red Hills and Bones*.

Imagine how her life, art, and visual language translates into other art forms. Consider what you would draw across into creative work of your own.

Red Hills and Bones, from O'Keeffe's years in her beloved New Mexico, highlights one of her most familiar visual motives, a skull, set in the foreground against an undulating landscape (Figure 6.8). Biographer Roxana Robinson describes how O'Keeffe

> set the bones of the body in splendid juxtaposition to the landscape, the gentle curves of the hills echoing the rounded contours of the bones. In *Red Hills and Bones* of 1941, a long thighbone and a set of vertebrae lie in the foreground against a background of hot rust-red hills. The narrow, jagged spaces between the vertebrae are echoed by the irregular crease in the hillside. The formal repetition, the tonal similarities, the long, sleek silhouettes, and the smooth, smooth textures all insist on the deep affinity between the two entities. (2021, p. 457)

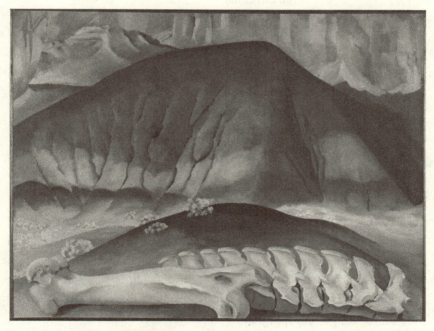

Figure 6.8 Georgia O'Keeffe, *Red Hills and Bones*
The Philadelphia Museum of Art / Art Resource, NY

PAUSE to pivot to Laura Kasischke's poetic response to *Red Hills and Bones*. What themes might be evoked in words after spending time with the painting?

Red Hills and Bones
Laura Kasischke

Where there are flowers, everything becomes a flower.
Without water, everything turns to water—the hills

are red water stirred by a hand, and will
always be. Bright light in the dull bones,
    Like
    the ladder
    of a spine
    laid down
    in the desert.
    You can climb

to the world you want. You can paint the world you see.

PAUSE to sketch out ideas for composition. Contemplate how artists use creative metaphors for translating ideas from one artistic medium to another. What might be explored—the curves of hills and bones? A wash of sound as a luminous background against crisp ladder-like figures in the foreground? Expansiveness? "Bright light in the dull bones?"

Consider these questions:

- What circumstances in educational settings, just as O'Keeffe heard music pouring from the studio of art professor Alon Bement, result in opportunities for students to pursue their fascinations?
- What artistic processes are involved in drawing inspiration from one art form to another? How does learning about this source of creativity spark interest in developing this way of looking at the world?
- Why are so many composers taken with the paintings of Georgia O'Keeffe?

A Group Profile as a Constellation of Connections

The basic premises undergirding the triptych strategy are straightforward: juxtapose works in multiple art forms based on their connections, whether shared themes, contexts, forms and elements, or expressive characteristics. Study these relationships. Set up an aesthetic puzzle of sorts by finding a gap to be filled. Create something—an interpretation, a description, a new work—that builds on and expands the relationships and fills the gap. The flexibility offered by this last "move" is nearly limitless. Although this chapter highlights groups of three works, the number of works can easily shift from two (a diptych) to four (a tetraptych) or any multi-section or multi-work grouping (a polyptych).

I have been inspired by the imaginative curricular projects that music teachers have designed using these premises as a springboard, translating them into vibrant explorations for elementary, middle, high school, and college students, and in general music, band, orchestra, choral, or other settings. One group of graduate students, primarily music teachers in a master's program, offered their ideas in the form of a state conference presentation titled "A Constellation of Curricular Explorations," showcasing their projects for other teachers.

The session began with a projection of stars: *Consider the lure of the night sky, the endless field of stars. Recall the magic when you first discovered—or someone explained to you—that stars could be traced in the patterns and shapes we call constellations. Orion, the hunter in the southern winter sky, can be located by finding the three stars that constitute his belt, which point to bright Sirius, the dog star. The imaginary lines that connect the stars form these shapes as we orient ourselves from our earth-bound positions to the night sky.*

Like the stars, endless possibilities can be explored in our music classrooms. The recognizable works we perform, study, and experience provide reference points for experience, but as teachers, we do not often know what invisible lines students draw to other realms of their personal and educational experience. We offer examples for you to consider that make those invisible lines visible, that welcome students to share the connections they bring their musical encounters.

The teacher/presenters distributed sticky notes to the participants, inviting them to add their own connections to large posters that lined the hall—one poster for each "lightning talk." At the end of the presentation, the teachers chose several of these "glimmering ideas" for comments. A brief description of these presentations conveys how the music teachers expanded on the basic idea of the triptych strategy to craft their own curricular projects:

- Graham Heise programmed Mussorgsky's "Gopak" from *The Fair at Sorochyntsi* for band, showing video of Russian dancers leaping across the stage to predict what the piece might sound like before ever playing through it. Citing Aaron Copland's exhortation that "What [the composer] desires above all is to encourage you to become as completely conscious and wide awake a listener as can possibly be developed,"[13] he spoke to the power of dance as central to this engagement.
- Rachel Palmer engaged orchestra students in playing "Ashokan Farewell," tied intimately to the Civil War through its use in Ken Burns's documentary. She asked students to read the letter of Sullivan Ballou, a heart-wrenching missive of a soldier writing to his spouse from the front lines, while also inviting them to question the provenance of the tune, which was written for a summer fiddle and dance camp in the 1980s, as a preface to studying songs from the Civil War era.
- Julianna Karvelius suggested alignments with English departments in her project based on Brian Balmages's "Nevermore," inspired by "The Raven" of Edgar Allan Poe. Her students composed their own pieces, thinking about the intensity, repetition of themes, and overall tone of Poe's writing.
- Paul Meiste began with "Acrostic Song" by David Del Tredici, based on Lewis Carroll's *Alice in Wonderland*, the acrostic poem itself, "Alice Pleasance Liddell," and unexpectedly, Salvador Dali's *Down the Rabbit Hole*, to add an unexpected twist to the project.
- *River Valley Serenade* by Patrick Wilson was the impetus for Melissa Plaskota's project for middle school students inviting them to determine just what is meant by the concept "folk music," and how the narratives of folk songs, such as "Shenandoah," "Red River Valley," and "The Water Is Wide," can be told in musical form through arrangements.

As each presenter shared their projects and described some of the rich insights their students learned through the process, participants in the session began to fill the posters with connections of their own. An all-too-brief session lit up with a galaxy of ideas. Later, in reflecting on this project, the music teachers spoke about shifts in their curricular approaches prompted by this work. Julianna shared that the connective potential of repertoire is now a primary criterion for selection for her band. Paul's students told him how they appreciated the change from the typical routine and the chance to share their insights about the art works and current events. Melissa was inspired to reframe her approach to planning, centering students' engagement and creativity. Rachel discovered the value of slowing down to foster deeper understanding.

Through projects such as these, alongside countless other curricular inspirations, I imagine students' "invisible lines" coming into focus, their rich associations and funds of knowledge made visible. Music educators' curricular imagination awaits these avenues for the pursuit of relational knowledge as webs of connections connect music, art, and poetry to life experiences in multiple dimensions. Some of these connections come into view by studying the works and their histories, but many more fall into place through the intricate weavings of sense and meaning that individuals bring as interpretations develop. The elastic generosity of the triptych strategy invites playful searches and thoughtful odysseys of learning.

7
Bridges of Inspiration
Synergy between Music and Art

The family of human expression known collectively as the arts has many members, and to extend the familial metaphor, has sometimes been called the "sister arts," although "cousins" might be a better substitute. Traditionally, music, painting, sculpture, dance, and architecture have been prominent, while also welcoming film, videography, photography, and literary arts into the fold. In twenty-first-century terms, we might add performance art, digital art, and a host of other blended forms, which intermingle in new generations of expression thanks to the boundlessness of the human imagination.

Although membership in this family expands and contracts depending upon the time, place, and purpose, music and art nearly always feature prominently in the family portrait. They share some fascinating bonds. One remarkable example is the phenomenon of *synaesthesia*, a "union of the senses" described generically as when a stimulus of one perceptual sense triggers a reaction in another unstimulated sense (Curwen, 2018, p. 94). Curwen notes that synaesthesia is rare, occurring in "approximately four percent of the population." There are many types of synaesthesia, among them *chromaesthesia*, the "phenomenon of seeing color when one hears certain sounds" (Strick, 2005, p. 15). Also called "color hearing," this capacity leads persons to associate certain colors with particular keys, tonalities, or timbres, and sometimes even composers' styles. I first learned about synthaesthesia when performing Scriabin's *Prometheus*, singing with the chorus behind a scrim on which colors—specified by the composer—were projected. Dutton (2015) reports that many musicians claim to experience this association between sound and color, including Pharrell Williams, Mary J. Blige, Lady Gaga, and Tyshawn Sorey.

In 2005, the Smithsonian Institution mounted an exhibition, "Visual Music," which explored chromaesthesia as well as the work of visual artists who emulated the abstract and spiritual qualities of music in their work. The exhibit featured installation art, digital projections, keyboard instruments that played colors, and other captivating pairings. The animating purpose was to "trace the history of a revolutionary idea: that fine art should attain the nonrepresentational aspects of music" (Rifkin & Strick, 2005, p. 7). Artists I expected to encounter were represented—Wassily Kandinsky, Paul Klee, Piet Mondrian, Georgia O'Keeffe, Arthur Dove—while others were new to me—Stanton Macdonald-Wright, František Kupka, Mikalojus Konstantinas Čiurlionis. These artists were compelled by similarities and differences between art and music, seeking to escape visual art's representational forms for more abstract means of expression as in music. Kandinsky's impression in 1914 that the arts were approaching one another seemed just as relevant in the twenty-first century as it was at the beginning of the twentieth. Wandering through the exhibit made me dizzy with ideas for cross-arts exploration.

In school settings, I have traced at least seven different purposes for bringing art and music into the curriculum as complementary pairs (Barrett, 2006b). Unsurprisingly, incidental mentions, such as the use of art as an illustration in music books, are most common. Music teachers often use drawing while listening to music as an opening for students' free expression. During the 1970s and 1980s, general music courses often featured lessons associated with a curricular movement called the *related arts*. Music textbooks contained lessons that focused on shared elements such as texture, variation, repetition and contrast, and other parallels. As one example, the preface to the *Silver Burdett Music* series offered a rationale: "The purpose of the lesson is to show how that quality or process operates distinctively in each art. The focus is always on the unique way each art uses that particularly aesthetic quality" (Crook et al., 1978, p. xi). The use of music as subject matter in art by including portraits of musicians or representations of musical events or symbols is another pattern.

Perhaps less frequently, visual art has been used as the impetus for creative expression in music through composition and improvisation, paralleling the same impulses found in contemporary artists' communities. Occasionally the curriculum addresses the specific study of notable artists and musicians inspiring one another's work through shared friendships, collaborations, and large-scale projects. Of particular interest in this chapter are educational experiences centered on works that "cross over"—art inspired by music and music inspired by art.

Crossing the Bridge of Inspiration

Consider the bridge of inspiration that travels from music to art and back again. What carries across from one art form to another in fueling the creative process? This impulse, *ekphrasis*, is commonly described as the "verbal representation of a visual representation." Keats's classic poem, "Ode on a Grecian Urn," is frequently cited as an illustrative example of an ekphrastic work in which a poetic text honors an art object. The poem captures both a description of the object, musings about its creation, and insights about broad phenomena such as beauty. Ekphrasis frequently refers to verbal description of a visual image in this classical sense.

Although the origins of the term refer most often to poetry, Bruhn (2000) applies the notion of ekphrasis more broadly, encompassing music as well as photography, film, dance, and even mime. In this expanded view, an artist re-presents or captures some aspects of one art form in another by using one medium to pay tribute to the other. This bridge of inspiration spanning art forms is particularly applicable to the fertile collaboration of visual art and music. Bruhn describes *musical ekphrasis*, distinguishing the concept from program music, in that it "narrates or paints stories or scenes created by an artist *other* than the composer of the music and in another artistic medium" (p. 554).

Many fruitful questions spring to mind once you start recognizing examples of this artistic interplay. What captures the imagination of artists, composers, or poets when they land upon a work from another artistic medium as their inspiration? As they create, what elements or ideas from one medium carry across to the other? Does this "carrying across" make any difference in the way we respond to a musical work inspired by another artistic medium? What could we learn as teachers/composers ourselves about this ekphrastic process in order to create playful, meaningful educational experiences for our students?

Perhaps a good starting place is to position yourself on the lookout for bridge-crossers. In the early twentieth century, the composer Arnold Schoenberg and artist Wassily Kandinsky infused their friendship with these "crossover" tendencies. Schoenberg created paintings and Kandinsky musical compositions so they would be able to talk to one another across their art forms and correspond about their means of expression. Kandinsky wrote about the rich possibilities of juxtaposing the arts, noting how they complement one another but also enhance their distinctive ways of expressing artistic ideas:

> At different points along the road are the different arts, saying what they are best able to say, and in the language which is peculiarly their own. Despite, or perhaps thanks to, the differences between them, there has never been a time when the arts approached each other more nearly than they do today. (Kandinsky, 1914/1977, p. 19)

Kandinsky's statement at that time of early modernism reflected a surge of interest from artists who strove to propel visual art toward the abstraction that music affords. Numerous examples can be found in the work of the painters Arthur Dove, Georgia O'Keeffe, Marsden Hartley, and Piet Mondrian, as they were drawn to music's non-representational character. Composers, including Claude Debussy, Duke Ellington, and Igor Stravinsky, were in turn inspired by art. In the mid-century, a creative colony at Black Mountain College sprang up, placing artists Josef Albers, Jasper Johns, and Robert Rauschenberg in creative juxtaposition with John Cage. Peter Vergo's *The Music of Painting* (2010) is a treasury of examples, insights, and potential avenues for curricular development, as is a discography compiled by Gary Evans, *Music Inspired by Art* (2002).

These artifacts of imagination—compositions and paintings in particular—create a provocative zone for expanding perceptive and responsive capacities in the arts. In addition, just as artists and composers have been inspired to move across one form to another, this pairing can prompt artistic production and creation. Creating a zone for this sort of artistic mash-up in school settings motivates interdisciplinarians to action.

An Exploration Both Deep and Wide

In Chapter 6, the triptych strategy highlighted multiple artists, multiple works, and numerous triptych groupings. In contrast, the remainder of this chapter delves more deeply into the astonishing curiosity and prodigious output of one particular artist, Paul Klee,[1] and his affinity for music. This artist's works have captivated my attention for decades as well as the curricular imagination of music teachers who have explored his oeuvre. First,

I provide a brief introduction to Klee's life (1879–1940) and work. This serves as a preface to a comprehensive curriculum project that illustrates pedagogical principles described in Chapter 5. I encourage readers to sample ideas liberally from this project. Although it is presented in a sequence, the content, strategies, and ideas for assessment could be rearranged in many configurations and for many classroom contexts. My aim is to illustrate a pedagogy of connections in extended form.

Panoramic Excursions Inspired by Klee

Paul Klee's art was heavily influenced by his own musical interests. He might well be considered as one of the most musical painters of the twentieth century. Klee's relationship to music has been the source of numerous scholarly investigations (Düchting, 1997; Kagan, 1983; Vergo, 2010; Weber, 2009). Similarly, his paintings have served as an inspirational springboard for many composers. Evans lists eighty-six composers who have drawn upon Klee's paintings in his discography of music inspired by art (2002).

One particular work, *The Twittering Machine*, an image of birds on a wire suspended over a pit or a platform, appears on Evans's list sixteen times, and certainly there are more recent examples than those Evans noted. Klee was inspired by his appreciation of Bach and Mozart to develop theories of art pedagogy using music's abstract qualities as he challenged his students to develop their practices of visual representation. He wrote in his diary, "Mozart and Bach are more modern than the nineteenth century" (Klee, 1964, p. 374). He developed artistic manifestations of musical rhythm (the layers of which he termed *dividual* and *individual* rhythms, corresponding roughly to metric and figural patterns), form (counterpoint and fugue), and harmonic/textural layering (what he called "visual polyphony"). These relationships are addressed in Klee's lecture notes from the Bauhaus, the famous German art school that served as an incubator for modern design. Once a musician knows about the way that music served as a driving force for Klee, these visual analogues to sound influence interpretation of works such as *Highway and Byways*, *Fugue in Red*, and *Ad Parnassum* (Düchting, 1997). Untangling these intriguing relationships between art and music brings us to an experience of Klee's art, and the musical reverberations that inspired its subject matter.

A Starting Place for Exploring Art and Music through the Work of Klee

Take a journey through three encounters with art works. First, consider two of Klee's paintings: *Rose Garden* and *Highway and Byways*.

> PAUSE to access Klee's *Rose Garden* (*Rosengarten*, 1920).
> PAUSE to access Klee's *Highway and Byways* (*Hauptweg und Nebenwege*, 1929).

View these two paintings and note the ways you perceive and respond to these works during your first encounter with them. Mindful engagement with the paintings will underscore essential points, so you are encouraged to make note of ideas that come to you during each of the three encounters that follow.

First Encounter with *Rose Garden* (1920) and *Highway and Byways* (1929)

The title *Rose Garden* draws our attention immediately to the swirling floral figures on leafless stalks scattered throughout the painting. These stand in contrast to the geometric rectangles and triangles that evoke a landscape of buildings rather than vegetation. Triangular shapes create tension in the center of the painting as the tower-like images advance and recede along diagonal lines. *Highway and Byways* seems less representational as horizontal and vertical planes intersect to form rectangles of varied sizes. The eye is drawn to the central vertical column of graduated lengths that stops just short of the horizon near the top of the painting. Curved lines and diagonals stand in contrast on either side of the center path. Subtle gradations of color create rhythmic patterns of pink, green, blue, and yellow. Which elements and features of the paintings did you describe in your first encounter?

Klee's art holds special interest for musicians given his lifelong involvement in musical performance and analysis. Music formed a central motive throughout his life; Klee's father was a music professor and his mother a singer. Before he settled on painting, he played violin in the Berne Municipal Orchestra and continued performing in chamber groups as an adult. His wife, Lily Strumpf, taught piano to support the couple. Throughout his prodigious career (it is estimated that he created nearly 10,000 works), he was fascinated by the relationships of music and visual art, often drawing upon musical ideas in painting. His diaries and pedagogical writings give plentiful evidence of his fascination with music and its workings (Düchting, 1997; Kagan, 1983; Weber, 2009). Klee believed that music had already reached its most sophisticated expression during the Baroque and Classical eras; reportedly, he had little interest in the contemporary musical output of his time. A caricature Klee made in 1909 reveals what he thought of Bruckner, Wagner, Mahler, and Richard Strauss. He provocatively titled it *Pianist in Distress—A Satire: Caricature of Modern Music*. Take note of the ways he provides visual commentary on this music!

> PAUSE to access Klee's *Pianist in Distress—A Satire: Caricature of Modern Music* (1909).

In this watercolor, Klee takes aim at what he thought was the unintelligible sound of contemporary music, preferring instead the balanced forms of earlier composers. Klee sought to capture in visual images the contrapuntal and polyphonic interplay of textures, rhythms, and melodic lines that he found most satisfying. Knowing what Klee thought of his musical contemporaries and knowing his preference for the forms and characteristics of Baroque and Classical styles, examine the two featured paintings again, this time speculating on the ways that the paintings might parallel musical works or concepts.

> PAUSE again to access Klee's *Rose Garden* (1920).
> PAUSE again to access Klee's *Highway and Byways* (1929).
> What parallels to music do you notice?

Klee often used music as a metaphor for painting. Many of his paintings have musical titles, such as *Fugue in Red* (1921), *Nocturne for Horn* (1921), and *Polyphonic Setting in White* (1930). In his lecture notes from the Bauhaus in Weimar, he mapped out rhythmic and melodic relationships to illustrate principles of visual design. Düchting describes how throughout his lectures for young painters:

> Klee investigated the structure of musical compositions.... In [this excerpt from his lecture notes], Klee focuses on two bars taken from a section of

Bach's sonata no. VI in G major for violin and piano, scored for three parts. Below the musical notes, he mapped out a graphical system for registering the pitch of the notes over three octaves. (Düchting, 1997, p. 35)[2]

Klee developed a theory of rhythm that distinguished between what he called "dividual" components (what we might think of as metric figures) and "individual" rhythms (melodic or figural rhythms), seeking to translate their rhythmic functions to the picture plane. He was especially interested in thinking about the interplay of rhythmic layers through what he called "*cardinal progress* by dividing vertical fields into two halves, four quarters, eight eighths, sixteen sixteenths" (Düchting, p. 43).

Aware of Klee's intention to represent rhythmic relationships in spatial form and knowing that he held Bach and Mozart as the pinnacle of musical achievement, return to the paintings once more. This time, however, find a recording, or play or recall a Bach piece as you study the paintings. I have paired the First Invention in C Major from the Two-Part Inventions with *Rose Garden* and a recording of Sonata in G Major No. 6 for Violin and Harpsichord (first movement) with *Highway and Byways*.

PAUSE a third time to access Klee's *Rose Garden* (1920) while listening to Bach.
PAUSE a third time to access Klee's *Highway and Byways* (1929) while listening to Bach.

In what ways does knowledge about Klee's involvement in music and his explicit use of musical elements as a source of ideas carry across as you view *Rose Garden* and *Highway and Byways* while listening to Bach? Although there is no specific historical evidence that Klee was influenced by any particular musical work of Bach for these two paintings, there is plentiful evidence that he was intrigued by the challenge of representing musical relationships in visual forms. Knowing that Klee was interested in how the picture plane could be divided and subdivided into parts that were analogous to the divisions and subdivisions of rhythm changes our focus as listeners and perceivers. The interplay of the metrical underpinnings with the foreground of the melodic rhythm invites us to shift fields of attention from one to the other as we view the painting while simultaneously listening to the rhythmic figures and metrical organization of Bach. Other musical and visual relationships may become apparent, such as perceiving the rose figures as the ornamented pitches in an otherwise scalar pattern or thinking about the texture of any given part of the painting or a line of music in relationship to the whole work. The crux is that knowledge of the artist's intentional use of musical elements as inspiration for the creation of a painting becomes an inviting avenue for understanding the work, and perhaps a bridge of inspiration for classroom encounters with a work. One might argue that this phenomenon would also be particularly informative for art educators who seek to broaden students' study of art technique and art history.

Inspiration can flow in the other direction just as easily—from art to music. This principle of reciprocity is best illustrated by another painting of Klee's, *Twittering Machine* of 1922 (Figure 7.1).[3]

One of Klee's most famous sayings (repeated frequently by art educators) was that "a line is a dot that goes for a walk." Here you see four birds outlined in angular profile in this whimsical painting (or is it whimsical at all)? Klee juxtaposes nature and the machine age through the handle, which we imagine produces a chorus of chirping when turned. Bruhn calls the painting "deceptively childlike and innocently witty at first glance" (2000, p. 362), before cautioning the viewer that other interpretations lurk in the shadows. Below the birds, for example, lurks peril or safety depending upon whether you view the pink rectangle as a yawning pit or a safe stage or platform to catch them should they fall.

Klee scholar Hugo Düchting must see the pink figure as a pit, given his interpretation:

In the famous *Twittering Machine*, the viewer is confronted with a bizarre visual joke not without tragic overtones. Operating the crank handle starts the "song" of mechanical birds, perched in a row like the notes of a musical scale. This song resounds in the infinity of cosmic space as a symbol for human, or animal, impotence against unknown cosmic forces. (Düchting, 1997, p. 54)

Music education scholar Jerry L. Jaccard, who shares Swiss heritage with Klee, reminded me of Swiss artistry in crafting complicated yet elegant mechanical devices, such as watches or music boxes featuring singing birds on a perch. From his perspective, the painting evokes a rather different interpretation:

Modern Switzerland is a conglomeration of languages, dialects and cultures. I was a volunteer in the Swiss National Olympic Team Office during the 2002 Winter Olympics here in Utah. The Swiss staff were always teasing each

BRIDGES OF INSPIRATION 143

Figure 7.1 Paul Klee, *The Twittering Machine*
© 2022 Artists Rights Society (ARS), New York

other that they couldn't understand each other's Swiss German dialects, so they spoke High German, French or English instead! I looked again at Klee's rendering to see if my hunch had any merit and indeed, I think it does. There are four birds in the Klee work, and there are four national languages in

144   SEEKING CONNECTIONS

Switzerland. Everything—money, stamps, official signs, tourist brochures, etc., is always printed in the four languages. So, a plausible interpretation of Klee's *Twittering Machine* is a joke about the complexities of living in a country with four languages. And he so cleverly uses the double metaphor of one of the machines for which Switzerland is so famous, the mechanical bird music box. (Personal communication with author)

Exploring multiple dimensions of the painting demonstrates how a work of art can call up a range of personal, social, historical, and political meanings in addition to its structure and origins. The *Twittering Machine*, with its mix of playful and portentous overtones, fascinates us with its ambiguous and fascinating meanings. Just as the multidimensional nature of musical works can be explored using the Facets Model, paintings, drawings, or sculptures can also be represented in this way. Figure 7.2 is a visual representation of

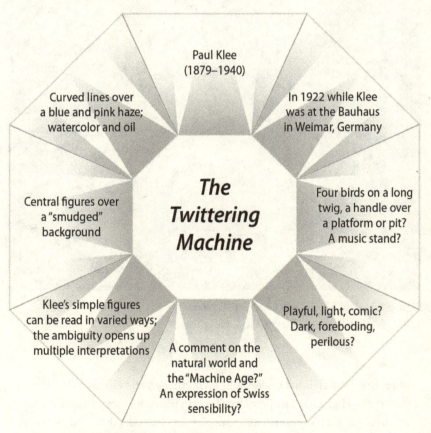

Figure 7.2   Facets Model: Paul Klee, *The Twittering Machine*

various dimensions of Klee's art work as a reminder that encountering a work from multiple dimensions may lead to curricular openings from many angles and perspectives.

Twittering Machine has also captured the attention of a host of composers, including Gunther Schuller, Tan Dun, Peter Maxwell Davies, Cindy McTee, Brian Balmages, and others. Studying Klee's painting while comparing how various composers have set the *Twittering Machine* to music could be an excellent exercise for cross-disciplinary analysis or the introductory premise for composition in the classroom.

From Art to Music: Cindy McTee

Cindy McTee composed *California Counterpoint: The Twittering Machine* for an accomplished wind ensemble. Rather than watercolor and ink on cardboard, McTee's materials are drawn from a palette of sounds—flute, oboe, clarinet, bassoon, horn, trumpet, tenor trombone, harp, piano, strings, and a host of percussion instruments. As you listen, keep the painting in mind, and speculate about the parallels between the artistic inspiration and McTee's lively work.

> PAUSE to listen to a recording of McTee's *California Counterpoint: The Twittering Machine*.

Very often, even when one artistic work has been inspired by another, we may not know which aspects inspired a composer to create an entirely new composition based on an encounter with a visual work. In McTee's case, however, we are fortunate in that she provided liner notes to unpack why she chose the title, and what she found compelling enough about the painting to take up the challenge of writing for symphonic wind ensemble. These notes allow us to consider what she saw and how she was moved to create:

> Klee's *Twittering Machine* is both a drawing and a painting of four birds perched on a crank shaft. The drawn images are whimsical, puppet-like, mechanistic, ironic, and playful, reflected by the faster sections of my composition. These are set against a lyrical field of transparent color, represented by the slower sections of my piece.
>
> I was especially drawn to the painting's biting humor; imagine what would happen to the birds if the crank shaft were turned! In my piece,

I make attempts at humor through the use of repeated structures and denied expectation—rhythms are displaced, passages are suddenly transposed or textures juxtaposed.

There are elements of danger in Klee's painting: arrows piercing some of the birds, a gaping hole or ditch the birds might fall into, and the presence of an exclamation mark which is a recurring symbol in Klee's work meant to suggest impending doom. The danger elements in my piece consist of many large silences, or musical holes, which the players risk falling into if they're not attentive.

Most important is my intention that the work, like Klee's *Twittering Machine*, convey movement—that it engage the body as well as the mind—that it dance! (McTee, 1993)

McTee's symphonic work is an example of musical ekphrasis; in these notes, she explains what she carried across from Klee's painting to her work for wind ensemble. Performers, conductors, and audiences gain access to her processes of noticing certain elements in the painting, wondering about their meanings, as she reveals interpretations that she subsequently realized in sonic form. Her realization, though, is not a copy of what she sees; instead, she playfully transmutes, or changes the spatial form of a painting into the temporal form of a musical work. Just as the Facets Model of Klee's painting is helpful, so might the diagram of McTee's work shown in Figure 7.3 lead to instructional possibilities for exploration.

Even when parallel works share a theme or rely upon the manipulation of image or sound in a similar way, disciplinary differences stand out. Fortunately *and* paradoxically, Klee's desire to push art to attain the abstract perfection of music, impossible to reach, also underscores why the spatial relationships of visual art are fundamentally different from the temporal relations of music. Including art that aspires to music helps students clarify the distinctive qualities of each form.

A Panoramic Curriculum Project Inspired by *The Twittering Machine*

A curriculum project illustrates the various ways that classroom experiences can be designed using these works and others as springboards for composition, perception, response, creative writing, and artistic exploration in

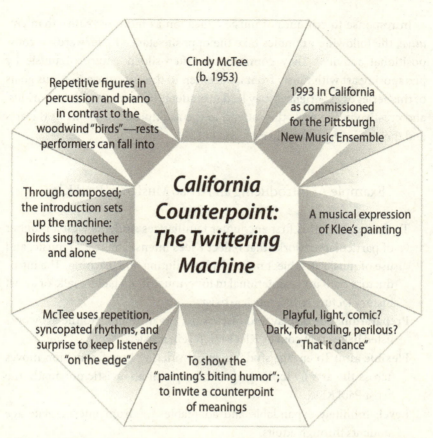

Figure 7.3 Facets Model, Cindy McTee, *California Counterpoint: The Twittering Machine*

general. Although readers may draw parallels to lesson plans and units, I have incorporated aspects of soft planning and more flexible design to encourage adaptation, modification, and creative curriculum-making in ways that may be of interest to teachers and students in many different settings and at many different ages. I think of Eisner's observation that "good curriculum materials both educate and emancipate teachers" (1990, p. 65). In that spirit, these examples have been used in a variety of contexts (workshops, conference presentations, university classes) and with students from elementary children through experienced teachers. The reader is encouraged to consider how they illustrate the rich interplay of music and art using the work of Paul Klee as the catalyst for design.

In response to critiques of music education as more *recreative* than *creative*, the following examples take the opposite stance by forwarding compositional activity.[4] They confront the often-siloed nature of music by juxtaposing art with music front and center. In this way, the ambitious goals of this series of experiences may lead to students who are confident, curious, and creative in the ways they attend to the multiple dimensions of the arts and their meanings in our lives.

Example A: Introducing an Artist/Musician, Paul Klee

To the teacher: This first encounter familiarizes students with a number of particular artworks that reflect Klee's intense interest in music, and use of music as subject matter in his painting and teaching. The introductory path is presentational in tone, much like a gallery talk, or an art history lecture with a musical twist.

Preparation: For display and discussion, organize links to the art works listed below that convey Klee's interest in music.

Flexible aim: To engage students in considering how fascination moves across the arts by looking at an example of an artistic polymath, the artist Paul Klee.

Level: Infinitely expandable and adaptable . . . from intermediate-age students through adults.

Entry Points
- For older students and adults, challenge them to think about persons who are recognized for their knowledge or expertise in more than one area, called a *polymath*. Who comes to mind? A "Renaissance person," such as Leonardo da Vinci, perhaps? For a polymath, interests in one area of curiosity may transfer to another. Ask students to name examples of well-known figures, such as actors who are painters, politicians who perform, and others. Include familiar persons in the immediate classroom context as well.
- Encourage students to reflect on their own areas of expertise when learning something new or creating something. *Have you ever found yourself using your skills and interest in one area to help you in another— athletic skills in dancing, for example, or mathematical skills in designing*

an object or the layout of a room? How does it feel to use your abilities in one area to solve problems or create something new in another?

Developing and Expanding

Introducing the artist. Paul Klee is known first and foremost as a visual artist, but he grew up in a Swiss household filled with music, studying the violin from an early age. He was also keenly interested in art and poetry and had a hard time deciding what path to pursue when it came time to choose. The photograph of Klee depicted in Figure 7.4 shows how he blended his passions together.

The string quartet is made up of art students, who used their easels as music stands. Paul Klee is on the right.[5]

In addition to this photograph, we have evidence of his delight in music in the way he used music as subject matter and titles in his paintings:[6]

Figure 7.4 Quintet in the Studio of Heinrich Knirr's Art School, Munich, 1900
Zentrum Paul Klee, Bern, Image Archive

- *Nocturne for Horn*, 1921.
- *In Bach's Style*, 1919 (featuring a fermata and other figures that resemble musical symbols).

Klee even tried to capture the distinctive sounds of musical forms and musical elements in painting. (Ask the students to guess these forms and support their answers):

- *Ad Parnassum*, 1932, an example of what he called "visual polyphony."
- *Fugue in Red*, 1921. (Play a few measures of Bach's "Little" Fugue in G minor).

He would have enjoyed the music that I paired with the *Fugue in Red*, since Bach was one of his favorite composers, perhaps next to Mozart. Klee had very strong opinions about the music that would have been more contemporary during his time (recall the nasty cartoon he drew to show what he thought of Mahler, Bruckner, Strauss, and Wagner).

- *Pianist in Distress: A Satire: Caricature of Modern Music*, 1909.[7]

Klee taught at a very famous German art school called the Bauhaus (first located in Weimar, then in Dessau). He kept all of his lecture notes, which were later published. Here are the notes he used to teach art students to think about musical relationships while painting. *Can you figure out what he is trying to teach?*

- Lecture notes from the Bauhaus to show the rhythmic relationships in Bach's Sonata no. VI in G Major for violin and piano.

Klee was explaining his theory about *dividual* and *individual* rhythms, which divide time into equal parts, like metric subdivisions, while also featuring melodic rhythms of short and long durations for the figural line of the music. Illustrate the difference by using musical examples the students already know.

As an experiment in perception, listen to a Bach two-part invention while you take a look at one of his works that suggests these rhythmic layers, *Highway and Byways*.

- *Highway and Byways*, paired with Bach's *Two-Part Invention in C Major*.

- Can you switch back and forth from listening to the "dividual" and "in-dividual" rhythmic layers as you look at the painting?

Reflecting and Synthesizing
Not all of Klee's paintings are this closely tied to music, especially since he created over 9,000 works in his life (and numbered them all)! Consider these questions, however:

- If you were to visit an art museum in which Klee's paintings from this period in his life were displayed, would your experience of the works shift, knowing about his interest in music?
- Why do you think that Klee was fascinated by Bach and Mozart more than the composers of his time?
- How would you approach changing sounds into images? What kinds of sounds would make the most interesting paintings, for example? Why?

Encourage students to pose other questions that come to mind after this introductory experience. What else would you like to know about Klee and his musical imagination?

Extending This Experience
- Invite students to locate examples of the music/art crossover. Look for historical and contemporary examples of individuals who enjoy the interplay of art and music.
- Encourage students who are similarly interested in several arts to describe their curiosities and to share examples with the class as they wish.

Assessing Student Responses
This introductory lesson is more a "lecture burst" than a more participatory experience, but look for student-initiated questions, connections to prior experiences with art or music, and particularly the quality of the discussion in the "reflecting and synthesizing" mode.

Example B: Interpreting *The Twittering Machine* (1922)

Preparation: Locate a reproduction of Klee's *Twittering Machine* to display.

Flexible aim: To engage students in constructing personal interpretations of Klee's *Twittering Machine*, as well as to inform them about the inspirations and curiosities that inspired Klee.

Level: Infinitely expandable and adaptable . . . from intermediate-age students through adults.

Entry Points
- If this lesson was preceded by the introduction to Paul Klee, ask students to compare notes in duos or trios on the ways that Paul Klee showed his interest in music through visual art. *What if the situation were flipped? How might visual art influence music? Can you think of examples?* (Mussorgsky's *Pictures at an Exhibition* may be a familiar example. Invite others.)
- This experience could easily be preceded by a focus on Mussorgsky's *Pictures*. Anna Harwell Celenza's book of the same name is useful as an introduction to the story of Victor Hartmann, Mussorgsky, and art critic Vladimir Stasov, and how the multi-movement composition was created (Celenza, 2016).

Developing and Expanding

Today, if we have a conversation about twittering, you are likely to pull out your cell phones. The focus of today's exploration is about twittering of a different sort . . . this art work by Paul Klee called *The Twittering Machine* (*Die Zwitscher-Maschine* in German). As I show it to you, first take a good long look [take time before proceeding].

- Let's take turns asking questions that describe the painting (later, we'll think about what it might mean and how it feels to us—the questions listed here are suggestions). *What do you notice?* (Encourage questions about lines, shapes, colors, figures). Look closely at the birds and describe each one. Look closely at the wire mechanism and describe it. Describe the muted colors of the background.
- Can you pose some questions that will pique our curiosity about the art work [such as] *What is the figure that looks like a music stand or microphone stand? Might the pink rectangle resemble a pit or a platform? What differences do you notice from bird to bird? What would happen if we could turn the crank? What sounds do you think you would hear?*

- How does this painting feel to you? If you were to choose one word that captures this feeling, what would it be?
- What might this image be trying to convey? Can you think of any themes that come to mind for this art work? What other questions might we ask about this painting?

Inviting the Translation of the Image into Sound (a Pivot to Composition)
- Just as Klee drew inspiration from music when he was painting, other composers have drawn inspiration from *Twittering Machine* to improvise or compose pieces for soloists, small groups, and large groups.
- Take a moment to jot down three to five ideas as you look at *Twittering Machine* and imagine possibilities for creating some music. What kind of timbres would you choose? How might these distinctive sounds convey the mood or expressive feeling of Klee's work? What could you do to turn this source of inspiration into sound?
- Would it be possible to convey something unexpected about the painting through sound? Ask for questions. Sketch your ideas.

Reflecting and Synthesizing
As you think about this invitation to compose, invite students to noodle around to prompt an entire range of ideas before settling in on a particular plan. Students may compose individually or in groups after capturing some preliminary ideas for the next compositional puzzle.

Extending This Experience
Gather up multiple interpretations of this art work from art historians and others to distribute.[8] Choose a few to read aloud. What do these excerpts tell you about the way that the writer is interpreting the work?

Assessing Student Learning
- The ways that students describe the art work will demonstrate how closely they are perceiving the various dimensions of the work. Listen for the vocabulary they use. Notice their descriptive nuances.
- Listen for the extensiveness of ideas among the students' interpretations. Can they articulate multiple perspectives on the work?
- When students pose questions about the composition exercise, listen for evidence of their imaginative scope of ideas. Encourage playfulness, fluency of ideas.[9]

Example C: Compose Your Own *Twittering Machine*

Preparation: Invite the use of classroom instruments, the students' own instruments, voices, found sounds. Gather up multiple reproductions of Klee's *Twittering Machine*, particularly if student groups spread out to nearby spaces or practice rooms for the composition exercise.

Flexible aim: To work with the artistic process of turning ideas and images into sound through composition; to express multiple interpretations of a painting through group discussion as they present their creative resolution of the artistic problem.

Level: Infinitely expandable and adaptable . . . from intermediate-age students through adults.

Entry points: Draw attention again to Klee's painting *The Twittering Machine*, reviewing some of the qualities that students noticed previously. Spend a little time thinking about why this painting is of interest to composers, perhaps because of some of the paradoxical contradictions or tensions that it evokes (humankind vs. nature; optimism vs. pessimism; anxiety about the Machine Age and fears that machines will take over, etc.).

Set up the composition task:

- Review your notes from yesterday about the creative ideas you generated to turn this painting into sound. As you get into groups, spend some time playing around with these ideas before you settle on an interpretive path to develop into a composition. Make use of instruments, voices, found sounds. Audition many different possibilities.
- Create a two-minute composition with a clear beginning, middle, and end. *Will you represent some bird sounds and some machine sounds in your composition?*
- As you work through the possibilities, make note of your compositional decisions so that you can explain them to others later.
- Take plenty of time to develop and refine your ideas until you are satisfied with your composition. If it helps you to write down these ideas in some fashion, please do so. You can also record your ideas in progress so that you can capture your compositional drafts that way as well.[10]
- Set expectations for the time students will have to work in groups (either on one day or over multiple work sessions depending upon the circumstances).

Developing and Expanding
As individuals or groups work on this compositional task, make yourself available for assistance and clarification as needed.

Presenting ideas: When it is time to students to share their compositions in progress, prompt others to notice the qualities that the composers highlight in their Twittering pieces. Ask composers to describe their decision-making processes and what they most wanted to convey in sound.

Reflecting and Synthesizing
Questions such as these can be used for individual writing or group discussion:

- How did you draw inspiration from one art form—painting—to create a work in another art form—music? What ideas did you most want to carry across?
- As you listened to other creative realizations of this Twittering puzzle, what did you learn about the variety of ways that this puzzle can be "solved?"

Extending This Experience
Depending upon the interests of the group, explore other compositions inspired by *The Twittering Machine*. Now that the students have had a chance to think through their creative processes in this lesson, they may be more curious about how other composers have set up similar tasks for themselves.[11]

- Consider Cindy McTee's *California Counterpoint: The Twittering Machine* for wind ensemble, and her program notes that speak directly to her inspiration and intentions.
- Brian Balmages has written a work for school bands, *Twittering Machine*, commissioned by middle school instrumental educator Chris Gleason, of Patrick Marsh Middle School in Sun Prairie, Wisconsin. In 2009, Gleason launched an ongoing project, *ComMission Possible*, for engaging contemporary composers to write specifically for his middle school band. The middle school students created projects prompted by this collaboration with Balmages, including contemporary dances, historical interpretations, and even animations in the style of a video game.
- Elementary school students have also composed their own versions of *Twittering Machine* using classroom instruments, voices, and movement. For one group, I simplified the task further for students who were

compositional novices by asking them to create rhythmic machines while I provided bird sounds (whistling, vocally, or playing a soprano recorder).

Assessing Student Learning
- Record the presentation of the compositions or compositional drafts. What do these convey about students' imaginative use of their musical materials, elements, and the organization of sound to convey their ideas?
- Consider making notes on students' compositional processes so that you can identity any recurring stumbling blocks or difficulties they encounter.
- If students write program notes, collect these to look for ways that they articulate qualities in the painting that they are representing in sound. What do these writing samples tell you about their creative intentions, and their knowledge of Klee's life and painting?
- Record the group discussion after the presentation of ideas, or collect student writing, to examine responses to the synthesis questions.

Example D: Beyond Twittering...

To the teacher: The intent of this lesson is to provide further choice and continued practice in composing to art works. This lesson refers to the introduction of Paul Klee in the opening, using his fascination with capturing musical elements in visual form as a different example from *Twittering*. This new example will serve as the springboard to a second round of composition in which students will choose their own paintings, investigate their history and characteristics, and express a greater range of creative ideas and interpretations.

Preparation: Provide websites that offer high-quality reproductions of Klee's paintings, or if available, gather books and reference materials with reproductions. Again, provide classroom instruments; encourage the students' own instruments, voices, found sounds.

Flexible aim: To examine a composition based on Klee's *Highway and Byways* that utilizes multiple rhythmic durations and overlapping phrases inspired by his theory of *dividual* and *individual rhythms*. This speech piece is the entry point for students to launch out in multiple directions to choose their own paintings and develop compositions according to those choices.

Level: Infinitely expandable and adaptable . . . from intermediate-age students through adults.

Entry Point

Gather students close by so they can view the score for a speech piece, *Soundways* (Figure 7.5). Follow this sequence for the performance directions, which uses 5 groups and a soloist:

- Ask the entire group to chant the line "fragment, fragment, tidbit, tidbit" in steady rhythm. Once this is established, assign the line to a small group to repeat throughout.
- Layer in the next two repeating lines: "o-ver-lap-ping" and "lap-ping o-ver" following the displacement suggested by the score—again assigning each line to another group. Sustain the voice through the boxes to the next syllable.
- Add in "Far Horizons," emphasizing the syncopation.
- For the fifth group, "Continuous," practice repeating the phrase in a loop.
- Listen to the balance of the interlocking parts, adjusting register or timbre of each part for clarity, if necessary.
- Ask for a volunteer to realize the solo line, which involves speaking various words in whatever tempo and register and order the performer

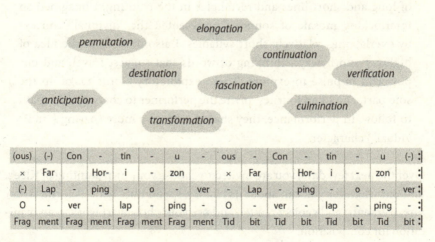

Figure 7.5 Soundways

chooses: "anticipation, permutation, destination, elongation, continuation, fascination, verification, culmination, transformation."
- Let the performers know that once the rhythmic underlayers are established, the soloist will begin. Invite the soloist to finish the piece in a dramatic way, signaling the entire group to watch for the ending. Rehearse and ask for students' ideas to make the speech piece as interesting as possible for listeners.
- Perform and enjoy! Generate alternate titles for this speech piece, as you wish.

Developing and Expanding
This piece was composed specifically to illustrate an idea that fascinated Paul Klee so much that he used it to instruct his art students at the Bauhaus in Weimar. Can anyone recall what idea this might be?

- Remember Klee's lecture notes (perhaps displaying them again), specifically playing with the idea of dividual and individual rhythms.
- Try locating these durational ideas in the painting *Highway and Byways*.

Could these be the composer's notes?[12]

My inspiration for this sound piece was Klee's *Highway and Byways*. Since Klee was intrigued by the interlocking layers of "dividual" and "individual" rhythms, which are represented in the interplay of long and short lines and rectangles in the painting, I imagined an interlocking mosaic of sound. I represented the "dividual" concept by overlapping relatively short syllables. I also drew from the idea of highway and byways, thinking of words that suggest travel, and our powerful impulse to explore. These exploratory words make up the solo part, and like a journey, invite the performer to choose which path to follow. In performance, they should take on a more soaring ("individual") character.

Over the next few days, you are invited to choose your own painting of Klee's, find out whatever you can about its history, spend time with its form, structure, elements, and subject matter, and use your chosen art work as an inspiration for composition.

Use the same processes that you drew upon to compose *Twittering Machine* to create your own distinctive composition and composer's notes for this new work.

After [several days], you will be asked to perform your piece, or find performers to perform it instead. You will also participate in a concert/exhibition of paintings and compositions, providing either a short lecture/demonstration or composer's notes to show how you moved across the bridge of inspiration from painting to sound.

A Repertoire of Possibilities for Reflecting and Synthesizing
As you think about this invitation to compose, remember to entertain many ideas before settling in on a particular plan. Choose others to compose with you, or work by yourself to create a solo based on the painting you chose.

Extending This Experience

- If students are interested in seeing additional examples of music inspired by art, consult triptychs from Chapter 6 or search online.

Assessing Student Learning
- The ways that students describe the art work will demonstrate how closely they are perceiving the various dimensions of the work. Listen for the vocabulary they use. Notice their descriptive nuances.
- Listen for the extensiveness of ideas among the students' interpretations. Can they articulate multiple perspectives on the work?
- When students pose questions about the composition exercise, listen for evidence of their imaginative scope of ideas. Encourage playfulness, fluency of ideas.

Example E: The Exhibition and Performances

To the teacher: This exhibition serves as the culmination of this entire sequence of experiences. Be sure to invite those who might be interested and informed by the work that students have produced and created.
Preparation: Make sure there is a suitably generous space to display the paintings (on easels, if you can find them) and performance spaces for

160   SEEKING CONNECTIONS

the individuals and groups, along with projection capabilities to display titles and composers' notes.

Flexible aim: The intent of this lesson is to showcase the myriad connections created through composition, interpretation of paintings, and composers' notes.

Level: Infinitely expandable and adaptable . . . from intermediate-age students through adults.

Starting Points

Thank composers and guests for their participation in this event and set up the process for exhibiting and performing:

- Introduce the members of your group, tell us the title and artist for your painting, the title of your composition (unless that gives away key surprises).
- Perform your composition.
- Ask participants what they noticed as they connected the music and the painting.
- Describe your intentions as your composers' notes are displayed.

Developing and Expanding

- Celebrate each group in sequence.

These questions may be useful to generate conversation:

- What relationships can you see and hear between the music and the painting?
- How are the two works similar? Different?
- Is there anything about the painting that echoes in the music?
- What are some of the most obvious relationships between the music and the painting? What are some more subtle relationships?
- What are some of the strongest connections between music and the painting? Do any relationships feel puzzling to you? Why?
- If you could ask the composers one question about their ideas, what would you ask?

A Repertoire of Possibilities for Reflecting and Synthesizing

Either on this same day, or on a subsequent day, share impressions of what was learned through this landscape of works. Encourage students to speak to one another about the ways that their compositions inspired new ways of thinking and feeling. Alternately, provide students with prompts for writing.

Assessing Student Learning
Across the entire project, consider the following:

- What evidence demonstrates that students have learned about the artists, contexts, works, and artistic dimensions of music and other related examples? Can you find evidence of the ways students have informed their work as they discuss, write about, or describe particular examples?
- What evidence demonstrates that students have gained skills in describing, interpreting, and evaluating works of art? In making new works through creative processes? Look for signs of their relational knowledge as they work within and across multiple art forms.
- What evidence demonstrates that students have formed personal understandings of art works and the connections to their lives? In what ways do they respond deeply to the affective dimensions of art works?
- How does this work point to the generative synthesis of multiple meanings students bring and take from this kind of exploration?
- In what ways might this exploration serve as an educationally vibrant experience?

Seeking Generative Impact

The lasting impact of this panoramic set of experiences, or others like it, can be seen in the way that students sustain and extend their curiosities beyond the boundaries of the experiences themselves. The generative power of interdisciplinary work, particularly in this context of creative affordances between music and art, may be seen in students' interest in interviewing composers about the ways they draw from disciplines outside of music as they compose, as they further their own compositional paths, and as they stay "on the lookout" for new sources of creative inspiration. In crossing back and forth from one art form to another, students may extend their artistic sensibilities as they develop greater understanding of the distinctive qualities of the arts, and their interplay in our lives.

8
Connecting Contexts
Music and History

I open this chapter with a paradox made apparent through personal reflection. Throughout my formal music education, history has remained mostly dormant as I have studied voice and piano, played oboe and sousaphone in bands, sung in choirs, and prepared to teach. With the exception of music history surveys and a few graduate courses, I cannot recall many instances when the origins of the music—its grounding in time and place, the composer's life, the events of the time, the sociocultural surrounds—were mentioned in more than perfunctory ways, often as an introduction to the primary goal of learning to perform the piece. It was as if "background information" surfaced briefly before quickly receding to the background again, leaving me with an odd free-floating sense of the past, untethered from any rooted insights that might make the music even more vivid or deepen its significance.

My formal study of US and world history, sadly confined to my elementary and secondary education, remained nearly free of music, or art, or literature, or any of the expressive streams of human activity that would have animated what seemed to me like a lengthy exposition of dates, figures, battles, and tallies of the victorious—the stuff of political history. In response to this instruction as a student inspired by the arts, I retreated to the background, keeping my distance from cultivating an interest in history until later when I came to realize what I had missed during my intellectual conversion to an interdisciplinary approach.

My educational history should not be held up as typical, but nonetheless, these insights lead me to question why these subject matters—so promising in their intersections—remain largely separated, their relationships underexplored. The "culprit" is not the subject area teachers or the schools I attended. Instead, I believe this gap can be explained by the very structures of schooling in which disciplines are separated, taught by subject matter specialists, and sequestered in courses and departments. In this chapter, I encourage disruption of these patterns, especially in pursuit of the benefits that

Seeking Connections. Janet Revell Barrett, Oxford University Press. © Oxford University Press 2023.
DOI: 10.1093/oso/9780197511275.003.0008

music, and the arts in general, bring to historical understanding, and that greater historical awareness can bring to the study of the arts. Viewing works contextually, *situating* them in time and place, and *relating* music to the social surrounds of the milieu, strengthens their capacity for communication and expression. I argue that these processes are inherently bound to music's significance in students' lives, rather than being incidental.

Urgency for bringing music and history in conversation with one another is palpable. At no time in recent memory have I witnessed more heated discussions and debates about the purposes of historical knowledge in schooling. I am reminded daily that the school subject we name as "history" is not settled and fixed, and that a more apt way to think of its multiple dimensions would be "histories" instead. In the 1990s, I followed the "history wars" that sprang up regarding the National History Standards and their rejection by the US Senate, which historian Jill Lepore attributes to a misguided perception by some legislators as "politics masquerading as history" (2012, p. 13). Fast-forward from that turbulent period to heated school board meetings in the 2020s related to spurious debates about Critical Race Theory and efforts to ban books related to diversity and racial justice. Ideological divisions have brought related curricular initiatives and the content of textbooks to the forefront of the nightly news. During this same period I have noticed a resurgence of interest in historical matters, perhaps ignited by the popularity of *Hamilton* among schoolteachers and the general public, catapulting the processes of teaching and learning history onto the public sphere. The music curriculum is inextricably linked to this groundswell of interest in history education and uprising of related controversies. Interdisciplinary work in this realm is needed now more than ever.

The aims of the chapter are twofold, aligning in large part with two cases of practice as prominent profiles of these complementary disciplines. The first illustrates how music is taught with its roots showing in a multidimensional way that implicates history. The case involves the story of a music educator whose interdisciplinary curriculum unit for students in an upper elementary classroom led to a lively examination of a song as an historical text. After addressing some of the implications from this case, some promising avenues from current initiatives in social studies and history education are described. The second case highlights the role of music in constructing historical understanding in performance settings, here as experienced by the members of a university orchestra and a large symphonic choir. This case highlights the benefits of opening music study to a gallery of historical sources integrally related to the work at hand. The two profiles, or curricular case studies, bring to light key issues through music teachers' practices.

Follow the Drinking Gourd: Questioning Historical Accounts of Music in Children's Literature

Examine lists of children's books frequently used to inspire elementary school curriculum projects involving music and you will likely see Jeanette Winter's *Follow the Drinking Gourd*, widely praised as a "fine rendering of history in picture book format."[1] The book intersperses the lyrics of the song within a story about Peg Leg Joe, an "old sailor who did what he could to free the slaves" (Winter, 1988, n.p.). Peg Leg Joe teaches the song to Molly and James, enslaved persons who hear a quail calling in the night as a sign to set out with their extended family on a perilous route to escape, using the North Star and the Big Dipper for navigation. Winter's bold illustrations, with repetitions of the refrain—*"for the old man is a-waiting for to carry you to freedom"*—woven through the text, have enchanted many children as they listened to their teachers read this book. Often paired with recordings by Pete Seeger, the Weavers, and other folk musicians, the song is frequently included in children's song collections, and has been arranged for choirs and orchestras as well. Program notes typically mention its use as a coded song to guide safe passage.

> PAUSE to obtain a copy of Jeanette Winters's *Follow the Drinking Gourd*. Listen to recordings of the song by folk musicians or as arranged for ensembles.

A brief review of curricular materials for music teachers will show how frequently *Follow the Drinking Gourd* has been included as a link to history, particularly the Underground Railroad, and even, via astronomy, to the use of the song by a planetarium.[2] The Underground Railroad, with its mention of secret tracks, secret messages, disguises, safe houses, conductors, and stars to guide the way to safety, enrobes the song in a cloak of mystery and adventure for children, who are often shielded via these book-based representations from the terror, violence, and hardships encountered by enslaved persons who risked their safety to pursue freedom. The complexities of the human network, with its clandestine stations and courageous persons who chose to harbor or guide others to points beyond, are seldom developed.

Katherine (Katie) Seybert set out to learn more about this well-loved melding of music and history for a master's project. In her role as an elementary music and beginning band teacher at a parochial school, her intention was to engage fourth and fifth grade students in building historical empathy while promoting the integration of curricular ideas across subjects. Katie started with her interest in the use of spirituals during the period of the Underground Railroad, an emphasis well suited to the religious aims of the school. She selected six spirituals for students to study and sing, developed profiles of historical figures such as Frederick Douglass and Harriet Tubman, and gathered instructional materials for the unit. With this general framework in mind, Katie searched for scholarly resources to deepen her understanding of the songs themselves. She wove these sources throughout her project, such as excerpts from *The Life and Times of Frederick Douglass* in which he spoke of the song "O Canaan, Sweet Canaan" as a pilgrimage not to heaven, but to a free state instead, or Harriet Tubman's singing of "I'm Bound for the Promised Land" as a way of signaling her plans for escape to her family.

Katie ran across several sources that questioned the widespread assumption that *Follow the Drinking Gourd* belongs to this period. Among them was the inclusion in the Smithsonian Folkways archive of a letter from Lee Hays to Pete Seeger in 1941 in which he recounted hearing fragments of the tune as a child. Hays added the signature line "for the old man is awaitin' for to carry you to freedom" to these fragments, publishing the song in 1947 as it is frequently sung (Kelley, 2008). Katie searched further, finding one of the first known documents to mention the song, a narrative written in 1928 by folklorist H. B. Parks who recalled hearing phrases of the song sung throughout the South in the early 1900s, long after the Antebellum period (Parks, 1928). A cultural history of the song traced some of its path of transmission from folklore to the classroom, raising concerns about its historical veracity (Bresler, 2008).[3]

After questioning how the song has been used in children's literature and in classrooms as an historical account, Katie decided to use her reading as an opportunity to involve the students in a discussion of songs as historical texts. She raised inquiry questions with the children, asking them to write reflections as they realized that historical accounts often change over time, and may contain elements that may not be trustworthy reflections of historical periods. One student wrote: "Some of the story of the Underground Railroad isn't real. I am pretty mad about it because we don't know much about the Underground Railroad but that doesn't mean you have to make it up!"

Katie realized the need for a culminating project that would enable the students to express their musical responses to the unit, particularly after their discussions of the contested origins of *Drinking Gourd*, one student writing, "If history was distorted I would probably feel tricked if I found out the truth. I would never distort history or anything because I want people to trust me." She located another children's book, Shane W. Evans's *Underground: Finding the Light to Freedom* (2011), which opens with "The darkness... the escape... We are quiet," conveying the passage to freedom in a series of short phrases and declarative sentences. The artistic impact of the spare and simple text is carried through illustrations in muted blues and blacks, with an occasional hint of yellow as a window or a flame before the last few pages erupt in golden tones, heralding "the sun... freedom." Katie worked with the children to develop a sound collage that would accompany a reading of the book. In small groups, using their band and classroom instruments, the students improvised musical textures to enhance the feeling tone of the text.

On the last day of the project, Katie led the children in singing the selected spirituals they had studied for their classroom teachers and a few invited guests. Katie slowly read *Underground*, leaving space for the children to fill with their own improvisatory soundscapes, evoking an atmosphere of fear, anticipation, and finally the relief of arrival. Serendipitously, I was visiting her school that day as a witness to this vibrant moment, speaking with Katie later about the significance of the project for the children as well as her beliefs and practices as a teacher. She reflected: "This process was very enlightening to me as an educator. Teaching music through an interdisciplinary approach that included historical empathy not only led to excellent classroom discussions but also led to musical compositions that conveyed emotions. This in turn led to the students having a much deeper musical experience than if we would have focused on music alone." The students' creative interpretations, alongside their study of the historical period and the richness of the spirituals, rounded out this experience, with generative potential to set down roots of understanding and empathy.

Questions Arising from This Case

At the heart of Katie's story sit fundamental questions related to the historical period and the children's capacity to answer questions such as: What was the Underground Railroad? What do we know about the experience of those enslaved persons who traveled the Underground Railroad—risking their lives to find freedom? Similar knowledge questions, epistemological in their nature, arose during Katie's search for sources and in her efforts to engage the children in questioning received accounts. What credible sources of information and insight can be accessed as a primary source? What is the role of folklore in conveying past lives? Can music serve as a credible source of historical information? What are the warrants for our beliefs that any given piece of music can claim to be an artifact of history?

Curricular questions follow. What are the aims we can hold in view in launching a project such as Katie's? How do music teachers probe what students know, and build on that knowledge? How do they approach the misconceptions students might have about the lives of those who lived in the past? What is lost when children are taught about the perils and paths of escape from slavery with music contributing to the soft mythology? What are the forms of engagement that uphold the integrity of musical aims and historical aims as well as their intersections? How does a multidimensional approach inform curricular possibilities? (Figure 8.1).

Strengthening the Educative Value of This Project

As she launched her search, Katie rather quickly confronted a problem shared by historians and educators alike—the notion of historical veracity, as the song shared only a tenuous filament of its historical relation to the period of slavery. In current initiatives forwarded by social studies and history educators, secondary accounts of history featured in textbooks are being replaced, or at least supplemented, with a focus on primary sources, documents, and artifacts that offer a more robust account of lived experience. Her use of quotes attributed directly to historical figures, and the thoughtful choice of spirituals, stood to establish this emphasis.

Not only was Katie involved in the process of searching for clues to examine the trustworthiness of stories, she also engaged students in thinking about these matters. It is clear from students' journals that this approach to

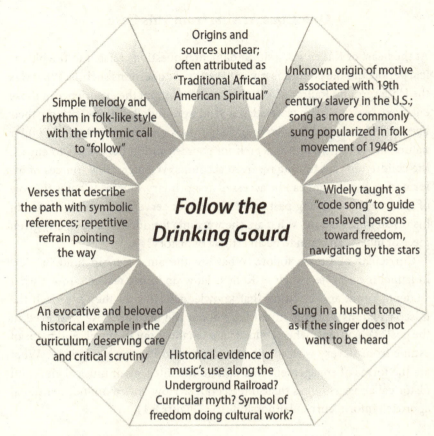

Figure 8.1 Facets Model: *Follow the Drinking Gourd*

inquiry captured their imaginations and their passions. In her desire to involve the students, Katie was mirroring initiatives in social studies and history education to promote historical thinking. Perhaps these students may be prone to question static accounts in the future, knowing that there are more voices, greater nuances, multiple perspectives waiting to be encountered.

Until such time that a body of historically informed curricular materials are developed for music teachers and classroom teachers alike, Katie was prompted to embark on her own search, digging through available scholarship and curricular materials to follow the trajectory of *Follow the Drinking Gourd* as best she could. To be on the search is fascinating, yielding small discoveries that throw received knowledge into question, and that spiral into more questions. The search fuels restless curiosity about matters that will not sit still. Thinking about the Facets Model questions, "Who created it?" and

"When, where, what, and for whom was it created?," you can imagine that what Katie discovered was not a tidy set of facts that pinned the song to the Antebellum period, but an unfolding chain of more ambiguous clues and attributions.

The curricular project Katie designed draws attention to the myths of curriculum, the limits of materials used for teaching, the pedagogical traditions that perpetuate inaccuracies, misconceptions, and biases if not subjected to critical scrutiny. Katie sensed that a culminating event ferreting out these misconceptions would feel unsatisfactory, so she made use of students' creativity as they improvised their own interpretations of the feelingful progression of events subtly suggested by the telegraphic text and evocative illustrations in *Underground*. Katie's curricular inventiveness and flexibility in responding to her students' needs led to an artistically expressive "resting place," knowing that historical understanding of the period of enslavement will continue to deepen over time.

Searching for Scholarship

Fath Davis Ruffins is the curator of African American History and Culture for the Smithsonian Museum of American History. Her talk "Symbol and Reality: The North Star in American Culture (Follow the Drinking Gourd)" establishes some important points about the history of this song (National Museum of the American Indian, 2019). The North Star, she explains, has been an enduring symbol of the search for freedom in African American culture. Abolitionist Frederick Douglass established an antislavery newspaper in 1847 called *The North Star*, in reference to Polaris, guiding enslaved persons to freedom. Later during the Harlem Renaissance and beyond, Black artists such as Jacob Lawrence and Aaron Douglas incorporated this cultural symbol in their paintings.[4]

But amid this symbolic importance, Ruffin unpacks historical details of the period that complicate naïve understanding of the routes to freedom. Displaying a National Geographic Society map, she explains that the route north was but one of many options for escape,[5] even noting that some enslaved persons ventured south in hopes of connecting with ships headed to British territories, since the British had outlawed slavery in 1830. Between 1800 and 1860, historians estimate that approximately 60,000 enslaved persons ran away, but many were recaptured to be "sold south." Ruffins clarifies that the most likely to escape were young men between thirteen and thirty-five years old. Her talk shines light on the ubiquity of "escape stories" in children's literature; historical scholarship suggests these instances were rare indeed.

Ruffins notes the popularity of *Follow the Drinking Gourd* as the subject of many children's books, mentioning several of the sources that Katie found in her search, and troubling the chronology that situates it in the nineteenth century rather than the twentieth. In early published collections of spirituals and "slave songs," including the repertoire of the Fisk Jubilee Singers, Ruffins concludes that there is "no evidence that this song was actually sung during the Antebellum period." However, she observes that the song still does cultural work as a symbol of freedom and freedom-seeking persons.

History educators have also raised questions about the myths and misconceptions surrounding this song. A particularly curious instance relates to its use in educational testing. Wineburg criticized an item on the 2010 US History National Assessment of Educational Progress (NAEP) in which fourth graders read the lyrics, "Follow the drinking gourd/for the old man is awaitin' for to carry you to freedom," before selecting their response to the question, "Why did African Americans originally sing this song?" The NAEP points to the choice "It gave directions about how to escape from slavery" as the correct answer, leading Wineburg to exclaim: "How is it that our national history test uses an interpolated section of a dubious 'coded' song—a text that *historians* have shown to be a fiction of the twentieth century—to quiz kids?" (Wineburg, 2011, emphasis in original, n.p.). Citing this *Drinking Gourd* item as an example, Breakstone criticizes test preparers for an especially "haphazard approach to writing standardized test questions" (2014, p. 458).

Picture Books as Bridges between Disciplines

The fusion of a compelling text, vivid illustrations, the intimacy of the storytelling circle in which the teacher's voice becomes animated in the telling of a story, and the embodiment of singing create moments of expressive power in the daily rhythm of the classroom. Reflect for a moment on the visceral response of stumbling across an illustration from a book that was read to you in childhood, and the way the image immediately registers as familiar. Music teachers are drawn to picture books, sensing this immediacy. Elementary music teachers in particular hunt for songs set in picture book format, biographies of musical persons, and stories about music. Reviews appear in pedagogical journals; purveyors of curricular materials display the latest resources at conferences for music teachers' browsing.

The critical appraisal of picture books in the curriculum parallels music education's current attention to song literature. In journals, conferences, and classrooms, music educators are calling teachers to decolonize the curriculum (Hess, 2015), adopt antiracist teaching practices (Hess, 2021), and scrutinize the origins of song literature that has been the mainstay of music classrooms for decades (Howard, 2021). The groundswell of calls for critical scrutiny of the music sung and played in classrooms is fueled by those who take responsibilities for justice seriously, and who intend to unveil racist practices and reconsider oppressive pedagogical strategies. Especially germane to this discussion is the need to analyze curricular materials for misrepresentations, both intended and unintended.

Elementary generalist teachers are drawn to children's trade literature as well, selecting biographies, songbooks, and narrative nonfiction as means to incorporate social studies instruction into the classroom. Social studies textbooks have been criticized for being "a mile wide, an inch deep, devoid of the intellectual disagreements, and replete with inaccurate and misrepresentative information, leaving young readers with intellectual backpacks overflowing with dubious, disconnected facts" (Bickford & Rich, 2014, p. 67). Children's literature often attempts to close that gap, serving as a main source of curricular material for teachers, especially in the elementary years.

Picture books, then, are a shared curricular territory of interest for music specialists and generalist classroom teachers alike. Although they may be chosen with different aims in mind, their use fulfills important curricular aims for young students. Imagine, for example, what subject matter and social connections are fostered when children hear books read by classroom teachers and sung by music teachers. The use of these picture books may serve as one area of curricular integration for students in visible and visceral form, as those that aim to contribute to children's civic and historical learning provide vivid forms of representation of lived experience for children's learning.

Historical Misunderstandings, Misrepresentations, and Interpretations

Social studies educators have studied what children learn from commemorations of the lives of historical figures, such as Martin Luther King

Jr., especially during the holiday observed widely in schools. Researchers have observed how teachers' well-intentioned inclusion of books about his early years become tangled up in far-ranging associations students make with films, television programs, and other media they have encountered, sometimes leading to misunderstandings of historical events and figures (Wills, 2005). Children's understandings are also "not emotionally neutral" as they are influenced by their families and social groups (Halvorsen, 2017, p. 389). Children generally rely on what sources tell them in what has been called "encyclopedia epistemology" (VanSledright, cited in Halvorsen, 2017, p. 391), but now that the encyclopedia has been replaced by the nearest browser, perhaps this term might be replaced with "search engine epistemology." In an age drenched with information, the question of media literacy arises—how to prepare students to sort through questionable sources in search for more reliable information about the past. Teaching students how to question this information is at the heart of civic literacy. Wineburg's analogy comes to mind: "reliable information is to civic intelligence what clear air and water are to public health" (2018, p. 159).

Enslavement is a particularly fraught case, as the portrayal of "enslaved people in inaccurate and simplistic ways . . . may distort students' understandings of history" (Hughes, 2021, p. 8). A controversy surrounding a children's book, *A Birthday Cake for George Washington*, energized a debate about the representation of enslaved persons in picture books (in this case a chef, Hercules, smiling through the birthday preparations with his daughter Delia as witness).[6] The controversy fueled additional scholarly critique of children's books as historical texts.

Patterson and Shuttleworth analyzed the text and illustrations in a cross-section of children's books to develop a framework for three "stances of historical interpretation" (2020, p. 14). Books in a *selective tradition* offer simplified versions of historical events and persons as a singular account. These books "minimize or exclude the violence of enslavement, show masters and enslaved person working happily together as equals, or omit enslaved persons from events in which they played prominent roles" (p. 15). A second category, *social conscience books*, present mixed portrayals of enslavement as a "joyless, painful experience, but subtle misrepresentations pervade the narrative text, or illustrations, or both." References to violence may be framed in a passive voice, or merely alluded to, contributing to readers' impressions that "enslavement 'happened upon people,'" thereby masking the perpetrators' responsibility for heinous acts. *Culturally conscious books* acknowledge these acts while also relating them to the economic and political structures that perpetuated enslavement, using active voice in describing systems of oppression and naming oppressors. Books in this category may also show acts of resistance that speak to the ingenuity and bravery of enslaved individuals in their quest for freedom.

These scholars acknowledge teachers' dilemmas in selecting books (and I would add music) to convey these hardships and terrors in ways that children can understand. They also acknowledge parental and community concerns. Thomas underscores the importance of teachers' principled "chaperoning" during the reading of books on difficult subjects.[7] An understanding of these categories, or stances, is also helpful in sorting through the growing body of literature for children for use in educational settings. In their listing of resources, Patterson and Shuttleworth include Shane Evans's *Underground* as an example of a social conscience approach. Thinking back to Katie Seybert's curriculum project, this book conveyed, albeit in subtle uses of text and illustration, the fear that accompanied the journey, and although the slavecatchers' menacing presence is depicted, the narrative is told from the perspective of the fleeing family. It may be that the interpretive space created by thoughtful books from this social conscience category provide educative openings for the arts to fill, a theme explored below.

What the Arts Bring to Social Studies and History

What can the arts do? When well informed, the arts can bring forward humanistic elements, the sense of lived experience, and openings for empathic understanding. I have long appreciated the way art educator Elliot Eisner captured what the arts can bring to the social studies:

> What students can learn about a culture, past or present, is both constrained and made possible by the forms of representation in which they have access and are able to "read." When social studies carries its messages to students mainly or solely through textbooks, it inevitably and severely limits what students are able to learn. Thus, attention to the arts, to music, and to literature in social studies programs is not a way to "gussy-up" the curriculum, it is a way to enlarge human understanding and to make experience in the social studies vivid. (1991, p. 553)

History educator Sam Wineburg lends weight to Eisner's call for vivid experience. "Every encounter with the past [hinges on] the tension between the familiar and the strange, between feelings of proximity and feelings of distance in relation to the people we seek to understand" (Wineburg, 2001, p. 5). He advocates, "an encounter with the past can be mind-expanding in the best sense of the term" (p. 6) as historical accounts prompt us to reconceptualize who we are in the present. Working between the tensions of proximity and distance gives us a constructive space for generating understanding, and the arts in particular belong in that space.

Music, with its evocative and symbolic power, engages students' minds and voices and fingers and breath, inhabiting their bodies as well as their imaginations. Curricular choices are far from trivial as "the images, tastes, and values that [students] encounter in school play a role in the construction of social identities and worldviews" (Woodford, 2005, p. 70).

The concept of *historical empathy* provides a useful framework I have explored in considering, for example, which children's biography of Ella Fitzgerald music teachers might choose if they prioritize empathic understanding, how they might teach the Great Migration through the arts in middle school, or question historical accounts of school desegregation through stories of the Little Rock Nine in inquiries for high school students (Barrett, 2022). Jason Endacott and colleagues posit that forming historical empathy involves: (a) *historical contextualization*, which involves developing understanding of the time and place, the "social, political, and cultural norms," and knowledge of concurrent events; (b) *perspective taking*, involving understanding other persons' "lived experience, principles, positions, attitudes and beliefs in order to understand how that person might have thought about the situation in question"; and (c) *affective connection*, in which knowing about the historical person's affective response to the situation may speak to similarities or differences with aspects of students' lives in the present (adapted from Endacott & Brooks, 2013, p. 43). Endacott's study of students' engagement with historical figures and events illustrates the power of these affective connections as potent avenues for sense-making (2014). Strongly integrated curricula place crucial ideas in proximity. When the arts are infused in historical study, the past feels closer and more relevant to the emerging identities of young persons. When history is infused in music classrooms, deeper understandings of time and place, expressions of feeling, and evocative meanings become accessible and audible. Through intersecting realms of experience, these human capacities are foregrounded in educational settings.

A Groundswell of Curricular Energy—Music and History at This Moment

The contentious debates, heated school board meetings, and pending legislative efforts focused on what sort of history should be taught in schools and how it should be taught compel teachers to respond. The historical underpinnings of music taught in schools are also scrutinized as communities look at traditions and repertoires that have long remained at the center of music classrooms. At a time when so many curricular issues point to deep public divisions in ideological, political, religious, and ethical matters, I am grateful for historians, journalists, educators, and professional organizations that inspire teachers toward justice in this difficult climate. I look to initiatives such as Facing History and Ourselves, which "uses lessons of history to challenge teachers and their students to stand up to bigotry and hate."[8] I look to the work of Rethinking Schools, committed to "sustaining and strengthening public education through social justice teaching and education activism."[9]

In preparing this chapter, I consulted Learning for Justice, whose "Teaching Hard History" project sponsored by the Southern Poverty Law Center provides thoughtful curricular frameworks for addressing difficult topics (Shuster et al., 2019). Music is incorporated in this framework in integral ways. In the K–2 curriculum on teaching enslavement for Teaching Hard History, for example, an essential principle of knowledge, "Students should know that enslaved people tried to maintain their cultures while building new traditions that continue to be important," follows with a related focus: "Music was very important in the lives of enslaved people, and the music they created shapes popular music today." The intention here is to instill in young children the idea that alongside the perils and hardships of enslavement, certain practices and beliefs provided stability and outlets for expression, among them, music. From those incipient ideas, the framework develops in upper primary grades through secondary school, maintaining music as a throughline.

Another prominent initiative, positioned unexpectedly at the center of state legislative efforts to ban its teaching in schools, is the 1619 Project.[10] Conceived to mark the arrival of enslaved persons in Virginia on the *White Lion*, and to tell a different origin story that evolves through ongoing histories of oppression over 400 years, the 1619 Project is an outgrowth of a report published in the *New York Times* led by Nikole Hannah-Jones and her colleagues. Since its publication in 2019, the project has expanded to include professional development opportunities for teachers, as well as the publication of curricular guidelines and books (Hannah-Jones et al., 2021). Again, music is an integral part of the story. Wesley Morris, one of the authors, speaks of the ingenuity, creativity, perseverance, and spirit that characterizes Black American music "born of feeling, of play, of exhaustion, of uncertainty, of anguish. Of essential introspection" (2021, p. 378).

Parallel movements in higher education also focus on revising static historical narratives. Music history pedagogy, for example, is undergoing a period of expansion and revision to link the composers, performers, works, and eras under study to social history, politics, and related developments in art and literature (Natvig, 2017). In the wake of the murder of George Floyd in 2019, schools of music began long overdue conversations to scrutinize the pedagogies and processes of preparing musicians, scholars, and teachers that have far-reaching implications for music education at large. In hope that these efforts will result in reimagining possibilities for music to play a role in ameliorating social inequities, may it be so. An example in close alignment with these aims follows in this second case of practice.

Historical Engagement with a Historically Significant Work for Ensembles

It was a Tuesday evening unlike any other. More than 250 singers and instrumentalists assembled for rehearsal, prepared to shape, polish, and refine their music making, the performance only weeks away. They expected to launch immediately into a productive rehearsal, guided masterfully by the conductor of this university orchestra and symphonic choir as they worked with the especially complex score. This particular Tuesday, though, began in an unexpected way. Upon their arrival, the singers and instrumentalists were invited to move to nearby rooms where subject matter experts were poised to give short lectures and demonstrations related to history, painting, and poetry, drawing from various media and historical artifacts as examples. For an hour, the musicians sampled from these offerings before returning to rehearse the piece with heightened awareness of its expressive power and artistic responsibility for communicating its historically significant dimensions.

The work at hand that evening was a symphonic oratorio that brackets one day in the life of a US president, a day in which the fragile progress of the Civil Rights Movement was compromised by a tragic discovery, a day in which—operating on what he thought was credible intelligence—the president made a decision that would catapult the country toward a long and protracted war. What could music possibly lend to the story of two landmark events in a day marked by such grief, suffering, and anxiety, fraught with the consequential weight of leadership? How might a work of art juxtapose these tensions, their emotional intensity, their historical gravity?

Steven Stucky was commissioned by the Dallas Symphony Orchestra to compose a piece to commemorate the centenary of Lyndon Baines Johnson's birthday, who served from 1963 to 1969 as the thirty-sixth president of the United States. Stucky collaborated with lyricist Gene Scheer to create an oratorio for soprano, mezzo soprano, tenor, and baritone soloists with choir and orchestra.[11] They decided to base the entire work on one day in LBJ's presidency, augmenting the confluence of two critical events. Early on August 4, 1964, the president received reports from Secretary of Defense Robert McNamara that US ships in the Gulf of Tonkin were under torpedo attack from North Vietnam. That evening, Johnson appeared on national television to say: "It is my duty to the American people to report that renewed hostile actions against United States ships on the high seas and the Gulf of Tonkin have today required me to order the military forces of the United States to take action in reply."[12] Historians now mark this moment, based on intelligence that was later shown to be unreliable, as questionable justification for the country's escalation in the Vietnam War.

Johnson also received a telephone call that evening to learn that the bodies of three civil rights workers, Michael Schwerner, James Chaney, and Andrew Goodman, who were believed to have been murdered in Mississippi, had been found. For weeks that summer, the country had been consumed with their disappearance. The three young men had signed up to work for CORE, the Congress on Racial Equality, as part of the Freedom Summer Project to register Black voters in the South. Johnson called the families of the men to speak with them directly before he would allow the FBI to release the news. Public outcry at these murders set the stage for the Voting Rights Act of 1965.

178 SEEKING CONNECTIONS

Scheer drew from transcripts of recorded conversations from the Oval Office, speeches, interviews, applications to CORE, and entries from Johnson's diary to craft the libretto for the concert drama. Stucky employed characteristic musical figures or gestures that underscored the identities and struggles of each historical figure (Swanson, 2014). The soloists represent two mothers of the slain civil rights workers, Mrs. Chaney and Mrs. Goodman (soprano and mezzo soprano), Secretary of State Robert McNamara (tenor), and President Johnson (baritone). A poem found on Andrew Goodman's apartment wall, Stephen Spender's "I think continually of those who are truly great . . . what is precious is never to forget," is sung by the choir throughout the work. The emotional trajectory of the twelve movements moves through the grief of the mothers, the escalating anxiety at McNamara's insistence that Johnson retaliate, the hope for change expressed in the applications for CORE, and the enormous burden of executive decisions that would have lasting consequence for the country. The tenth movement is a "lamentation for the unnecessary deaths of both the Civil Rights workers and the victims of the Vietnam War" (Megill, 2016).

> PAUSE to access and sample various movements, taking note of their intensity:
> "The Saddest Moment" (Mrs. Chaney, Mrs. Goodman, McNamara)
> "I Wish to Be a Part of that Fight" for Chorus (from Michael Schwerner's application)
> "Had We Known" (McNamara)
> "Elegy" for orchestra.

Alex Underwood, a doctoral student in choral conducting, was inspired to organize a gallery of events for the musicians in these ensembles, which extended beyond the evening of the rehearsal exploration to include other opportunities, such as a screening of the film *Mississippi Burning*, as well as pre-concert talks on the night of the performance with librettist Scheer (sadly, Steven Stucky died earlier in the year this performance occurred). Months before, Alex had begun investigating the oratorio, as well as a host of other contextually salient events and works of the time, as he planned to engage the musicians and the audience in a multidimensional experience (Figure 8.2). For the performance, he designed projections, supertitles, images, and video that drew the audience more viscerally into the historically significant time and place.

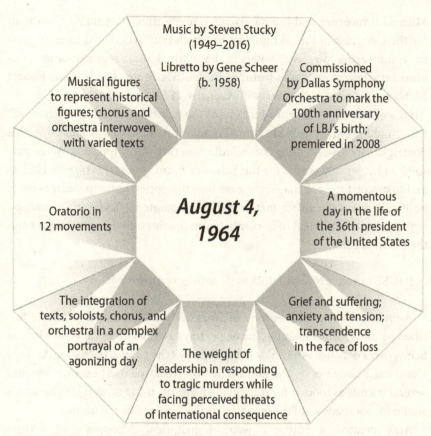

Figure 8.2 Facets Model: Steven Stucky, *August 4, 1964*

A Gallery of Evidence

The carousel of speakers was particularly powerful. Alex invited persons to speak to various related aspects of this historical event and the period in general. In one room, musicologist Gayle Magee contrasted media coverage of the murders from expected sources such as the *New York Times* and the *Washington Post* with examples of journalistic coverage from the *Philadelphia Tribune* and the *Chicago Defender*, targeted more specifically to African American readership. In another room, conductor Andrew Megill provided a poetic analysis of the Stephen Spender poem, "I think continually of those who were truly great," which Andrew Goodman had displayed in his apartment. Another site introduced the musicians to the application essay of

180 SEEKING CONNECTIONS

Michael Schwerner and the handwritten application of Andrew Goodman for the Congress of Racial Equality, in which they articulated their reasons for volunteering to register voters in the south. A short segment of the documentary *Fog of War* was featured in another room. In the film, Robert McNamara discusses the events of August 4, 1964, from his perspective.

One center featured reproductions of the paintings of Norman Rockwell, who might seem an unlikely contributor. While Rockwell is known for his nostalgic narrative paintings of "middle America," most typically White persons, in his weekly covers for the *Saturday Evening Post*, his hire in 1963 as an illustrator for *Look* magazine gave him the opportunity to address more politically infused subject matter. Rockwell painted *Murder in Mississippi*, which depicts a moment of horror between the three civil rights workers and the Ku Klux Klan.

PAUSE to access Norman Rockwell's *Murder in Mississippi*.

Although *Look* published one of Rockwell's studies rather than the finished painting, the dramatic scene he portrays in sepia tones captures Michael Schwerner's defiance as he holds James Chaney, who has just been shot; Andrew Goodman's body lies on the ground nearby. Rockwell used his own son and several friends as models for staging the painting, using powerful lights in his studio to cast shadows of the menacing posse just outside the frame.

Alex created a complex web of historical accounts and artistic interpretations to enrich the performers' understanding of the music and deepen their engagement with its historical premise. Later, he reflected: "After creating this project, it serves as a model for my educational, community, and professional ensemble performances. Because music is not created in a cultural, social, or political vacuum, there are always rich contexts to explore. I find that performers bring their own life experiences, curiosities, and knowledge to the inquiry process, which builds community, understanding, and makes the performance more expressive because the artists are more deeply connected to the music."

Implications from This Historically Infused Performance

Although an oratorio of this scope and heft may be beyond the reach of school groups for performance and study, consider what might be learned from this particular case of practice. What elements are likely to leave a trace in the hearts and minds of those who participated, those who witnessed, those who informed this project? Consider the selection of works that could sustain this kind of inquiry. Which works that are both musically and historically complex would be suited to such a comprehensive and multimodal exploration? Think about the various forms of scholarship that went into the planning of these multifaceted event, as well as the many forms of representation—news accounts, documentaries, paintings, poetry—that complemented the study and performance of the work at the center of the project. Scan your community to locate collaborators who can lend their expertise or suggest connections to other experts and resources. Remember that the composers and librettists/poets/authors of texts used in musical works are often pleased to respond to inquiries about their aims, purposes, and processes in creating the work.

As I witnessed this expressive project unfold and attended the moving performance, I noticed an especially profound shift regarding what it means to prepare for a complex undertaking of this sort. Ensemble rehearsals are often governed by the expectation of efficiency, which typically means prioritizing time spent singing and playing. The use of the rehearsal time for Alex Underwood's enrichment gallery was a departure from this usual practice, yielding layers of meaning for the performers that set the entire evening and subsequent performance apart as *an* experience. The depth of insight that comes from these explorations may encourage others to create similar opportunities for learning in ensemble settings.

Calling for Context

"Context, from the Latin *contexere*, means to weave together, to engage in an active process of connecting things in a pattern" (Wineburg, 2001, p. 21). Schools are sites in which the musical and historical patterns of the past and present are made available to the young. Schools are also memorial spaces in which the politics of remembrance (Wills, 2005) define who is in view and how tributes to notable persons are woven into student experience. Music educators are often called to participate in commemorative ceremonies or celebrations that speak to these generative aims. More often than the heart can bear, music educators find themselves called to organize community events in which music plays a healing role in the aftermath of tragic events and losses. Through informed preparation, varied forms of engagement, and empathic concern, music teachers join with their colleagues in related disciplines to promote critical and creative approaches "essential to understanding and personal and civic responsibility" (Woodford, 2005, p. 21). They strive to weave together communities of brokenness and division.

Individual teachers can be catalytic forces for this work, but the collaborative power of shared expertise will certainly enrich potential impact. I dream of patrons, associations, or organizations who would sponsor large consortia of music teachers and arts educators to collaborate with social studies and history teachers whose work is at the forefront of a sea change in historical inquiry and interpretation. Imagine what could be accomplished if journal articles, conference presentations, and university coursework in music education were aligned more closely with contemporary curricular movements in history and social studies education. Leadership in the preparation and design of readily available curricular materials is a crucial first step.

Collaborating with musicologists is another fruitful approach. They can guide music educators as they develop expertise in tracing the trajectories of musical invention and reception. This sort of music-related archaeology is intense but satisfying, particularly given plentiful access to online resources. Adopting the strategies and sensibilities of musicologists, music teachers can build their capacities to model historical thinking as they develop areas of curiosity into curricular inquiries.

Toward Historical Inquiry in Music Classrooms

The following guidelines can serve as starting points while music educators and others build a stronger infrastructure for innovative curricular work and professional development. Whatever your interest or personal experience with integrating music and history, these recommendations for a context-savvy music classroom can be readily implemented once a commitment to teaching music with the roots on is made.

Engage students as "song detectives" as they trace the history of a song and search for its point of origin, the ways that is has been adopted by individuals and groups, its reception history, and its relationship to contemporary experience. Collect multiple versions and interpretations that will shed light on the way music has been woven into the social fabric of community life. Musicologist Jeff Magee describes a particularly useful method, a *song profile*, which is a "selective but in-depth exploration of a song's composition and performance history that makes apparent how variable meanings are socially constructed through time." Any music—whether a song or an instrumental piece—could prove valuable; the Facets Model might be useful in approaching such a search. Imagine what students might learn if this strategy replaced static "composer reports" that tend to restate what is known rather than produce new knowledge. Magee points to these benefits: "Such studies draw their power and relevance from following a familiar, apparently simple piece through a long path of sources until the piece itself reemerges as a complex document of American music and culture" (Magee, 2000, p. 537). Use the trajectory of the song as a means for learning about the social, political, educational, personal, and collective ways that songs move through the world.

Triangulate your sources; tell more than one story. Just as journalists and historians must be sure their sources are reliable, encourage students to evaluate sources of information. Search with vigor, and with attention to credibility. Resist telling a single story of the origins or transmission of a work since history involves interpretation, multiple perspectives, evidence of the nuanced richness of human experience. As a field, it might be wise for music educators to cultivate scholarly skepticism regarding program notes, websites, and other quick sources of contextual information about the musics we bring into the classroom. A discontinuity—some facet that does not quite fit or make sense—can trigger more searching to see what else can be discovered. Students can be invited to expand brief program notes, for example, into more compelling, and perhaps more robust, profiles of the music.

Gather multiple forms of representation. In planning for a presentation, a performance, or an exhibition, gather engaging artifacts and documents to be used in crafting the experience through direct encounters with photographs, journal entries, historical documents, paintings, poems, newspaper entries, and other forms that might enhance your musical study. Involve students in making aesthetic decisions about these forms, and the ways they can be grouped and juxtaposed for expressive purposes. Adopt the stance of a documentarian as you surround the focal works with social, artistic, and contextual artifacts.

Infuse historical understanding throughout your curriculum. In the opening to this chapter, I mentioned the frequent practice of providing "background information" as an introduction to study. If this is the only time that contextual understanding surfaces, however, it is likely that this practice will have little impact on students' understanding. Bring context to the foreground by asking thoughtful questions throughout the unit or overall plan. *How does this music reflect the time and place it was created? What other questions might be raised to deepen our understanding? What will we bring to our understanding or performance of this music?* Consider how bracketing entire cultural groups in certain times of the year, such as Black History Month, Hispanic American Heritage Month, Asian American Pacific Islanders Month, Indigenous Peoples' Day, and other emphases highlight cultural contributions while confining such contributions to timebound parcels.

Make use of informants. History is an enormous panorama of human enterprise; history education is a far-reaching field. Rely on those who can help you to convey history in vivid, grounded, and as much as possible, historically complex ways. I spend a lot of time browsing journals in history education and social studies education for constructive strategies. Consult with your colleagues in your school or district who can provide insight into what their curriculum offers. Broaden your search to the community to find others who can speak with authority and passion to your project. Remember that students in your music classroom may be intensely interested in history and may be encouraged to contribute their energies and insights.

Consider the impact of these investigations on students. Challenging commonplace accounts of history and music's role in these events and movements may also challenge students' unexamined beliefs and shed light on long-standing patterns of inequity and oppression. Exercise ethical concern and care in framing these inquiries and be vigilant in supporting students who may feel vulnerable or at risk. Strive to establish classroom environments that can sustain courageous conversations while supporting students' varied levels of understanding and diverse perspectives. Much wisdom can be gleaned from guidelines provided by organizations such as Facing History and Ourselves and the Teaching Hard History project for building climates of trust and clarity, and fostering open and civil discussion.

Become attuned to context without becoming overwhelmed. When I showcase the work of music educators who are "context-savvy" to other teachers, I encounter a common response: "I do not have time to do the kind of scholarly homework that this approach seems to require!" The power of the particular shapes my reply. If you can identify one musical example in your curriculum that calls out for greater contextual exploration, start there. Once you identify a certain song or instrumental piece as a good candidate for historical inquiry, launch into a search. Many teachers find that once they embrace this mindset, their curiosities take flight as the inquiry takes off. Over time, as the Venn diagram circles of music and history move closer together and overlap, you may find this groundedness becomes central to your teaching practice. Over time, you will develop a portfolio of projects that could be expanded and reanimated in your classroom.

9
Assessing the Strength of Connections

Assessment. The term itself kindles strong reactions. Whenever I hold a conversation with teachers about this topic, a complex mix of opinions and feelings tumble forth. Assessment is often a site of struggle for teachers—with local expectations, with pressing challenges of keeping track of students' progress, with philosophical stances about what matters as music educators. Even when commonplace terms and common problems related to assessment surface, conceptual confusion arises, too, and especially so in an interdisciplinary context. How might we think about assessing the strength of connections that students form in a music classroom that prioritizes relational thinking? Is this possible? Is it necessary? The purpose of this chapter is encourage teachers to sharpen their attention to the connections students construct in music classrooms, leading to greater alignment of curricular content and instructional strategies with relational thinking.

Before proceeding, though, I invite you to bracket a set of issues related to assessment that often cloud and complicate understanding. If possible while thinking through the ideas in this chapter, try to set aside concerns related to grading, meeting district or state standards, documenting students' progress and conveying the results to others, and even evaluating teacher performance. Although all are consequential matters, this bracketing should permit approaching interdisciplinarity assessment from a different vantage point, unencumbered, at least for the moment, by these concerns.

I will illustrate briefly with grading as an example. For many, assessing is nearly synonymous with grading, but this merging calls out for questioning and uncoupling. Alfie Kohn has written persuasively on the ways that common emphases on grading overtake more comprehensive questions about students' learning, exhorting teachers "who care about learning . . . to do everything in their power to help students forget that grades exist" (Kohn, 1993, p. 206). As one of the foremost critics of grading practices in schools, Kohn argues that they deflect teachers' and students' attention from more substantive pursuits, such as seeking to understand content worth learning, collaborating with others, and making choices that foster inquiry and autonomy. Elliot Eisner explains that "grading is a data reduction process used to symbolize the merits of student work. Grades are supposed to represent the pooled judgments teachers make about student work" (2002, p. 181). He explains that much is lost in the reductive processes of grading that minimizes much richer evidence of learning, especially in the arts.

Following this line of thought as it pertains to interdisciplinarity, a chain of questions appears. What would happen if teachers suspended their concerns about reducing judgments to a single letter or number? What if teachers dwelt longer and more attentively to multiple dimensions of students' work? If grades are an inevitable responsibility for teachers, what might be done to minimize their prominence? What cultural shifts need to transpire to support teachers' authority in gauging student progress? What new dimensions of students' progress come into view if music teachers take an interdisciplinary turn?

In another bracketing move, I often advise students in my courses to box up their worries about grading and put them under their chairs in preparation for a more substantive discussion of the promises of assessment of a different sort. In this chapter, I intend to describe alternative ways of approaching assessment, still crucial to teaching and learning, while allaying anxiety about the technical processes and pressures of assigning grades (Barrett, 2006a). This adjustment seems especially necessary to free up more space for identifying and drawing attention to connections.

Stretching Exercise (of a Philosophical Sort)

Spend time to think through a philosophically oriented exercise involving if/then statements. Consider how you would respond to these statements, or if you wish, use them as prompts for journal entries or conversations with others.

- If I value the connections students make in music class, then how do I demonstrate this value through my classroom practices—what I typically do?

- If I value the connections students make, then how do I draw attention to them by commenting or responding directly to these associations and ideas?
- If some of the most memorable moments of classroom life arise in unexpected and serendipitous expressions of meaning, then how might I invite more serendipity?
- If I take care to document students' musical growth in my classroom, then how do I capture their growing capacities to relate music to other subjects and aspects of their lives?
- If I intend to create more opportunities for connections in my pedagogy, then how do I plan for these connections? Is that possible?
- If communicating the breadth and depth of students' relational thinking is important to me, then how often and to whom do I communicate this growth?

After you move through your responses, step back to notice patterns, appreciating how your beliefs and practices align, and also where alignments might be strengthened. If/then statements function as "truth serum," shedding light on the congruence of teachers' beliefs and practices.

At the heart of an interdisciplinary perspective on learning and teaching is a desire to foster connected thinking. Realizing this desire requires teachers to realize their values in action, which this stretching exercise illuminates. Recall Parsons's principle that "integration occurs when students make sense for themselves of their varied learning and experiences, when they pull these together to make one view of their world or their place in it. It takes place in their minds or not at all" (2004, p. 776). I am reminded of fundamental challenges and possibilities in bringing these generous and seemingly abstract aims into view. How is this kind of integrated thinking made manifest, tangible, public for others to witness? What happens if teachers fail to attend to the sense students make for themselves, relying instead on a more general hope that classroom activities have an impact on their perspectives? What if alongside this notion that students create one view of their worlds, we acknowledge that connectedness leads to plural views, complex understandings, multiple vistas for experience? Assessment can serve as a great clarifier for sorting through these questions and forging ahead. It is fundamental to teaching, inescapable, as Eisner notes: "To abandon assessment and evaluation, regardless of the field, is to relinquish responsibility for one's work" (2002, p. 179).

Music Teachers' Judgments in Assessing Connections

One of the most generous definitions of assessment I have collected—in the sense of being all-encompassing of its broad scope in teachers' work—is framed by Martin Fautley and Richard Colwell:

> Assessment consists of designing, conducting, interpreting, and communicating the results of an investigation into learning. One assigns value, one describes the meaning of data and observations, one synthesizes experiences, and the resulting judgments indicate the merit, worth, and significance of the educational venture. (2012, p. 477)

This view of assessment is superordinate to many other descriptions by encompassing many uses for assessment across the landscape of teachers' work. Its central aim is the investigation of learning. In contrast with common assumptions that assessment is what happens at the end of instruction, this perspective suggests that assessment is in play from the moment teachers begin to frame an educational experience. Fautley and Colwell's emphasis on values and describing meaning seems critical especially in interdisciplinary contexts where teachers' capacities to respond to students' interpretations and personal meanings are paramount. Teachers' judgments are integral to the assessment process, a theme worth developing.

Fautley and Colwell's broad view is complemented by another definition that feels even more grounded in teachers' intentions to gauge students' growth: "Authentic assessment means looking closely and continuously at students' work and efforts in order to be a better, more relevant, and more finely tuned teacher" (Ayers, 2019, p. 53). Music educators might find this notion of being "finely tuned" as a particularly fitting disposition toward attentive, purposeful, and student-oriented teaching. The mutuality of teaching and learning is at play in Ayers's statement, in a recursive loop of noticing students' efforts and refining teachers' actions, and then noticing and refining again.

Eisner underscores the importance of teachers' judgment in assessment as well, tracking its pervasiveness across moments that occur daily in classrooms:

> Judgments are made each time a teacher determines if a student understands an idea. Judgments are made when a teacher decides if a

student is engaged in [their] work. Judgments are made when a teacher chooses what to emphasize in [their] comments to a student. Judgments are made when a teacher determines the progress a student has made over time. (2002, pp. 179–180)

Eisner situates these judgments in specialized professional contexts, describing them as *connoisseurship*, the "art of appreciation. Connoisseurs notice in the field of their expertise what others may miss seeing. They have cultivated their ability to know what they are looking at" (p. 187). To approach assessment from the perspective of a connoisseur suggests that music teachers develop capacities to describe the qualitative dimensions of learning—the moments when students' sense-making appears to shift in meaningful directions, revealing nuances of thought, clear signs of growth. In my view, this qualitative focus enables assessment in arts education more fittingly than a quantitative approach, in which observations are turned into some form of measurement—a grade, a score, a level on a rubric. Eisner's marvelous chiasmus, "not everything that matters can be measured, and not everything that is measured matters," comes to mind (p. 178). His concept of connoisseurship pertains especially well to a search for connections. Do we know what we are looking at and looking for when it comes to students' relational thinking?

A Heuristic for Attending to Connections

To pay attention is to notice, to name, to make public. I suspect that in any given class or rehearsal, teachers and students pay attention in many ways to what is happening in the moment. Some of these associations are no doubt fleeting, others deeply meaningful. Observation is one of the most powerful instruments for growth in teaching, and an essential precursor to making judgments about the depth and breadth of learning. How often do teachers or students pause the action for a moment to capture how the music at hand is related to other musics, or subjects outside of music, or the pressing issues of the day? I also suspect that in the name of efficiency, bound to the ever-insistent clock, many moments go unrecognized. As I have witnessed the preparation of music educators, I have often thought that the "tuning" of attention is brought to bear first and foremost by identifying and correcting errors in musical performance—necessary for some aspects of music learning, but not the point here.

After searching far and wide for helpful models or heuristics, I created one of my own. Figure 9.1 is a conceptual model designed to heighten music teachers' awareness of multiple dimensions of relational thinking. The model also addresses criteria that might be used in strengthening music teachers' judgments as they craft their comments, responses, encouragements, and critiques of students' work in turn.

For explanatory purposes, the model assumes that students are engaged in the study of closely related works, either within music or across art forms.

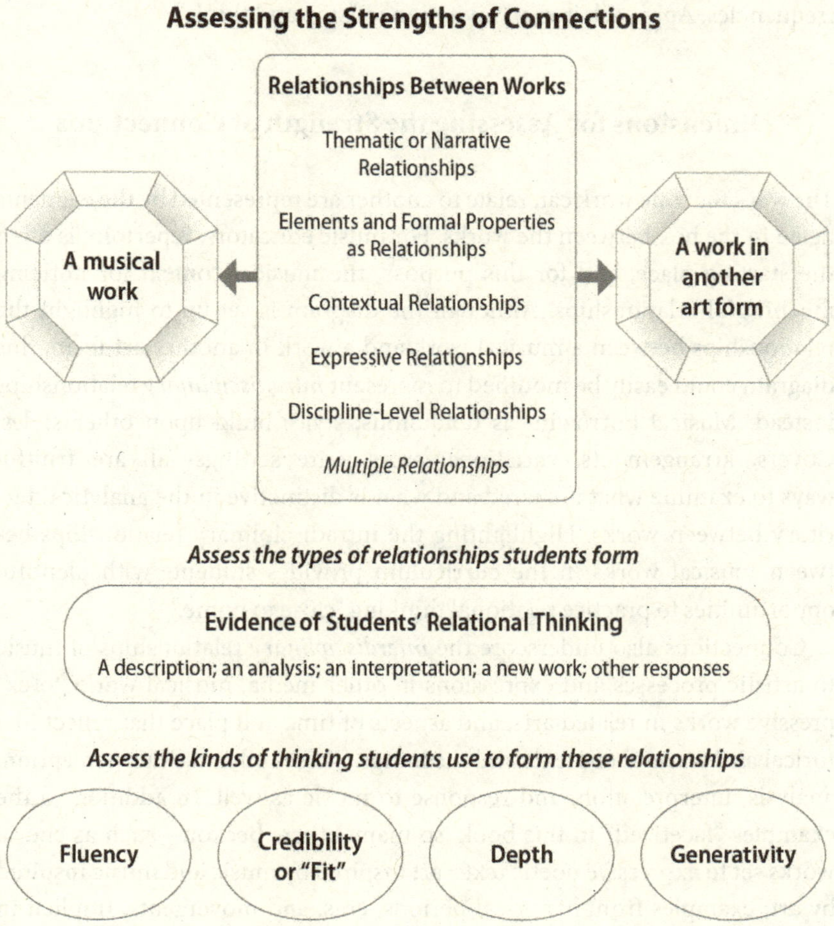

Assessing the Strengths of Connections

Relationships Between Works

Thematic or Narrative Relationships

Elements and Formal Properties as Relationships

Contextual Relationships

Expressive Relationships

Discipline-Level Relationships

Multiple Relationships

A musical work ← → A work in another art form

Assess the types of relationships students form

Evidence of Students' Relational Thinking
A description; an analysis; an interpretation; a new work; other responses

Assess the kinds of thinking students use to form these relationships

Fluency   Credibility or "Fit"   Depth   Generativity

Figure 9.1 Assessing the strength of connections

As you work through the model, pair a work from your portfolio of examples with another work (recognizing that many of the examples included in this book, such as the triptychs, involve more than two works). Please note that this model will be useful for examining multiple dimensions, but that it is not intended to be used as a template for assessment for a specific assignment, although it might be handy for examining collections of work in exhibitions or portfolios. Imagine, for example, using the model for reflection on the kinds and types of connections that are named and set apart in your classroom, and for branching out to be more attuned to dimensions that sit under the radar.

Think of this diagram, perhaps, as an app that might trace your typical habits and practices while tuning your attention to seldom-heard frequencies. Approach it as an invitation to "stop and think."

Dimensions for Assessing the Strength of Connections

The ways that one work can relate to another are represented by the elements listed in the box between the works. For music educators, repertoire is often the starting place, and for this purpose, the musical context for noticing meaningful relationships. Although the diagram is set up to highlight the relationships between a musical work and a work in another art form, this diagram could easily be modified to represent *intradisciplinary* relationships instead. Musical borrowing is ubiquitous; styles build upon other styles. Covers, arrangements, variations, cross-genre settings—all are fruitful ways to examine what is shared and what is distinctive in the analytical territory between works. Highlighting the intradisciplinary relationships between musical works in the curriculum provides students with plentiful opportunities to practice relational thinking "close to home."

Connections also underscore the *interdisciplinary* relationships of music to artistic processes and expressions in other media, musical works to expressive works in related arts, and aspects of time and place that reflect historical and cultural contexts and meanings. These influence our perception, analysis, interpretation, and response to music as well. In addition to the examples "facetized" in this book, so many others beckon—such as choral works set to expressive poetic texts; art inspired by music and music inspired by art; examples from historical periods, eras, and movements. Implicit in this model is the notion of integrity between disciplines, reflecting a balance of attention between the music and the related discipline.

After selecting two works for juxtaposition, the model moves through two additional interrelated sets of ideas. First, teachers can assess the *types of relationships students form*, which are essentially descriptive categories that center on relationships between works—the similarities and distinctive qualities of one work to another and the distinctive attributes of disciplines as well. Six of these categories are described below. The other set of ideas—*criteria for assessing relational thinking*—will follow.

Noticing the Types of Relationships Students Form

Thematic or narrative ideas are often used by artists in the creation of works that forward some key idea in sound, image, gesture, or text. Young students often pick up on these topical relationships, and the music curriculum for young children is frequently organized around simple themes as well, such as animals, the seasons, or celebrations. Interdisciplinary arts educator Joanna Cortright calls such songs-by-theme *fingertip connections*, a starting point.[1] At more advanced levels, themes take on a more abstract nature, such as justice, freedom, metamorphosis, grief, or transformation. Huib Schippers and colleague Adri Schreuder developed an approach for a world music course organized by themes, among them music and the supernatural, music and travel, music and fusion, music and technology, music and love, music and death, music and nature, music and place, music and dissent, music and commerce (Schippers, 2010, pp. 175–179). Connections between the abstract themes and the particularities of works following this approach would be bolstered by multidimensional investigation. Music conceived as programmatic lends itself to narrative exploration, the "story" of the music taking prominence. A path of extramusical ideas through the exposition, rising action, climax, and resolution of a narrative intertwined with the temporal unfolding of the music offers imaginative possibilities for interpretation and creativity. Noticing these connections, then, involves attending to topical subjects and themes and the ways that students engage with them. Attending to these connections may also trace how surface-level associations deepen with experience.

Elements and formal properties of a work can be compared and contrasted with the elements and formal properties of another. Such an emphasis requires that students perceive distinct qualities, label those qualities, and then consider how they are manifested across works. When students identify similarities and differences in the use of elements, focusing on sound, image, gesture, and text; focus on general principles of design (unity, variety, emphasis, balance, proportion, contrast); or concentrate on the architectural structures of form, they sharpen their awareness of the way artistic ideas are shaped through the manipulation of elements into satisfying artistic wholes. Recall the focus on artistic properties and elements as features of multidimensionality, and the ways that music education has privileged ways of analyzing music that align with Western European systems. Noticing the ways that students attend to the properties of music and other art works can expand when teachers are vigilant to observe ways that students name what they hear, see, and perceive outside of these conceptual categories.

Noticing *contextual connections* in music as they link to contextual connections in other arts and disciplines moves us into regions of culture, style, and historical era. Forming connections goes far beyond merely naming the composer of the work to showing curiosity about the history of the work itself as well as the general milieu in which the work was created. Students can situate a musical example within a family of works connected by style or cultural practice, and act on that knowledge through informed performance practice. *Informing* is salient here. Teachers take note of the ways that fixed facts about art works, which are relatively inert, transform into useful contextual knowledge that changes students' perceptions, impressions, performance, and interpretation of the work.

Affective meanings come into play when teachers and students seek the *expressive characteristics* of the music linked to expressive characteristics of other arts, the province of mood, emotion, and feelingful response. Attending to the vast realm of expressive meanings of music and other arts works parallels the vast realm of responses students may form. Noticing and naming these meanings is a frequent challenge when words fail to capture subtle shades and movements, yet teachers and students attempt to do so nonetheless. Affective dimensions may indeed be captured verbally, but also through gestures, movement, visual representations, and musical performance itself. When students explore how art works embody feeling, they become more sensitive to the expressive potentials of works, and the various interpretive levels of response they evoke. Journal writing often brings affective dimensions to light, providing access to expansive realms of feeling.

Discipline-level relationships have surfaced rarely in my teaching experience without direct elicitation, yet they deserve keen attention. This dimension of connectivity refers less to the qualities of the art works themselves and more to the ways that disciplines function. Noticing students' thinking about these relationships requires them to think rather abstractly about the fundamental nature of music, art, poetry, dance, and other arts. Beyond useful distinctions such as "music uses sound; poetry uses words; art uses images; dance uses gesture," students must grapple with the distinctive qualities of art forms as complex and complicated disciplines, going far beyond surface-level replies.

I recall hearing about a teacher who asked students to compare and contrast disciplines as school subjects, receiving the answer that "music happens before lunch, and art after lunch." In more sophisticated ways, students can be encouraged to identify the sensibilities that shape a discipline, the ways that disciplines share common ideas, the ways they are distinct, and instances of work at the borders where disciplinary conceptions have been challenged or expanded. Seeking to understand these discipline-level relationships requires sophisticated thought. I am reminded of Bennett Reimer's observation that these interrelationships help us "to recognize music as part of a larger world of human values and therefore to understand it as precious in and of itself while also kindred to other values that are also distinctive and precious" (2003, p. 293). Following Reimer's lead, I hold that teaching the arts in tandem makes attention to their distinctive powers more likely.

Synthesizing *multiple relationships among music and other disciplines*. One of the signs of intellectual development may be found in students' capacities to think about multiple intersections between one work and another, or one discipline and another. Music teachers can attend to (and celebrate) these overlaps of curiosity and coordinated thinking. Synthesis provides a wide berth for interpretive play, since students can draw upon some or all of the categories above to show how these multidimensional aspects of art works cohere and interact in the experience of two or more works. Students can describe how the relationships between music and another art or art forms influence the performance, creation, analysis, interpretation, or evaluation of the work or works. These categories must be used descriptively to draw attention to the types of relationships that are worth pursuing and ways we could encourage students to connect works within music or between music and other disciplines.

Forms of Evidence

Evidence of students' relational thinking could take many forms, including a description, an analysis, an interpretation, a new work, or some other kind of response that makes thinking apparent and tangible. Boix Mansilla (2005) and her colleagues at Harvard Project Zero have studied the relational thinking of college students who participate in interdisciplinary research centers and educational programs. She calls assessment the "black hole" of interdisciplinary programs since so many are befuddled by it, recommending that enlightenment can be found by looking at student work that sits at the intersection of deep disciplinary grounding melded with integrative leverage from related disciplines. The definition of interdisciplinary understanding she offers points strongly toward the synergistic insights that result from combining disciplines (and therefore the criteria used in evaluating such insights) to generate varied responses: "the capacity to integrate knowledge and modes of thinking drawn from two or more disciplines to produce a cognitive advancement—for example, explaining a phenomenon, solving a problem, creating a product, or raising a new question—in ways that would have been unlikely through single disciplinary means" (p. 16). Signs of growth revealed through descriptions, interpretations, new works, and performances allow us to see if the connections have prompted changes in thinking, and whether students have reorganized what they know and feel.

Criteria for Assessing Relational Thinking

Assessing the kinds of thinking students use to form these relationships can involve criteria that involve the extent and quality of relational thinking. Applying these criteria to students' interdisciplinary work gives us evidence of students' overall facility in drawing meaningful connections across works or disciplines and allows teachers to evaluate the relational thinking of individual students through the development of their work. Some of these criteria are drawn from creative thinking literature, helpful here to concentrate on the kind of divergent thinking that also characterizes interdisciplinarity. These include fluency, credibility or "fit," depth, and generativity. Each will be described in turn.

Students demonstrate *fluency* in their relational thinking when they can make multiple connections between works or disciplines, and when they make numerous connections with ease. Teachers can attend to fluency by asking, "How extensive are the connections students incorporate in their work?" With practice, relational thinking should become more fluent as students develop facility in thinking about multiple relationships and contexts. However, merely counting the number of connections that students list will feel unsatisfying if the connections themselves are not plausible.

Evaluating *credibility or "fit"* is a matter of evaluating the quality of the connections, and the bases students use to form associations. The key idea here is that student work should be supported by evidence. We typically think of evidence as citing details that show how relational thinking is informed by contextual knowledge of the work—who created it, for what reasons, and in what times and places. The evidence that stems from students' perceptions of the works and how they articulate those perceptions also informs relational thinking. Teachers can attend to credibility or fit when they ask, "Do the connections make sense? Can students articulate the bases on which they draw associations between and among works?" Evidence, then, can stem from this sense-making.

Depth is a matter of moving from the superficial to the sophisticated. Some connections are more straightforward than others (prominent themes, for example), but others require that students look beyond the obvious to deeper levels of thinking. Although I wonder if a taxonomy of relationships would be useful, teachers readily recognize when students' products and responses prompt meaningful connections to their lives, moving beyond surface-level first impressions to substantive insights.

Finally, student thinking can be evaluated according to its *generativity*, or its capacity to lead to further exploration of the works at hand and works and ideas beyond the immediate context. This criterion has roots in Bruner's notion that "the first object of any act of learning ... is that it should serve us in the future. Learning should not only take us somewhere; it should allow us to go further more easily" (1960/1977, p. 17). Teachers attend to generativity when they ask how the connections formed by students lead to meaning beyond the moment and the particular instance of relational thinking. How do students draw upon connections to form new knowledge, products, and explanations, or to conduct inquiry across the disciplines? What is the significance of this educational experience for the next encounter students have with multidimensional works? Unlike the other three criteria of fluency, credibility, and depth, which can be captured by examining the evidence of students' relational thinking in the products and processes of their work, generativity is more elusive to pin down, but fundamentally important to lasting impact.

Approaches to assessment should align with educative aims. The way that assessment focuses our attention on educative goals helps to clarify whether time and care spent gathering evidence of connections has moved learning closer to the realization of curricular intentions and purposes. In the spirit of interdisciplinarity, this rich evidence might also move beyond what teachers initially hoped might transpire. Thinking back to the aims outlined in the first chapter, teachers might look for moments of sense-making, creative and critical thought, situating music in its time and place, depth of understanding, interpretive richness, and engagement that spills over into other classrooms and spaces outside the school.

Multiple Methods of Assessment; Multiple Types of Learning

Professional development sessions about assessment have blossomed over the past decade at elementary, secondary, and tertiary levels. School, district, or university committees on assessment have proliferated. Expectations for more frequent and detailed progress reports have escalated. Witnessing this surge (and being caught up in it in several ways) has prompted me to step aside to reflect on the purposes and practices of these initiatives. For example, while sitting in an assessment committee meeting several years ago, I was struck by the common recommendation for teachers and professors to create rubrics for all listed curricular outcomes in their educational programs. I noticed that this recommendation was so widespread that I began to think of rubrics as the Swiss army knife of assessment. In other words, rubrics are suggested as the solution for every assessment-related problem. Music teachers enrolled in graduate classes have told me that they are required to develop rubrics to match every one of their curricular goals. I began to reflect on this conundrum.

The use of multiple means of assessment counters this "one rubric fits all" situation. For interdisciplinary contexts, multiple strategies better provide ways of gathering, examining, and judging what students know, especially as two or more subject areas are combined in a unit or educational investigation. Table 9.1 provides constructive guidance for thinking through the types of assessment, and different forms of knowledge and understanding derived from educational psychology that may be of interest in processes of assessment. Teachers might consult this table after considering questions such as:

- What evidence of students' understanding will I be collecting?
- What types of knowledge or understanding might students demonstrate?
- How will I judge the quality of student work, the evidence of learning?
- How might this evidence be used to communicate growth to the student or others?

The table clarifies the distinction among different types of knowledge and understanding for interdisciplinary work (or for that matter, most any subject focus). In the first row, the focus is on *declarative knowledge*, knowing that something is the case. Teachers might be interested in students' acquisition of relevant facts or principles related to the educational unit or experience. They might also want to capture students' use of that knowledge. The assessment strategies or types that align with declarative knowledge include short response items, essays, dictation exercises, or listening exams. These strategies verify whether students possess this knowledge, as well as areas where they need more instruction. As part of an overall plan for assessment,

Table 9.1 Multiple methods of assessment to convey the depth and breadth of music learning

What students know	What are you looking for?	Assessment types
Declarative knowledge about music, such as facts or principles	Acquisition and use of knowledge	Selected response exams; essays, dictation exercises, listening exams
Procedural knowledge about music: knowing how to do something	Demonstration of complex products and processes—to perform, present, create analyze, synthesize	Rubrics that show levels of attainment as well as criteria for good work, checklists, rating scales
Personal knowledge about music: dispositions, reactions, insights	Affective aspects of students' musical experiences—attitudes, preferences, responses	Journal assignments, reflective writing recordings of discussions
"Habits of mind": qualities of students' work and interactions with others	The ways that students approach their work	Observation and description of students' contributions, difficulties, responsible habits, etc.

students could demonstrate their knowledge of art works, movements, eras, composers, and particular elements and techniques in this category. If declarative knowledge is the sole focus of assessment, however, this limits what teachers can learn about their students. Thinking of subject matter knowledge as a "resource, not a possession" (Kliebard, 2006, p. 120) places the emphasis on how students build on this base to construct meanings, make new works, and forge stronger connections.

The second row address procedural knowledge, *knowing how to do something*. The demonstration of complex processes often entails the degree to which students possess abilities or skills to perform, present, create, analyze, and synthesize. Making observations about these abilities demonstrates students' levels of attainment—from beginning efforts to more complex demonstrations. Further, these processes may involve multiple dimensions. Rubrics are often useful to capture these levels and dimensions, as are some rating scales and checklists. Imagine, for example, student compositions based on paintings. The rubric might address compositional criteria such as creative thinking, craftsmanship, and aesthetic appeal, augmented with composer's notes in which the student describes aspects of the painting that inspired the music.

Personal knowledge about music is a broad and revealing category encompassing student preferences, reactions, attitudes, and associations with music and matters beyond. Deeply personal and idiosyncratic, this sort of knowledge speaks directly to the affective dimensions of interdisciplinary exploration. In my classroom, these revelations have been the most illuminating, intriguing, and vivifying, providing access to students' meaning making in ways that speak to the heart of integrative work. Strategies for inviting the construction and expression of personal knowledge include journal assignments, reflective writing, recordings of discussions, video logs, audio commentaries on videos, and shared digital conversations between students.

The phrase "Habits of Mind" is often attributed to the work of Costa and Kalick (2008), whose typology I encountered decades ago, but here I use it in a more generic sense to refer to interdisciplinary dispositions, sensibilities, tendencies, and patterns of action and interaction with others. Music educators might take note of the ways that students "take" to interdisciplinary inquiry, paying attention to the generative power of curiosity, interest in broadening music study in productive dimensions, and collaborative tendencies to build on the ideas of others. Attending to difficulties, stumbling blocks, and areas of confusion may also inform next steps to dislodge barriers to interdisciplinary stances. In the pursuit of social justice, I might also attend to students' empathy, critical stances, and orientations toward activism and justice.

Consult this table when planning or conducting a project to think about the multiple ways you may gather evidence of students' growth, and to consider the kinds of knowledge or understanding that can best be captured by using various strategies, techniques, and types of assessment. The broader the scope of the work—through portfolios or exhibitions, for example—the more types of understanding can be noticed. In gathering this evidence, pay attention to the complementary relationship between or among disciplines. How do various strategies for assessment demonstrate that the "whole is greater than the sum of the parts," that "1 + 1 > 2?"

Aligning Curriculum, Instruction, and Assessment: The Braid

What is taught, how it is taught, and what students learn are inextricably bound together. To show the balance among these aspects, and the way that particular elements support one another, I turn to the metaphor of a braid. A well-woven braid consists of three strands of roughly equal weight intertwining as one strand alternates with another. The metaphor of the braid suggests that planning an interdisciplinary project entails articulating a flexible aim that also describes the primary areas of musical and related content for the project (the first strand); gathering up multiple instructional strategies to guide the pedagogical pathway for the project (the second strand); and planning for moments during the project and at its conclusion for assessing the depth of connections students form (the third). A related challenge here is to accommodate soft planning, providing enough structure to frame the project while also allowing for flexibility as the project shifts or expands during its implementation. To illustrate possibilities, I offer two examples. The first is based in a choral rehearsal setting in a high school and the second in a general music classroom at the middle or high school level.

Contre qui, rose

PAUSE to access and read a poem by Rainer Maria Rilke, "Contre qui, rose." PAUSE to access and listen to Morten Lauridsen's setting of "Contre qui, rose" for choir.

Imagine a high school chorus deep into learning Lauridsen's expressive setting of Rilke's poem. Rilke, a German poet who wrote in French in the last years of his life, fashioned a cycle of twenty-seven poems with roses as his central image. The composer Morten Lauridsen chose five of those poems as inspiration for a choral cycle, *Chansons des roses*. He was drawn to the poems as "especially charming, filled with gorgeous lyricism, deftly crafted, and elegant in their imagery" (cited in McCoy, 1994, p. 28). "Contre qui, rose" might be read as playful and teasing or more introspective as the speaker in the poem questions why the rose has developed thorns to keep others away.

Although it would certainly be possible to sing this beautiful French text without delving into the translation, concentrating solely on the melody, harmonies, and pronunciation, a choral music educator seeking connections could engage singers in exploring Rilke's poem to see how they draw multiple meanings from the text (relying on the translation provided in the score). They can look for the "music" in the language itself—Rilke's poetic artistry. The singers could be encouraged to "translate" the meaning of the poem by restating what they thought Rilke was expressing using their own words instead to show their comprehension. Singers could meet in small groups of two or three to discuss how the "sides" of our identities we show to the world keep others at a distance, and the thorn-like barriers we construct to keep them out. The choir could be guided to notice compositional choices Lauridsen made in setting Rilke's text for choir, such as the suspension that does not resolve at the end of the phrase "*Votre joie trop fine vous a-t-elle forcée de devenir cette chose armée*/Is it your too fragile joy to become this armed thing?"[2] Students could draw on their interpretive variations to suggest ways that the piece could be sung, performing each to arrive at an especially expressive choice.

The elements in the braid, then, include the flexible aim of teaching musical interpretation by connecting Rilke's poem as text and composer Lauridsen's setting of the text. Instructional moves in this example are numerous, including opportunities for singers to complete journal entries, work in small groups toward multiple interpretations, analyze the score to note the composer's compositional decisions, and negotiating a shared interpretation to guide performance of the piece. Assessment in this example is integrated closely using multiple methods and at multiple points. The music educator could gather journal entries, make note of group discussions as students share ideas, encourage students to mark the scores to note particularly interesting places for discussion, and guide the processes of arriving at a shared interpretation as students realize their thoughtful ideas in sound. The intertwining of the content focus and flexible aim, pedagogical approaches, and moments of assessment illustrate their alignment.[3]

Lincoln Portrait

Centennials and bicentennials often serve as the impetus for interdisciplinary collaboration as communities, associations, or other entities commemorate the anniversary of the birth of famous figures, or sometimes their passing. Such was the case in 2009 when the Ravinia Festival launched a professional development initiative for teachers focused on music that celebrated the life and times of Abraham Lincoln, and particularly Aaron Copland's famous orchestral work, *Lincoln Portrait,* with narration taken from Lincoln's speeches, messages to Congress, replies to Stephen Douglas in the debates of 1858, and phrases from the Gettysburg Address.

To expand the educative potential of this project beyond the Copland work, I organized a unit on the theme of portraits, guided by the inquiry questions: What is the purpose of a portrait? What makes a good portrait? How do artists in various art forms create portraits? What would you want a portrait of yourself to convey about you? The project began with a focus on a rather unusual portrait, *Lincoln for the Defense,* by Norman Rockwell.

PAUSE to access the image, *Lincoln for the Defense,* by Norman Rockwell.

Unlike many portraits of Lincoln, this one shows a young Lincoln standing. Rockwell accentuates his forcefulness at a decisive moment during a famous murder trial that Lincoln won in his early years, known as the "Almanac Case." The perspective of the viewer—looking up at his tall frame—heightens this effect. In his argument, Lincoln established that witnesses to the murder could not have seen the defendant since there was no moonlight at the time, which he substantiated with reference to an almanac (Walsh, 2000), held in his left hand while pounding his fist with other.

After deriving what could be "read" about Lincoln's character from this painting, students were asked a pivot question, "How would you create a portrait of Lincoln in words—through poetry?" Next, we read and interpreted a section from Carl Sandburg's book-length poem, "The People, Yes," in which Sandburg characterizes Lincoln as "a mystery in smoke and flags" (Sandburg, 1936).

PAUSE to access the poem from "The People, Yes" by Carl Sandburg.

In contrast to the decisiveness of the fist on the table shown in the Rockwell portrait, Sandburg shows Lincoln as malleable in his thinking, saying "yes" to the paradoxes of democracy and variability in his interpretation of the Constitution. At the celebration of Lincoln's sesquicentennial in 1959, Sandburg conveyed his complexity in this way: "Not often in the story of mankind does a man arrive on earth who is both steel and velvet, who is hard as rock and as soft as a drifting fog, who holds in his heart and mind the paradox of terrible storm and peace unspeakable and perfect" (in Peterson, 1994, p. 371). As students' interpretations of the poem and the painting correspondingly become more nuanced, the stage is set for the next pivot question, "How would you compose a piece of music in tribute to Lincoln?"

Aaron Copland's *Lincoln Portrait* was composed in the wake of Pearl Harbor when conductor Andre Kostelanetz invited Jerome Kern, Virgil Thomson, and Aaron Copland to create pieces as "a musical portrait gallery of great Americans" (Crist, 2005, p. 289), hoping to provide a source of strength for anguished audiences. In his inimitable style, Copland drew on several folk tunes for thematic material ("Springfield Mountain" and "Camptown Races") while writing a part for a narrator. Copland wrote: "I was skeptical about expressing patriotism in music—it is difficult to achieve without becoming maudlin or bombastic, or both. I was hoping to avoid these pitfalls by using Lincoln's own words" (Copland & Perlis, 1984, p. 342). From an impressive list of famous actors, politicians, journalists, and musicians as narrators, students decide to listen to a recording featuring James Earl Jones in this role.

PAUSE to access a recording of "Lincoln Portrait" with James Earl Jones as narrator.[4]

As students understand the historical context for Copland's work, trace its popularity, and understand how the narration and orchestral textures combine, they develop a sense of portraiture for this particular example (Figure 9.2). Lincoln's own words in the narration contribute historical gravity to the musical portrait, underscored by Jones's resonant voice. Copland's use of the

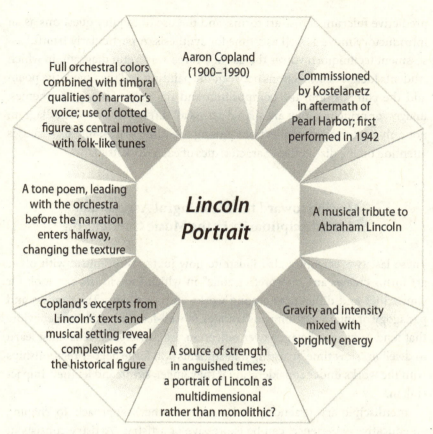

Figure 9.2 Facets Model: Aaron Copland, *Lincoln Portrait*

folk tunes harkens to Lincoln's upbringing and popular appeal. The dotted musical figure that acts as a unifying motive reminds students of the decisiveness of Lincoln's fist on the table in the Rockwell painting. As in the Sandburg poem, Copland portrays multiple sides of Lincoln's character, his folksy origins juxtaposed with decisive oratory. The unit then concludes with a return to the inquiry questions, although another excellent option would be to invite students to create portraits in the artistic medium of their choice.

In this exploration, using portraits as a theme—applied to a specific historical figure captured in multiple art forms—offers flexible aims for understanding the musical work, of course, but also meaningful juxtaposition of the ways that painters, poets, and composers approach the creative process of representing a historical figure. Pedagogical strategies include multiple moments of "noticing" in all three forms, the use of pivot questions as a predictive fulcrum across art forms, and the use of inquiry questions as an introductory move as well as a time for synthesis. A particularly fruitful assessment technique involves the use of a three-way Venn diagram, in which students look for connections between the painting and the poem, the poem and the composition, the composition and the poem, as well as themes, images, or principles that are shared across all three works. A Venn diagram not only explores the connections among the three works, but also focuses attention on the distinctive characteristics of each work itself.

Moving toward the Meaningful Assessment of Interdisciplinarity in the Music Curriculum

These last two examples also illustrate how juxtaposing music with other art forms creates an "interpretive zone" in which individuals can look for similarities and differences among works and art forms. The process and pedagogy of interpretation runs counter to well-learned teaching behaviors that tend to value efficiency over reflection. Interdisciplinarians must learn to dwell in "slow time," trusting that students will forge deeper relationships with the works under consideration if they linger, savor, and let their impact sink in.

Interdisciplinary practices, and even a teacher's approach to shaping an educative experience, can be expressive of artistry: "Artistry consists in having an idea worth expressing, the imaginative ability needed to conceive of how, the technical skills needed to work efficiently with some material, and the sensibilities needed to make the delicate adjustments that will give the forms the moving qualities that the best of them possess" (Eisner, 2002, p. 81). Teachers' curricular artistry is apparent in the ways such an inquiry is introduced, developed, and brought to a synthetic close.

Assessment (if shaken loose from its mechanistic moorings) involves keen listening, looking, thinking, responding, imagining, revising, and reflecting. I wonder what would happen if we could revitalize the term *assessment* to give it new life to refer to what teachers do when they are keenly inquisitive about the ways that students make sense of their experience. I suspect that it has become entangled in deterministic, reductive, and neoliberal discourse and that teachers are weary of talk about assessment. I suspect that the meanings of *growth* as in "growth measures" are very different from the Deweyan sense of taking something from the past that in turn is modified through experience toward resonance in the future. In its most generous form, assessment allows teachers to marvel at the networks of meaning that students form through their work in an interdisciplinary classroom, the networks made even more extensive and intertwined through interdisciplinarity. When this satisfaction is shared with students, with other teachers, with parents, with visiting artists, and with the community, integrated thinking is made public. Such efforts can be celebrated, recognized, and deservedly praised.

10
The Music Curriculum in an Interdisciplinary Landscape

A landscape calls up images of nearly limitless space, far horizons, verdant growth, and flourishing ecosystems of interdependent life. I evoke this image purposefully in this last chapter as an invitation to think generously and wisely about the promises of interdisciplinarity in the music curriculum. I imagine standing in a field (in both senses of the word) brimming with possibility for teachers' creativity, for curricular avenues both newly invented and revitalized, and for situations that encourage the crossing of boundaries. I imagine students' awakenings to vibrant forms of feeling, intersections of knowledge, and realms of meaning. I imagine a renaissance of support for and commitment to public schooling, recognizing its centrality to democratic living.

If this sounds like a utopian dream, I stand by the vision. So many others stand here, too, oriented toward promise. Among those curriculum scholars and philosophers, I draw hope from Patrick Slattery's statement: "we must recognize that, while the present is conditioned by the past, every moment is also full of future possibilities for change and new directions" (2013, p. 282). I take heart in Maxine Greene's admonition that "We also have our social imagination: the capacity to invent visions of what should be and what might be in our deficient society, on the streets where we live, in our schools" (1995, p. 5). I am challenged by Hannah Arendt's call to "prepare [our children] in advance for the task of renewing a common world" (Arendt, 1961, p. 196).

Yet I am deeply troubled as well, as challenges to teachers, school communities, and public education mount. Combined with the upheavals triggered by the worldwide pandemic, with its unspeakable losses and disruptions, tears in the fabric of our "deficient" society make teachers' lives more difficult than one can imagine. Music teachers have often cut through "white noise" in their school contexts—staying grounded in the face of competing initiatives, mandates, and various distractions. In this moment, though, the noise has intensified to a roar as we hear about efforts to silence teachers by imposing restrictions on what can be taught and learned, attempts to pass legislation banning curricular materials and books, pedagogical prohibitions against teaching about race, class, sexual identity, and gender. I am concerned about a growing inhospitable environment that compromises teachers' abilities to exercise their professional judgment.

Music education is inextricably implicated in these struggles, caught up in this raucous clamor and unsettling climate, as the musics we perform, study, and create bear the very markers of culture, identity, and group affiliation that some wish to ban. At a time when so many music educators are welcoming diverse repertoires and voices, they can be silenced as well. As they situate musical traditions in historical contexts and artistic movements, such as some of the examples portrayed in these pages, music educators teach powerful lessons about what it means to express human experience in sound. I hold hope that they will be given the freedom to align their values, beliefs, and practices toward these ends.

In this final chapter, I return to interdisciplinarity as a "version" of music education that might provide openings for moving forward, although of course, not as a panacea or a prescription. Just as Eisner names multiple visions and versions of art education, maintaining that these approaches are the "products not only of visionary minds and persuasive arguments, but also of social forces that create conditions that make certain aims congenial to the times" (2002, p. 25), I offer these ideas for consideration, development, and critique by the field if the underlying premises hold merit and if they are found congenial to the times, or even welcome in inhospitable times. Similarly, music teachers, including those who are yet to explore a more connected curriculum and those already sympathetic to these principles, must evaluate their potential.

The purpose of this chapter is to map spaces for interdisciplinarity across two landscapes: first, the broader field of music education, addressing initiatives for professional development and music teacher education. The second focus speaks directly to local contexts, offering insights for music teachers to consider as they take up, expand, or refine these ideas.

Toward Interdisciplinarity within the Field of Music Education

Music education is currently undergoing a transformation unlike any I have witnessed in more than four decades of teaching, enabled by lively philosophical discourse, critical scrutiny of practices and repertoires, greater emphasis on musical creativity, and reconfiguration of music teacher education programs. In this mix, I stay on the lookout for audible and visible signs that richly relational aspects of music teaching and learning are on the rise. What follows are some recommendations to strengthen an interdisciplinary emphasis in the field.

Philosophical inquiry along these lines might turn to the boundary-breaking work of artists who travel in many social contexts, and who sit at the nexus of the cross-fertilization of arts and their relevance to societal issues. The creative dynamism and collective energy they generate, alongside the prolific hybridization of art forms, seem particularly promising for those who want to explore the intersections of contemporary art making with elementary and secondary education. If there is indeed a "new renaissance" building in the twenty-first century, music education may be better served in developing interdisciplinary rationales by looking to these realms of innovation than rather than relying on questionable instrumental claims that the arts improve test scores. I look forward to the development of a plurality of aims for this boundary-crossing perspective.

As an editor of a research journal, I seldom receive studies that pertain to curricular matters. I call on more researchers to conduct systematic study of programs that illuminate how teachers, artists, and teaching artists occupy shared spaces between the arts and humanities on behalf of students' learning. Case studies that document the particularity and complexity of relational teaching and learning would be especially welcome. One area in particular that seems pressing has to do with interdisciplinary arts activity in middle school settings. Middle schools often claim interdisciplinarity as an organizational pillar of the middle school experience. In what ways do music teachers at this level contribute to this mission? Portraits of students' school experiences in richly connective environments, at any level, would offer narrative accounts of the ways they make sense and draw connections for integrated views of their worlds.

I have written elsewhere that this perspective is not a method, and especially not in the way that professional discourse in music education often labels philosophical and pedagogical systems as such (Barrett, 2016). There are no periodicals, annual meetings, professional associations, or membership dues for interdisciplinarians. Yet there is a need, in my view, to create networks or channels for music educators aligned with these ideas to converse with one another. There is a need for the thoughtful work of these teachers to be accessible to others through publication, presentation, or some other medium. In comprehensive views of the music curriculum (especially in what we call "general music"), pedagogical possibilities abound. The benefits of relational thinking should not be confined, though, to any particular branch of music education, so I suspect that those who are inclined to integrated perspectives are widely dispersed and would benefit from greater coordination, collaboration, and recognition.

Artistically conceived professional development fosters teacher learning. An altogether too common criticism of professional development for music teachers is that it all too often falls short of its aims. A recurrent problem is the format. "One-off" conference sessions or workshops that are mostly presentational are useful for planting seeds, but their limited scope is insufficient to sustain teachers' interests and explorations. In my view, short courses, networks or institutes, site-based and long-term projects, and especially graduate study provide more substantive ground for intellectual and collegial exchange, and thus are also more likely to lead to robust curricular growth.

I offer five criteria to consider in creating and critiquing professional development for music educators that facilitates curriculum integration. Such programs must ring true for musical processes (most often identified as creating, performing, responding, and connecting), as well as the diverse and dynamic musical traditions and practices emphasized in the curriculum. They must meet expectations of *disciplinary fit*. Second, offerings must enable meaningful, rather than superficial, connections between and among related subject areas in ways that make sense, including the arts and other disciplines. They must promote *interdisciplinary integrity*. Third, programs should meet the particular needs and characteristics of the *school contexts* in which the music teachers serve. There is no "one size fits all" in curricular work, so flexibility is critical if teachers are to adapt interdisciplinary ideas to the affordances and constraints of various school settings. I hold the fourth criterion as beneficial, but not essential, given that some music teachers make inventive curricular moves on their own without the benefit of collaborative engagement with others. However, the *collaborative capacity* of interdisciplinary initiatives enables teachers to form professional learning communities while drawing upon the expertise of disciplinary specialists and amplifying the collective wisdom of practice held within the group. Finally, the last criterion for consideration is the way that professional development initiatives address *teacher growth* through cultivating imagination, promoting inquiry, fostering educational critique, and making space for reflection. Of course, such an ambitious view of growth is more likely a lifelong project, but any proposal that claims to transform teachers' thinking must honor the expertise they bring with them, and justify its value in teachers' lives by acknowledging these crucial dimensions of teachers' work.

When I speak with other music teacher educators about interdisciplinarity, a frequent question is "Where does this fit?" in an undergraduate program. So often, any emphasis on curricular integration is but a cursory flash in a carousel of course topics and requirements. I understand this concern, particularly in light of "methods" courses that include so much "content" that teacher educators feel compelled to "cover" (every quotation mark intended). I find this an intractable dilemma. If music teacher educators value an interdisciplinary perspective, its exploration will have greater resonance and staying power if embedded within the curriculum, not just dropped in. I have been extraordinarily fortunate to teach courses dedicated to the curricular imagination at two universities. These courses have sometimes been required for undergraduate music education majors while open to all who are interested. This openness has brought such richness to the classroom conversations as students from many areas of study have contributed valuable insights and ideas.

At the graduate level, master's students in summer programs have found a course-long emphasis sufficient as an intellectual space to play with ideas, strategies, and techniques, to explore models, and to invent their own projects. Many have implemented these projects, returning to showcase their impact on students' learning in elementary, middle, and high school settings. Their enthusiasm for this work is palpable, as is my respect for the range of subjects and settings in which their work has taken hold.

Toward Interdisciplinary Stances for Music Teachers

The landscape as viewed by music teachers in their school settings has familiar, distinctive features. Communities influence schools, and the educational opportunities of those who inhabit them. Curriculum is not placeless, far from generic. Music teachers who come to understand the social relationships, community histories, shared traditions, and political character of a school community also understand the ways these elements shape, in part and in varied degrees, educative possibilities for teachers and students

(Campbell et al., 2021). They also navigate through the contingencies of the landscape, aware of local expectations and school policy, as they exercise curricular agency (Barrett, 2020). Music teachers who take on an interdisciplinary perspective do so while embedded in and knowledgeable about these context-bound elements of their school surroundings.

I imagine taking a grand tour of schools where the spirit of interdisciplinarity flourishes, and where students' educational experiences surge with the energy that the arts make possible. I imagine observing music teachers as they create the environing conditions that bring students' rich insights to the surface (Dewey, 1938). I want to interview these teachers to learn more from the wisdom of practice they have crafted as they foster integrated mindsets. Again, I hear Elliot Eisner's voice: "Anyone can "look in on schools. The trick is to see. Seeing requires an enlightened eye . . . through which different genres of teaching can be appreciated" (1992, p. 620).

With an enlightened eye, then, what might one see if intrigued by the teaching "genre" of an interdisciplinary perspective? How might you strengthen this stance in your own work if you find it compelling? In drawing these pages to a close (but never a conclusion, never a stopping point), I offer suggestions for those who are considering a more integrated stance, or who want to deepen their commitments.

Attend to your own artistic growth and sustenance by participating in the artistic life of your community and renewing artistic interests that may have been displaced by other responsibilities. When I achieved tenure at one of my universities, close friends and family staged an "intervention" to help me recalibrate my energies, suggesting that "I do something I have never done, but always wanted to do." Although I had a rich life of museum attendance and learning about artists, I returned to art making after decades away, taking classes in pastels, abstract art, and watercolor. The shift in roles from teacher to student was profound for me, yielding provocative insights that folded back into my music teaching, such as the feeling of beginning over, embracing vulnerability, following curiosities.

Another fertile catalyst for personal growth is to *create your own stretching exercises*. A particularly lively exercise is "make your own field trip," which invites teachers to branch out by participating in a community arts experience in areas "outside" what they would normally take in. Music teachers who have played with this idea have first immersed themselves in the experience without consulting outside resources, relying on their own sensibilities and curiosities in a less familiar space. Once they feel "immersed," they have often informed their experience by drawing on experts or consulting reference material, taking a metacognitive view to notice how their impressions shift or stand firm. Many have drawn on their musical sensibilities as pathways for encountering the unfamiliar, such as performance art, architecture tours, cultural dance festivals, and even fashion shows.

Start with manageable curricular projects before branching out. The demands and pressures of teaching are many. I often encounter teachers who find these ideas intriguing but overwhelming. A good starting place is to search for a work that falls into the category "works with a high IQ," and especially one that you have longed to explore with your students. As you engage with the work, take time to follow the paths that lead outward from the work, and then return again to the work to reflect on the way connected paths strengthen musical understanding, awareness, expressivity, and interpretation. After auditioning the work and finding it promising, introduce it to your students, keeping the pedagogical space as flexible and open as possible as they form connections of their own. Teachers often tell me that they begin with just one work as part of a concert cycle, or a quarter or semester.

Search for kindred souls with complementary sensibilities. If an interdisciplinary perspective is indeed a stance, a way of viewing teaching and learning (and perhaps life in general), look for others who share related aims for integrating thought, experience, and curricular initiative. Build an affinity group of music educators, arts educators, history and social studies teachers, composers, poets, improvisers, artists, and others, establishing a community for creative and critical exchange.

In collaborative teams, lead with examples. There are rich benefits to collaboration and shared expertise if your context and circumstances make joint effort possible. I have often found that initial conversations about curricular integration usually float around the table, with ideas circling overhead in fairly ambiguous ways as teachers first share ideas from their disciplinary home bases. Talk about the arts with others can feel nebulous and circular (which is probably one of the reasons that talk is insufficient). Memories of unsatisfactory prior encounters with integrated initiatives often cast shadows over the proceedings. It is helpful to recall how teachers are socialized to protect the home bases of their disciplines, so it may take time and trust to move forward. Looking at specific examples, much like a centerpiece in the middle of the table, often grounds teachers' curricular deliberations by providing clearer focus on possible aims and strategies, points of connection, and avenues of intersection.

Work across the borders of specialization. Think generously about those who might contribute to creating educative experiences. Look to students as co-constructors of the curriculum, for example. What ideas fuel their imaginations and what might be possible in bringing these ideas into a curricular moment? Challenge "subspecialties" of music education by pushing against boundaries established by teachers of general music, instrumental music, choral music, technology, popular music, composition, and other areas of emphasis. Look to other arts specialists in your schools, as well as "classroom" teachers in the corridors who have experience and interests in the arts. Community partnerships are fertile environments for interdisciplinary work, especially as orchestra leagues, community bands, museums, galleries, centers for the book arts, folk music societies, and other established groups seek ways to widen their circles of participation and reach.

Refine what it means to do this work well; gather examples of students' projects as compelling evidence and study them. Continue to refine the criteria for evaluating the potency of interdisciplinary projects, what they offer music education, what they offer more rounded views of students' growth. Vivid examples of student work and stories of educationally vital experiences serve as the most convincing and compelling rationale for a curricular emphasis. Look for ways to capture this evidence as students exercise their relational thinking and communicate these relationships in multiple forms of expression. I have been delighted by performances accompanied by exhibitions of students' writing, art works, and imaginative projects.

To Be on the Search

The primary goals of interdisciplinary work in music and the arts are to promote relational understanding, to invite and intensify expressive meanings, and to foster lifelong engagement. The role of the interdisciplinarian is to mediate students' meaning making, which is enabled by the breadth and depth of connections they form. Recall the opening metaphors, and the image of meaning carrying across permeable boundaries. Teachers take an interdisciplinary stance when they exercise their knowledge, craftsmanship, caring, and passion in the service of this integration and synthesis. I see this stance as an orienting compass, not a passing curricular trend. Music teachers' professional judgment is paramount so that learning experiences reflect the integrity of music study in complementary awareness of the integrity of related disciplines.

Teaching for connections also sets music apart as a distinct form of human expression, heightening the way students value music and participate in the pleasures and challenges it affords. Unless we are able to see interdisciplinary approaches as congruent with music education's visions of the curriculum, such efforts will be seen as peripheral to the field's primary purposes and aims. Starting with multidimensional works, and studying fewer of them more comprehensively, will also allow instructional space for the interpretation of those works, and for the germination of meaningful relationships. The satisfactions and joys that come from witnessing vibrant moments of connection have lasting impact on teachers, students, and communities.

"An interdisciplinary perspective" resists classification and rigid definition, while opening space for catalytic turns and openings. In my own teaching, shifting my thinking about music from a clearly defined subject area that needs to be patrolled and defended to a form of permeable human expression open to influence from other realms and capable of influencing other realms has been profound. This shift has altered the way I view curriculum and pedagogy, inviting more fluidity, flexibility, complexity, improvisatory play, and risk-taking. My understanding of integrated curriculum has become more provisional, nuanced, and supple than when I first started on this path.

The generative promise of an interdisciplinary perspective calls music teachers and others toward more elastic views of curriculum-making. As teachers create conditions that invite young persons to make sense of their worlds, experiencing the relevance and resonance of the arts in their lives, we can move nearer to the realization of education as an emancipatory force. In times that ask so much of teachers, that call for healing and compassion, the arts can shed light on areas of injustice by creating educative spaces in which empathy can take hold. May teachers' artistry in curriculum-making, pedagogical creativity, caring, and passion bring these integrated forms of feeling and understanding into young persons' lives.

Notes

Chapter 1

1. Jacobs attributes this definition to the noted Swiss psychologist Jean Piaget, citing *The Epistemology of Interdisciplinary Relationships*, 1972. This definition was developed for use in an international survey of teaching and research in universities reported in the same collection of papers as Piaget's, but cannot be attributed to him.
2. https://libbylarsen.com/works/song-concerto/.
3. https://www.nytimes.com/2013/12/29/arts/music/claire-chase-invites-young-musicians-to-create-new-paths.html.
4. https://www.music.northwestern.edu/news/2013/claire-chases-2013-convocation-address.
5. https://designcenter.illinois.edu.
6. Bernstein's groundbreaking Norton Lectures given at Harvard University in 1973.

Chapter 2

1. I have taken the liberty of changing pronouns to gender-neutral forms whenever possible.
2. One of the privileges of coauthorship is being able to attribute a particular idea to a particular person, in this case my cherished friend Claire Wehr McCoy (1954–2000).
3. Jackson engages many dimensions of Dewey's philosophy beyond what is presented here, including the principles of interaction and continuity, the consummatory aspects of experience, the qualitative immediacy, expressiveness of the arts, unity, temporality, objects as catalysts for experience, their qualitative immediacy, relation to emotion, AND intrinsic and extrinsic meanings, among others.
4. I readily acknowledge the privileges that enable this progression of persons through music in schools, recognizing that not all persons have access and not all communities provide these opportunities.

Chapter 3

1. https://www.musicbusinessworldwide.com/over-60000-tracks-are-now-uploaded-to-spotify-daily-thats-nearly-one-per-second/.
2. https://www.youtube.com/watch?v=9YS5xfA7MYg.

218   NOTES

3. https://libbylarsen.com/resources/on-music/.
4. The other two systems are the line and the sentence. Peacock may be drawing here from Ezra Pound's *melopoeia, logopoeia, and phanopoeia*, having to do with the rhythmic qualities, intellectual content, and imagery at work in most forms of poetry.

Chapter 4

1. Gandolfi's expansion has been realized in part through new movements for subsequent performances in Chicago ("The Cosmic Garden in Bloom," 2016) and in Atlanta ("Gardens Feed Also the Soul," 2017).
2. Musicmap, https://www.musicmap.info/#.
3. The basis for the streaming service Pandora.
4. https://www.silkroad.org/rhiannon-giddens-announcement.
5. https://www.fifth-house.com/mission-statement.
6. https://www.roomfulofteeth.org/roomful.
7. In 2019, Roomful of Teeth artistic director Brad Wells and composer Caroline Shaw published a statement acknowledging concerns expressed by Inuit artist Tanya Tagaq that the group had appropriated vocal traditions of the Inuit, *katajjaq*, in *Partita*. Wells and Shaw explained this was not their intent, outlining a number of future actions the group would take in support of Indigenous artists and in acknowledgment of these cultural practices. (Document found on *Scribd*, October 23, 2019).
8. https://massmoca.org/event/walldrawing305/.

Chapter 5

1. My involvement with this project was in the 1990s. BandQuest still continues today with innovative programming for young bands. The American Composers Forum added a ChoralQuest project in the 2000s.
2. My deepest thanks to Herb Dick, who has kept a vintage Mac alive to access the CD-ROM, and who was able to capture this screen shot of the dashboard. Kudos, also, to Laura Krider of the American Composers Forum, who had additional screen shots for *Old Churches* in her files. Joanna Cortright, Rebecca Tokke, and Tim Buzza were also involved in the development of the curriculum. Searching for evidence of this project reminds me of the importance of archival work to preserve the intellectual fruits of collaboration.
3. At the time of writing, a brief clip from this interview was available on the BandQuest site: https://composersforum.org/BandQuest/old-churches/. Other clips of Colgrass working with the middle school students were available on YouTube.
4. Composer's note on the Winona Drive project (unpublished, undated).
5. In the spirit of this project and its collaborative team, the students heard their compositions workshopped by the University of Minnesota's University Wind Ensemble. Imagine that!

Chapter 6

1. https://catalog.aclib.us/Mobile/BakerAndTaylor/Review?ISBN=0810943867&UPC=&position=1.
2. https://whitney.org/exhibitions/jasper-johns?section=3#exhibition-artworks.
3. Access available reproductions of this painting (and others throughout this chapter) to more fully experience color and texture.
4. Readers are encouraged to access multiple works by the artists named throughout this chapter, most readily accessible from museum websites.
5. https://theconversation.com/50-years-ago-jimi-hendrixs-woodstock-anthem-expressed-the-hopes-and-fears-of-a-nation-120717.
6. https://www.nytimes.com/2022/02/18/arts/music/tyshawn-sorey-rothko-chapel.html.
7. I use Christopher Rothko's first name here just to keep him straight from his father's name, which I list as Rothko.
8. From McGrath, "A Portraitist Whose Canvas Is a Piano," *New York Times*, April 22, 2005, https://www.nytimes.com/2005/04/22/arts/music/a-portraitist-whose-canvas-is-a-piano.html.
9. In 2017, allegations of sexual harassment were raised against Close, leading some museums to remove his paintings or cancel planned exhibitions. Upon his death in 2021, the art world grappled with the impact of these allegations on his legacy.
10. Other examples include Michael Daughterty's *Ladder to the Moon*, evoking New York City landscapes; John Harbison's *Piano Quintet* (1981); Steve Heitzig's score for the film *A Marriage: Georgia O'Keeffe and Alfred Stieglitz*; Dan Welcher's *Prairie Light*, based on three watercolors; and no doubt many others not listed here. A particularly interesting compositional and contextual history surrounds Samuel Hazo's *Blue and Green Music* for wind ensemble. This composition was commissioned by Patrick Marsh Middle School in Sun Prairie, Wisconsin, where Georgia O'Keeffe was born. Curiously, many of the middle school students were unaware of this famous painter's connection to Sun Prairie, so they toured her birthplace as part of the study.
11. Notes for "Black Birds, Red Hills," https://libbylarsen.com/works/black-birds-red-hills. A recording of this work can also be accessed on Larsen's website.
12. http://www.kevinputs.com/works/the-brightness-of-light.html.
13. Copland, "What to Listen For in Music" (1988).

Chapter 7

1. Pronounced in German with characteristic closed and tight "e" sound similar to "kleh" or "clay."
2. An excerpt from Klee's lecture notes showing how he mapped out this Bach sonata: http://www.kleegestaltungslehre.zpk.org/ee/ZPK/BF/2012/01/01/055/.
3. Access this art work online as well to note Klee's use of color.
4. I have used letters instead of numbers for the five lessons to suggest that teachers might easily think of a different sequence that more flexibly fits the needs and interests

of the students and the contexts in which they teach. These encounters may be read as a curricular unit, but I encourage the readers to forge their own path.
5. String teachers often comment on Klee's posture when they see this photo.
6. Throughout these lesson examples, I have drawn on the work of scholars and art historians named earlier in the chapter.
7. Not suitable for children!
8. Examples presented earlier in this chapter may be helpful.
9. This lesson can easily be adapted to younger children with some modifications. You might begin with *Paul Klee Animal Tricks* (Rümelin, 2002), asking them to name or spot the animals they see in *Fish Picture*, *Where Eggs Come From* (chicken and pig), *With the Brown* (camel), *Brocard Cat Washing*, and *Twittering Machine*. Invite them to describe the artist's style. *This book is called Animal Tricks . . . why do you think the author picked that title?*
10. Consider asking students to write "program notes" for their compositions that speak to their inspirations and intentions.
11. Maud Hickey's *Music Outside the Lines: Ideas for Composing in K–12 Music Classrooms* provides an entire curriculum and many open-ended strategies for teaching composition. A parallel lesson to *Twittering Machine* that may provide further ideas and guidance can be found in Activity 4F: Arts Together Inspire (2012, pp. 82–83).
12. Speech pieces in *Silver Burdett Music* in the 1970s were my inspiration for this sound piece.

Chapter 8

1. Winter's book is one of several children's books on this theme: http://www.followthedrinkinggourd.org/Appendix_Childrens_Books.htm.
2. *Follow the Drinking Gourd* is included in a lesson plan on layers of meaning in spirituals found in my own coauthored book, in fact (Barrett, McCoy, & Veblen, 1997).
3. See also "Song, Story, or History: Resisting Claims of a Coded Message in the African American Spiritual 'Follow the Drinking Gourd'" (Kelley, 2008).
4. See Jacob Lawrence, "Forward Together" (1997), depicting Harriet Tubman; Aaron Douglas, "Aspiration" (1936).
5. https://www.nationalgeographic.org/maps/undergroundrailroad/?utm_source=BiblioRCM_Row.
6. https://www.npr.org/sections/thetwo-way/2016/01/18/463488364/amid-controversy-scholastic-pulls-picture-book-about-washingtons-slave.
7. From Episode 5, Season 2, "Teaching Slavery through Children's Literature, Part 1: with Ebony Elizabeth Thomas, https://www.learningforjustice.org/podcasts/teaching-hard-history/american-slavery/teaching-slavery-through-childrens-literature-part-1.
8. https://www.facinghistory.org/about-us.
9. https://rethinkingschools.org/about-rethinking-schools/our-history/.

10. The 1619 Project has catalyzed especially strong opinions and responses from historians, politicians, educators, and community leaders, raising questions about the nature of historical fact and interpretation, objectivity, ideology, and curricular agency. For scholarly critique of the project and its reception, see Jamnah and Zimmerman (2022), Pickup and Southall (2022), as well as numerous reports and podcasts.
11. A short film by the 21C Media Group includes interviews with Steven Stucky, Gene Scheer, and the families of the slain civil rights workers: https://www.youtube.com/watch?v=WtSQ4PJTnrI.
12. Johnson's speech as transcribed from the film listed above.

Chapter 9

1. With appreciation to Joanna Cortright for this useful term.
2. English translation by Barbara and Erica Muhl, appearing in the score (Southern Music Publishing, 1994).
3. With appreciation to Stephen Dowling, who inspired this example.
4. The narrator begins approximately halfway through the entire work, which is approximately fourteen minutes in length.

References

Addonizio, K., & Laux, D. (1997). *The poet's companion: A guide to the pleasures of writing poetry*. W. W. Norton.

Akkerman, S. F., & Meijer, P. C. (2011). A dialogical approach to conceptualizing teacher identity. *Teaching and Teacher Education, 27*, 308–319.

Allsup, R. E. (2010). Choosing music literature. In H. F. Abeles & L. A. Custodero (Eds.), *Critical issues in music education: Contemporary theory and practice* (pp. 215–235). Oxford University Press.

Allsup, R. E. (2016). *Remixing the classroom: Toward an open philosophy of music education*. Indiana University Press.

American Composers Forum. (1997). *Blueprint for New Band Horizons*. American Composers Forum.

Arendt, H. (1961). *Between past and future: Six exercises in political thought*. Viking Press.

Ayers, W. (2019). *About becoming a teacher*. Teachers College Press.

Barrett, J. R. (2006a). Developing the professional judgment of preservice music teachers: Grading as a case in point. *Journal of Music Teacher Education, 15*(2), 8–20.

Barrett, J. R. (2006b). Highways and byways: Interdisciplinarity, teacher knowledge, and the comprehensive music curriculum. *Mountain Lake Reader: Conversations on the Study and Practice of Music Teaching, IV*, 24–36.

Barrett, J. R. (2007). Music teachers' lateral knowledge. *Bulletin of the Council for Research in Music Education, 147*, 7–23.

Barrett, J. R. (2016). Adopting an interdisciplinary approach to general music. In C. R. Abril & B. M. Gault (Eds.), *Teaching general music: Approaches, issues, and viewpoints* (pp. 168–182). Oxford University Press.

Barrett, J. R. (2020). Policy at the intersection of curriculum and music teacher agency. *Music Educators Journal, 107*(1), 37–42.

Barrett, J. R. (2022). Fostering historical empathy through music, art, and poetry. In C. R. Abril & B. M. Gault (Eds.), *General music: Dimensions of practice* (pp. 134–151). Oxford University Press.

Barrett, J. R., McCoy, C. W., & Veblen, K. K. (1997). *Sound ways of knowing: Music in the interdisciplinary curriculum*. Schirmer Books.

Barrett, J. R., & Veblen, K. K. (2018). Meaningful connections in a comprehensive approach to the music curriculum. In G. E. McPherson & G. F. Welch (Eds.), *Music learning and teaching in infancy, childhood, and adolescence* (pp. 141–159). Oxford University Press.

Barrett, T. (2000). About art interpretation for art education. *Studies in Art Education, 42*(1), 5–19.

Bates, M. (2014). *Alternative energy*. Aphra Music.

Bernstein, L. (1965). *The unanswered question: Six talks at Harvard*. Harvard University Press.

Bickford, J. H., & Rich, C. W. (2014). Examining the representation of slavery within children's literature. *Social Studies Research and Practice, 9*(1), 66–94.

Boix Mansilla, V. (2005). Assessing student work at disciplinary crossroads. *Change, 37*(1), 14–21.

Bond, J., & Wilson, S. K. (Eds.). (2000). *Lift every voice and sing: A celebration of the Negro national anthem.* Random House.

Breakstone, J. (2014). Try, try, try again: The process of designing new history assessments. *Theory and Research in Social Education, 42*(4), 453–485.

Bresler, J. (2008). Follow the drinking gourd: A cultural history. http://www.followthedrinkinggourd.org/.

Bresler, L. (1995). The subservient, co-equal, affective and social integration styles and their implications for the arts. *Arts Education Policy Review, 96*(5), 31–37.

Bresler, L. (2002). Out of the trenches: The joys (and risks) of cross-disciplinary collaborations. *Bulletin of the Council for Research in Music Education, 152,* 17–39.

Bruhn, S. (2000). *Musical ekphrasis: Composers responding to poetry and painting.* Pendragon Press.

Bruner, J. (1982). The language of education. *Social Research, 49*(4), 835–853.

Bruner, J. (1996). *The culture of education.* Harvard University Press.

Bruner, J. S. (1960/1977). *The process of education.* Harvard University Press.

Bruner, J. S. (2006). *In search of pedagogy* (Vol. II). Routledge.

Burton, J. M., Horowitz, R., & Abeles, H. (2000). Learning in and through the arts: The question of transfer. *Studies in Art Education: A Journal of Issues and Research, 41*(3), 228–257.

Cage, J. (1967). *A year from Monday: New lectures and writings by John Cage.* Wesleyan University Press.

Campbell, M. R., Thompson, L. K., & Barrett, J. R. (2021). *Constructing a personal orientation to music teaching: Growth, inquiry, and agency* (2nd ed.). Routledge.

Celenza, A. H. (2016). *Mussorgsky's Pictures at an Exhibition (Once upon a masterpiece).* Charlesbridge.

Cochran-Smith, M. (1991). Learning to teach against the grain. *Harvard Educational Review, 61*(3), 279–311.

Colgrass, M. (2002). *Old churches.* American Composers Forum.

Comita, J. (2007, October 31). Chuck Close: Portrait of the artist. *W Magazine.*

Copland, A., & Perlis, V. (1984). *Copland 1900 through 1942.* St. Martin's/Marek.

Costa, A. L., & Kallick, B. (2008). *Learning and leading with habits of mind: 16 essential characteristics for success.* Association for Supervision and Curriculum Development.

Crist, E. B. (2005). Copland and the politics of America. In C. J. Oja & J. Tick (Eds.), *Aaron Copland and his world* (pp. 277–306). Princeton University Press.

Crook, E., Reimer, B., & Walker, D. S. (1978). *Silver Burdett music: Teacher's edition.* Silver Burdett Company.

Crowe, T. R., & Watkins, N. (2008). *Rare birds: Conversations with legends of jazz and classical music.* University Press of Mississippi.

Curwen, C. (2018). Music-colour synaesthesia: Concept, context and qualia. *Consciousness and Cognition, 61,* 94–106.

Davids, B. M. (2002). *Grandmother song.* American Composer Forum.

Detels, C. (1999). *Soft boundaries: Re-visioning the arts and aesthetics in American education.* Bergin & Garvey.

Dewey, J. (1916/1944). *Democracy and education.* Macmillan.

Dewey, J. (1934). *Art as experience*. Perigee Books.
Dewey, J. (1938). *Experience and education*. Collier Books.
Düchting, H. (1997). *Paul Klee: Painting and music*. Prestel.
Dutton, J. (2015). The surprising world of synaesthesia. *The Psychologist, 28*, 106–109.
Eisner, E. W. (1990). Creative curriculum development and practice. *Journal of Curriculum and Supervision, 6*(1), 62–73.
Eisner, E. W. (1991). Art, literature, and music within social studies. In Shaver, J. P. (Ed.), *Handbook of research on social studies teaching and learning* (pp. 551–558). Macmillan.
Eisner, E. W. (1992). Educational reform and the ecology of schooling. *Teachers College Record, 93*(4), 610–627.
Eisner, E. W. (2002). *The arts and the creation of mind*. Yale University Press.
Endacott, J., & Brooks, S. (2013). An updated theoretical and practical model for promoting historical empathy. *Social Studies Research and Practice, 8*(1), 41–58.
Endacott, J. L. (2014). Negotiating the process of historical empathy. *Theory and Research in Social Education, 42*, 4–34.
Evans, G. (2002). *Music inspired by art: A guide to recordings*. Scarecrow Press.
Evans, S. W. (2011). *Underground: Finding the light to freedom*. Roaring Brook Press.
Fautley, M., & Colwell, R. (2012). Assessment in the secondary school classroom. In G. F. Welch & G. E. McPherson (Eds.), *Oxford handbook of music education* (Vol. 1, pp. 478–494). Oxford University Press.
Francis, R. (1984). *Jasper Johns*. Abbeville Press.
Freire, P. (1998). *Pedagogy of freedom: Ethics, democracy, and civic courage*. Rowman & Littlefield.
Gabriel, M. (2018). *Ninth street women: Lee Krasner, Elaine de Kooning, Grace Hartigan, Joan Mitchell, and Helen Frankenthaler: Five painters and the movement that changed modern art*. Back Bay Books.
Gardner, H. (1991). *The unschooled mind: How children think and how schools should teach*. Basic Books.
Gardner, H., & Boix Mansilla, V. (1994). Teaching for understanding in the disciplines and beyond. *Teachers College Record, 96*(2), 198–218.
Glass, P. (2015). *Words without music: A memoir*. Liveright Publishing Company.
Greenberg, J. (2001). *Heart to heart: New poems inspired by twentieth-century American art*. Harry N. Abrams.
Greene, M. (1995). *Releasing the imagination: Essays on education, the arts, and social change*. Jossey-Bass.
Grossman, P., Wineburg, S., & Beers, S. (2000). Introduction: When theory meets practice in the world of school. In S. Wineburg & P. Grossman (Eds.), *Interdisciplinary curriculum: Challenges to implementation* (pp. 1–16). Teachers College Press.
Halvorsen, A.-L. (2017). Children's learning and understanding in their social world. In M. M. Manfra & C. M. Bolick (Eds.), *The Wiley handbook of social studies research* (pp. 385–413). John Wiley.
Hannah-Jones, N., Roper, C., Silverman, I., & Silverstein, J. (Eds.). (2021). *The 1619 Project: A new origin story*. New York Times Company.
Hargreaves, A., Earl, L., Moore, S., & Manning, S. (2001). *Learning to change: Teaching beyond subjects and standards*. Jossey-Bass.
Hess, J. (2015). Decolonizing music education: Moving beyond tokenism. *International Journal of Music Education, 33*(3), 336–347.

Hess, J. (2021). Becoming an anti-racist music educator: Resisting Whiteness in music education. *Music Educators Journal, 107*(4), 14–20.

Hevner, K. (1936). Experimental studies of the elements of expression in music. *The American Journal of Psychology, 48*(2), 246–268.

Hickey, M. (2012). *Music outside the lines: Ideas for composing in K–12 music classrooms.* Oxford University Press.

Hill, J. (2018). *Becoming creative: Insights from musicians in a diverse world.* Oxford University Press.

Howard, K. (2021). Ethical song research for the general music teacher. *General Music Today, 34*(3), 42–44.

Howard, P., Becker, C., Wiebe, S., Carter, M., Gouzouasis, P., McLarnon, M., Richardson, P., Ricketts, K., & Schuman, L. (2018). Creativity and pedagogical innovation: Exploring teachers' experiences of risk-taking. *Journal of Curriculum Studies, 50*(6), 850–864.

Hughes, R. E. (2021). "What is slavery?" Third-grade students' sensemaking about enslavement through historical inquiry. *Theory and Research in Social Education, 50*(1), 29–73. https://doi.org/10.1080/00933104.2021.1927921.

Intrator, S. M. (1999). *"Spots of time that glow": Portraits of educationally vital experience.* [doctoral dissertation, Stanford University]. Stanford, CA.

Intrator, S. M. (2003). *Tuned in and fired up: How teaching can inspire real learning in the classroom.* Yale University Press.

Intrator, S. M. (2005). Preserving the beauty of learning: The qualities of an aesthetic curriculum. In P. B. Uhrmacher & J. Matthews (Eds.), *Intricate palette: Working the ideas of Elliot Eisner* (pp. 175–182). Pearson.

Jackson, P. W. (1995). If we took Dewey's aesthetics seriously, how would the arts be taught? In J. Garrison (Ed.), *The new scholarship on Dewey* (pp. 25–34). Springer.

Jackson, P. W. (1998). *John Dewey and the lessons of art.* Yale University Press.

Jacobs, H. H. (Ed.). (1989). *Interdisciplinary curriculum: Design and implementation.* Association for Supervision and Curriculum Development.

Jamnah, D., & Zimmerman, J. (2022). Policy dialogue: The war over how history is taught. *History of Education Quarterly, 62*, 231–239.

Jencks, C. (2003). *The garden of cosmic speculation.* Frances Lincoln Limited.

Johnson, J. W. (1933). *Along this way: The autobiography of James Weldon Johnson.* Viking Press.

Johnson, J. W., & Johnson, J. R. (1970). *Lift every voice and sing: Words and music.* Hawthorn Books.

Juslin, P. (2009). Emotion in music performance. In S. Hallam, I. Cross, & M. Thaut (Eds.), *The Oxford handbook of music psychology* (pp. 377–389). Oxford University Press.

Kagan, A. (1983). *Paul Klee: Art and music.* Cornell University Press.

Kajikawa, L. (2019). The possessive investment in classical music: Confronting legacies of white supremacy in U.S. schools and departments of music. In K. W. Crenshaw, L. C. Harris, D. M. HoSang, & G. Lipsitz (Eds.), *Seeing race again: Countering colorblindness across the disciplines* (pp. 155–174). University of California Press.

Kandinsky, W. (1914/1977). *Concerning the spiritual in art.* Dover Publications.

Katz, S. L., & Gardner, H. (2012). Musical materials or metaphorical models? A psychological investigation of what inspires composers. In D. Hargreaves, D. Miell, & R. Macdonald (Eds.), *Musical imaginations: Multidisciplinary perspectives on creativity, performance, and perception* (pp. 108–123). Oxford University Press.

Kelley, J. B. (2008). Song, story, or history: Resisting claims of a coded message in the African American spiritual "Follow the Drinking Gourd." *The Journal of Popular Culture, 41*(2), 262–280.

Klee, P. (1964). *The diaries of Paul Klee, 1898–1918*. University of California Press.

Kliebard, H. M. (2006). Dewey's reconstruction of the curriculum: From occupations to disciplined knowledge. In D. T. Hansen (Ed.), *John Dewey and our educational prospect: A critical engagement with Dewey's Democracy and Education* (pp. 113–128). State University of New York Press.

Kohn, A. (1993). *Punished by rewards: The trouble with gold stars, incentive plans, A's, praise, and other bribes*. Houghton Mifflin.

Langer, S. K. (1957). *Problems of art: Ten philosophical lectures*. Scribner.

Larchner, C. (2009). *Jasper Johns*. The Museum of Modern Art.

Lepore, J. (2012). *The story of America: Essays on origins*. Princeton University Press.

Lum, C.-H., & Campbell, P. S. (2007). The sonic surrounds of an elementary school. *Journal of Research in Music Education, 55*(1), 31–47.

Magee, J. (2000). Irving Berlin's "Blue Skies": Ethnic affiliations and musical transformations. *The Musical Quarterly, 84*(4), 537–580.

McCoy, J. (1994). Choral poetry: The extended works of Morten Lauridsen. *The Choral Journal, 35*(4), 25–30.

McTee, C. (1993). *California counterpoint: The Twittering Machine [program notes]*. Bill Holab Music. http://www.cindymctee.com/california_counterpoint.html.

Megill, A. (2016). *Program notes, "August 4, 1964."* University of Illinois at Urbana-Champaign School of Music.

Morris, W. (2021). Music. In N. Hannah-Jones, C. Roper, I. Silverman, & J. Silverstein (Eds.), *The 1619 Project: A new origin story* (pp. 359–379). New York Times Company.

National Museum of the American Indian. (2019). *Symbol and reality: The North Star in American culture (Follow the Drinking Gourd)*. Retrieved December 21, 2021, from https://www.youtube.com/watch?v=AjzmcaC9vJ4.

Natvig, M. (Ed.). (2017). *Teaching music history*. Routledge.

O'Keeffe, G. (1976). *Georgia O'Keeffe*. Viking Press.

O'Toole, P. (2003). *Shaping sound musicians: An innovative approach to teaching comprehensive musicianship through performance*. GIA.

Oxford University Press. (2021). *OED Online*. Oxford University Press. www.oed.com/view/Entry/59412.

Page, R. N. (2006). Curriculum matters. In D. T. Hansen (Ed.), *John Dewey and our educational prospect: A critical engagement with Dewey's Democracy and Education* (pp. 39–65). State University of New York Press.

Palmer, P. J. (2011). *Healing the heart of democracy: The courage to create a politics worthy of the human spirit*. Jossey-Bass.

Parini, J. (2008). *Why poetry matters*. Yale University Press.

Parks, H. B. (1928). Follow the drinking gourd. *Publications of the Texas Folklore Society, 7*, 81–84.

Parsons, M. (2004). Art and integrated curriculum. In E. W. Eisner & M. D. Day (Eds.), *Handbook of research and policy in art education* (pp. 775–794). Lawrence Erlbaum.

Patterson, T., & Shuttleworth, J. M. (2019). The (mis)representation of enslavement in historical literature for elementary students. *Teachers College Record, 121*(4), 1–40.

Patterson, T. J. (2020). Teaching hard history through children's literature about enslavement. *Social Studies and the Young Learner, 32*(3), 14–19.

Peacock, M. (1999). *How to read a poem . . . and start a poetry circle*. Riverhead Books.
Perry, I. (2018). *May we forever stand: A history of the Black national anthem*. University of North Carolina Press.
Peterson, M. D. (1994). *Lincoln in American memory*. Oxford University Press.
Peterson, R. A., & Kern, R. M. (1996). Changing highbrow taste: From snob to omnivore. *American Sociological Review, 61*(5), 900–907.
Phenix, P. H. (1964). *Realms of meaning: A philosophy of the curriculum for general education*. McGraw-Hill.
Pickup, A. J., & Southall, A. B. (2022). A critical discourse analysis of the 1619 Project controversy and its implications for social studies educators. *The Social Studies, 113*(5), 223–236.
Pierce, K. M. (2005/2006). Posing, pretending, waiting for the bell: Life in high school classrooms. *The High School Journal, 89*(2), 1–15.
Pope, D. C. (2001). *"Doing school": How we are creating a generation of stressed-out, materialistic, and miseducated students*. Yale University Press.
Reimer, B. (1991). Criteria for quality in music. In R. A. Smith & A. Simpson (Eds.), *Aesthetics and arts education* (pp. 330–338). University of Illinois Press.
Reimer, B. (2003). *A philosophy of music education: Advancing the vision* (3rd ed.). Prentice Hall.
Rifkin, N., & Strick, J. (2005). Foreword. In K. Brougher, J. Strick, A. Wiseman, & J. Zilczer (Eds.), *Visual music: Synaesthesia in art and music since 1900* (pp. 7–9). Thames & Hudson.
Robinson, R. (2021). *Georgia O'Keeffe: A life*. Brandeis University Press.
Rose, L. S., & Countryman, J. (2013). Repositioning "the elements": How students talk about music. *Action, Criticism & Theory for Music Education, 12*(3), 44–64.
Rose, T. (1994). *Black noise: Rap music and black culture in contemporary America*. University Press of New England.
Ross, A. (2007). *The rest is noise: Listening to the twentieth century*. Farrar, Straus and Giroux.
Rothko, C. (2015). *Mark Rothko: From the inside out*. Yale University Press.
Rümelin, C. (2002). *Paul Klee animal tricks*. Prestel Verlag.
Samson, J. (2001). Reception. In *Grove music online*. Retrieved 6 Oct. 2021, from https://www-oxfordmusiconline-com.proxy2.library.illinois.edu/grovemusic/view/10.1093/gmo/9781561592630.001.0001/omo-9781561592630-e-0000040600.
Sandburg, C. (1936). *The people, yes*. Harcourt, Brace and Company.
Schippers, H. (2010). *Facing the music: Shaping music education from a global perspective*. Oxford University Press.
Schubert, E. (2003). Update of the Hevner adjective checklist. *Perceptual and Motor Skills, 96*, 1117–1122.
Scott, J. (2010). Music review—Black birds, red hills: A portrait of six paintings of Georgia O'Keeffe. *The Clarinet, 37*(4), 79.
Shuster, K., Jeffries, H. K., McCoy, M. L., Newell, M., Shear, S. B., Snyder, C., & Thomas, E. E. (2019). *Teaching hard history: A K–5 framework for teaching American slavery*. Southern Poverty Law Center.
Slattery, P. (2013). *Curriculum development in the postmodern era: Teaching and learning in an age of accountability* (3rd ed.). Routledge.
Small, C. (1998). *Musicking: The meanings of performing and listening*. Wesleyan University Press.

Strick, J. (2005). Visual music. In K. Brougher, J. Strick, A. Wiseman, & J. Zilczer (Eds.), *Visual music: Synaethesia in art and music since 1900* (pp. 15–21). Thames & Hudson.

Swanson, E. (2014). August 4, 1964: 50 years later. *Choral Journal, 55*(1), 50–55.

Tepper, S. J., & Ivey, B. (2008). *Engaging art: The next great transformation of America's cultural life*. Routledge.

Turino, T. (2008). *Music as social life: The politics of participation*. University of Chicago Press.

Vergo, P. (2010). *The music of painting: Music, modernism and the visual arts from the Romantics to John Cage*. Phaedon.

Wade, B. (2009). *Thinking musically: Experiencing music, expressing culture*. Oxford University Press.

Walsh, J. E. (2000). *Moonlight: Abraham Lincoln and the Almanac Trial*. St. Martin's Press.

Weber, N. F. (2009). *The Bauhaus group: Six masters of modernism*. Alfred A. Knopf.

Wills, J. S. (2005). "Some people even died": Martin Luther King, Jr., the Civil Rights movement and the politics of remembrance in elementary classrooms. *International Journal of Qualitative Studies in Education, 18*(1), 109–131.

Wineburg, S. (2001). *Historical thinking and other unnatural acts: Charting the future of teaching the past*. Temple University Press.

Wineburg, S. (2011). Can educators even answer these lame questions? *History News Network*. https://historynewsnetwork.org/article/140055.

Wineburg, S. (2018). *Why learn history (when it's already on your phone)*. University of Chicago Press.

Wineburg, S., & Grossman, P. (Eds.). (2000). *Interdisciplinary curriculum: Challenges to implementation*. Teachers College Press.

Winter, J. (1988). *Follow the drinking gourd*. Dragonfly Books.

Woodford, P. G. (2005). *Democracy and music education: Liberalism, ethics, and the politics of practice*. Indiana University Press.

Index

For the benefit of digital users, indexed terms that span two pages (e.g., 52–53) may, on occasion, appear on only one of those pages.

Tables and figures are indicated by *t* and *f* following the page number

Abeles, H., 10–11
Allsup, Randall, 80, 92
Alternative Energy, 78–79, 79*f*
American Composers Forum, 89, 95–101, 97*f*, 102
America Windows, 23
Anderson, Benedict, 62
Angelou, Maya, 61–62
Appalachian Spring, 42
Arendt, Hannah, 208
Art as Experience (Dewey), 21
arts, the, 86, 134
   bridge of inspiration between, 136–37
   cross-arts inspirations, 127–30
   Dewey on, 21–22, 23
   interdisciplinarity in, 8–10, 19–20, 89–90
   interpretation in, 105–6
   juxtaposition in, 107
   Kandinsky on, 128, 136–37
   monoaesthetic curricula in, 26
   nature of experience in, 21–23
   pedagogy of mutuality in, 91–92
   in social studies and history education, 173–74
   triptychs across art forms, 108–9, 110–11
   visual art in music curricula, 135
arts education, 10–11, 21, 30, 31, 40, 190
assessment, 156, 186–87, 188
   of connections, 190–93, 191*f*
   curriculum and, 201–7
   interdisciplinarity and, 187, 188, 189, 206–7
   multiple methods for multiple learning types, 198–201, 199*t*
   by music teacher judgment in, 189–90
   of relational thinking, 195–98
   of relationships formed by students, 192–95
August 4, 1964, 179*f*
Autumn Rhythm, 22–23
Ayers, W., 81, 189

Bach, J. S., 141–42, 150–51
Balmages, Brian, 155
BandQuest project, of American Composers Forum, 95–101, 97*f*, 102
Barrett, J. R., 15, 41–42, 46
Barrett, Terry, 106
Bates, Mason, 78–79, 79*f*
Beers, S., 12
Bement, Alon, 127
Bernstein, Leonard, 14, 54
Black Birds, Red Hills, 128
Black history and community, 44, 47–49, 57–58, 63–65, 175–76
Black Violet, 75–76
Blue and Green Music, 128
Boix Mansilla, V., 195–96
Bond, Julian, 61, 62
boundary-crossing sensibilities, 73, 74–77, 208
Breakstone, J., 170
"Brightness of Light, The," 128
Bruhn, S., 136, 142
Bruner, Jerome, 89, 90–92, 107
Burton, J. M., 10–11

Cage, John, 99, 112
California Counterpoint: The Twittering Machine, 145–46, 147*f*, 155

Chagall, Marc, 23
Chaney, James, 177–78, 180
children's literature, 164–66, 167–69, 170–71, 172–73, 174
chromaesthesia, 134–35
Clague, Mark, 116
Close, Chuck, 122–27, 125f
Clyburn, James, 49
CMP. See Comprehensive Musicianship through Performance
Colgrass, Michael, 89, 97f, 97–99, 101f, 102
Colwell, Richard, 189
Comiskey, Miles, 87–89
Comprehensive Musicianship through Performance (CMP), 103–4
Concerning the Spiritual in Art (Kandinsky), 127–28
connections, 82, 131–33, 190–95, 191f
contemporary performers and composers, 77–80
context, 45–49, 181–82, 184–85, 194
"Contre qui, rose" (Rilke), 201–3
Copland, Aaron, 42, 116, 132, 203, 204–5, 205f
Cortright, Joanna, 193
Costa, A. L., 200–1
Countryman, J., 51
COVID-19 pandemic, 82, 83, 208–9
Crauwels, Kwintin, 72
culminating activities, 102
Culture of Education, The (Bruner), 90
curation, 109, 111–17
curriculum, 15–16, 26, 92, 216. See also music curriculum
curriculum planning
  in BandQuest example, 95–101, 102
  context in, 46–47
  Facets Model in, 42–43
  interdisciplinary, 94, 103
  linear and prescriptive, 93, 94
  risk-taking in, 92–93
  soft planning, 89, 93–94, 95–100, 102
  triptych strategy in, 110

Daniels, Ezra Claytan, 75–76
Davids, Brent Michael, 99–100
Desert Island Discs Challenge, 82

Detels, Claire, 12–13
Dewey, John, 16, 94, 217n.3
  on the arts, 21–22, 23
  on environing conditions, 28, 104–5
  on experience, 19–20, 21, 23, 24, 26–27, 35, 40–41, 65, 206–7
"Diamante for Chuck" (Greenberg), 126–27
disciplinary depth, in music teaching, 28–30, 32
disciplines
  boundaries of, 8, 12–13
  interdisciplinarity of, 12–13
  music, 5–6
  permeability of, 12–13, 72–73
  relationships between, 194–95
Düchting, Hugo, 140–41, 142
Dutton, J., 134

eclectic week, 82–83
educationally vital experiences (EVEs), 26–28
educative experiences, 19–20, 71–72, 86, 90, 104–5
  miseducative experiences and, 24
  teacher intention, in crafting, 28
Eisner, E. W., 15–16, 93–95, 146–47, 173–74, 186–87, 188, 189–90, 209, 213
ekphrasis, 110, 112–15, 118, 136
Endacott, Jason, 174
environing conditions, 28, 104–5
ethnomusicologists, 46–47
Etudes
  Lifelong Musical Profile, 70
  Opus 1, Moments of Connection, 20–21, 24–25
  Opus 2, Lateral Knowledge, 33–34
  Opus 3, Arts-Related CV, 34–35
Eurocentricity, 37–38, 39–40, 50, 51, 52
Evans, Gary, 137, 138, 169, 173
Evans, Shane W., 166
EVEs. See educationally vital experiences
experience. See also educative experiences
  of the arts, 21–23, 59–60
  Dewey on, 19–20, 21, 23, 24, 26–27, 35, 40–41, 65, 206–7
  nature of, 21–23
Experiential Facets Model, 65–66, 66f

Facets Model, 41, 43f
   Alternative Energy in, 78–79, 79f
   August 4, 1964 in, 179f
   BandQuest project and, 100–1
   California Counterpoint: The Twittering Machine in, 146, 147f
   context in, 46–47
   in curriculum planning, 42–43
   Experiential Facets Model, 65–66, 66f
   Follow the Drinking Gourd in, 168f, 168–69
   "Lessons from a Painting by Rothko" in, 121f
   "Lift Every Voice and Sing" in, 64f
   Lincoln Portrait in, 205f
   Map in, 116f
   "Map" in, 117f
   Old Churches in, 101f
   origins of, 41–44
   for song history research, 182–83
   Twittering Machine in, 144f, 144–45, 146
   Untitled 1953/1954 in, 122f
   updated version of, 43–44, 44f
Facing History and Ourselves, 175
Fautley, Martin, 189
Feldman, Morton, 120
Fifth House Ensemble, 74–75, 76–77
Floyd, George, 49, 176
Follow the Drinking Gourd (song), 164–66, 168f, 168–70
Follow the Drinking Gourd (Winter), 164–65
Freire, Paulo, 91
Fugue in Red, 150

Gandolfi, Michael, 68–70
Garden of Cosmic Speculation, 67–71
Garden of Cosmic Speculation, The (musical work), 68–70
Gardner, Howard, 55, 101–2
Giddens, Rhiannon, 73
Glass, Philip, 122–27, 125f
Gleason, Chris, 155
Goodman, Andrew, 177–78, 179–80
Grandmother Song, 99–100
"Great Gate of Kiev," 54
Greenberg, Jan, 109–11, 114, 126–27

Greene, Maxine, 22, 25, 86, 91–92, 103, 208
Grossman, P., 11, 12

Hannah-Jones, Nikole, 175–76
Hays, Lee, 165
Heart to Heart (Greenberg), 109–10
Heise, Graham, 132
Hendrix, Jimi, 116
heuristics, 65, 89, 94–95, 107, 190–92
Hevner, Kate, 58, 59f
high interdisciplinary quotient musical works, 95
high IQ musical works, 81, 83, 103–4, 214
Highways and Byways, 138–45, 150–51, 158
historical empathy framework, 174
history
   the arts and, 173–74
   children's literature on, 164–66, 167–69, 170, 172–73, 174
   historical engagement with historically significant work for ensembles, 176–78, 179–81
   misunderstandings, misrepresentations, and interpretations of, 171–73
   music and, 162, 163–64, 174, 175–76, 179–85
   toward historical inquiry in music classrooms, 182–85
Holst, Gustav, 75
Horowitz, R., 10–11
Howard, P., 92–93

interdisciplinarians, 20–21, 33–35, 77, 93–95
interdisciplinarity, 7–8
   aims of, 16–18
   in the arts, 8–10, 19–20, 89–90
   assessment and, 187, 188, 189, 206–7
   in curriculum planning, 94, 103
   of disciplines, 12–13
   high IQ works in, 103–4
   interpretive zones for, 104–6
   juxtaposition in, 109
   multidimensionality and, 80
   multiple entry points in, 101–2

interdisciplinarity (cont.)
  in music curriculum, 16–18, 71–72, 81, 103, 208, 211–12, 214
  in music education, 1, 5, 19–20, 209–12
  of music teachers, 19–20, 30, 211–16
  omnivorousness as prelude to, 71–73
  permeability and, 12–13
  pivot in, 102
  in schools, quest for more, 10–12
  triptychs in, 110
interdisciplinary pedagogy, 89–90, 92, 94–95, 210–11
interdisciplinary perspective, 14–16, 17
interdisciplinary relationships, 17, 39–40, 192
International Contemporary Ensemble, 8–9
interpretive zones, 95, 104–6, 206
intradisciplinary practice, 14
intradisciplinary relationships, 41, 192
Intrator, Sam, 26–27

Jaccard, Jerry L., 142–44
Jackson, P. W., 23, 217n.3
Jacobs, Heidi Hayes, 5–6, 217n.1
Jencks, Charles, 67–69
Johns, Jasper, 111–12, 113*f*, 114–15, 116*f*, 116
Johnson, James Weldon, 47–48, 53, 56–57, 63–64
Johnson, J. Rosamond, 47–48, 53, 63–64, 65
Johnson, Lyndon Baines, 177, 178
Journey LIVE, 75
juxtaposition, 106–7, 109, 110, 131, 193

Kaepernick, Colin, 49
Kajikawa, Loren, 39
Kallick, B., 200–1
Kandinsky, Wassily, 127–28, 134–35, 136–37
Karvelius, Julianna, 132–33
Kasischke, Laura, 130
Katz, Bobbi, 118–19, 120, 121*f*, 121
Katz, S. L., 55
Keats, John, 136
King, Martin Luther, Jr., 49

Klee, Paul, 137–38, 139–61, 143*f*, 144*f*, 149*f*
Kliebard, Herbert, 94
Kohn, Alfie, 186–87
Kooning, Elaine de, 120

Langer, Suzanne, 59–60
Larsen, Libby, 6, 52–53, 128
lateral knowledge, 32–33, 33*f*
Lauridsen, Morten, 201–3
Learning for Justice framework, 175
Lepore, Jill, 163
"Lessons from a Painting by Rothko" (Katz), 118–19, 120, 121*f*, 121
Levingston, Bruce, 123
Lewis, J. Patrick, 114–15, 117*f*
LeWitt, Sol, 77–78
lifelong musical profile, imagining, 70–71
"Lift Every Voice and Sing"
  affect and meanings of, 61–62
  Black history and community and, 44, 47–49, 57–58, 63–65
  in Facets Model, 64*f*
  properties and forms of, 53
  subject matter of, 56–58
  synthesis of dimensions, 63–65
Lincoln for the Defense, 203
Lincoln Portrait, 204–5, 205*f*
Lustig, Ray, 76

Magee, Gayle, 179–80
Magee, Jeff, 182–83
Map (painting), 112, 113*f*, 114–15, 116*f*, 116
"Map" (Lewis), 114–15, 117*f*
May We Forever Stand (Perry), 63–65
McCoy, Claire, 15, 21, 41–42, 46
McNamara, Robert, 177, 178, 179–80
McTee, Cindy, 145–46, 147*f*, 155
Megill, Andrew, 179–80
Meiste, Paul, 132–33
Mind/Mirror, 111–12
Morris, Wesley, 175–76
multidimensionality, 40–41, 65–66, 80, 89, 91, 104, 193, 195
Murder in Mississippi, 180
Musical Portrait of Chuck Close, A, 122–23, 124–26

musical works
    affective dimensions of, 58–60, 61–62, 194
    as cases for curricular exploration, 39–40
    connections of, 82, 193–95
    contexts of, 45–49, 181–82, 184–85
    forms and structures of, 51–53
    high interdisciplinary quotient, 95
    high IQ, 81, 83, 103–4, 214
    intradisciplinary relationships of, 41
    meanings of, 60–62
    multidimensionality in encounters with, 40–41
    in music curriculum, 37–38, 39, 103
    music students on, 37, 40, 193–95
    music teachers on, 36–40, 45–46, 82, 83–85, 181–82
    omnivorous approach to exploring, 71–72
    program notes for, 55
    properties and elements of, 49–51, 53, 193–94
    racism in, 38
    researching, 84–85
    subject matter of, 53–58
    synthesis of, 62–65
music curriculum, 37–38, 87
    assessment and, 201–7
    constellations of connections projects in, 131–33
    on history and music, 164–66, 167–69, 173, 175–76, 183–84
    interdisciplinarity in, 16–18, 71–72, 81, 103, 208, 211–12, 214
    multiplicity in, 69–70
    on musical elements, 50–51
    musical works in, 37–38, 39, 103
    panoramic project inspired by *The Twittering Machine*, 146–61
    picture books in, 170–71
    related arts movement, 135
    repertoire in, 103
    students in shaping, 81
    visual art in, 135
music educators. *See also* assessment
    aims of, 19
    background knowledge of, 45
    breadth and depth of musical preparation, 33*f*, 33
    breadth of knowledge, 31–32
    challenges to, 208–9
    in collaborative teams, 214
    on contexts of musical works, 45–49, 181–82, 184–85
    curriculum planning, in BandQuest example, 95–101, 102
    exercises for going deep, 83–85
    exercises for going wide, 82–83
    on high IQ musical works, 104
    on history, 163–64, 181–85
    on inspiration, 26
    interdisciplinarity of, 19–20, 30, 211–16
    interdisciplinary perspective of, 14–16
    lateral knowledge of, 32–33, 33*f*
    on multidimensionality, 65–66
    on musical works, 36–40, 45–46, 82, 83–85, 181–82
    musical worlds of students and, 72–73, 82
    music as discipline for, 6
    pedagogy of, 86–89, 90–91
    philosophy of, 80
    on repertoire, 36–37, 103–4
    specialization by, 6–7, 29, 30, 31, 33, 215
    on triptychs, 108, 115
Music Genome Project, 72
music history pedagogy, 176
Music Inspired by Art (Evans, G.), 137
"Musicmap" (Crauwels), 72
Music of Painting, The (Vergo), 137
musicologists and musicology, 9, 39, 46–47, 60–61, 182
music students. *See also* assessment
    in BandQuest project, 98–100, 102
    composition and improvisation by, 76–77
    curriculum shaped by, 81
    engagements with several arts, 86
    environing conditions of, 105
    on history, 182–83, 184
    interpretation by, 105–6
    on musical elements, 50
    on musical works, 37, 40, 193–95
    musical worlds of, 72–73, 82
    participation of, 29–30

music students (*cont.*)
   pedagogy and, 86–87, 88–89, 90–91
   relational thinking, 90–91, 195–98
   soundtrack assignments for, 82
   specialization by, 30
   on triptychs, 117
Mussorgsky, Modest, 54, 75, 132, 152
mutuality, 15–16, 88, 89–92, 93

National Association for the Advancement of Colored People (NAACP), 48–49
New, Trevor, 76
New Canons, 76
new music, 8, 55, 76–77, 79–80, 81, 123
Ngan, Melissa, 74–77

"Ode on a Grecian Urn" (Keats), 136
O'Keeffe, Georgia, 127, 128–30
Okpebholo, Shawn, 75–76
Old Churches, 89, 97f, 97–99, 101f, 102
Oliveros, Pauline, 76–77
O'Malley, Patrick, 75–76
omnivorousness, 71–73, 74

Page, Reba, 11, 15
paintings, 111–17, 127–30, 137–38, 139–61, 180
Palmer, Parker, 31
Palmer, Rachel, 132–33
pantoum, 119
Parini, J., 112–14
Parks, H. B., 165
Parsons, Michael, 7–8, 106, 188
Partita for 8 Voices, 77–78
Patterson, T., 172–73
Peacock, Molly, 57
pedagogies
   Bruner on, 89, 90–92
   challenges of shifting, 92–93
   of Comiskey, 87–89
   composition, 87
   curricula and, 92, 216
   folk, 90
   heuristics and, 94–95
   interdisciplinary, 89–90, 92, 94–95, 210–11
   models of mind in, 90–92
   of music educators, 86–89, 90–91

music history, 176
   of mutuality, 88, 89–92, 93
permeability, 5, 12–13
Perry, Imani, 47–48, 53, 56, 57–58, 62, 63–65
Phenix, Philip, 12–13
Phil (Fingerprint), 124, 125f
Pianist in Distress—A Satire: Caricature of Modern Music, 139–40
Pictures at an Exhibition, 75, 152
Pierce, K. M., 25–26
Pink and Blue I and *II*, 128
Planets, The, 75
Plaskota, Melissa, 132–33
poetry, 109–10, 130, 136, 201–6
   poetic portraits, 122–27
   portraits in poetic forms, 126–27
   in triptychs, 112–14, 118–22
Pollock, Jackson, 22–23
Pope, D. C., 25–26
Prall, David, 14
program music, 55, 136, 193
Puts, Kevin, 128

Questioning techniques, pivots, 95

Realms of Meaning (Phenix), 12–13
Red Hills and Bones (painting), 128–30
"Red Hills and Bones" (Kasischke), 130
Reimer, B., 103–4, 195
relational thinking, 17–18, 18f, 88, 89–91, 191, 193
   assessment of, 195–98
Releasing the Imagination (Greene), 22
repertoire, 36–38, 39–40, 103–4
repetition, 84
Rethinking Schools, 196–97
Rilke, Rainer Maria, 201–3
Rivers Empyrean, 75–76
Rockwell, Norman, 180, 203, 204–5
Rodeo, 116
Roomful of Teeth, 77–78, 218n.7
Rose, L. S., 51
Rose Garden, 139–45
Ross, Alex, 79–80
Rothko, Christopher, 120, 121
Rothko, Mark, 118–20, 119f, 121–22, 122f
Ruffins, Fath Davis, 169–70

Samson, J., 60–61
Sandburg, Carl, 203–5
Scheer, Gene, 177, 178
Schippers, Huib, 193
Schoenberg, Arnold, 136–37
school routines, as anaesthetic, 25–26
Schreuder, Adri, 193
Schwerner, Michael, 177, 178, 179–80
Seeger, Pete, 164, 165
Seybert, Katie, 165–69, 170, 173
Shaw, Caroline, 77–78, 218n.7
Shuttleworth, J. M., 172–73
1619 Project, 175–76, 221n.10
Slattery, Patrick, 22–23, 208
Small, Christopher, 38–39
social studies, the arts and, 173–74
Soft Boundaries (Detels), 12–13
soft planning, 89, 93–94, 95–100, 102
Sorey, Tyshawn, 120
Soundways, 157–58, 157*f*
Sound Ways of Knowing (Barrett, J. R., McCoy, & Veblen), 15, 41–42, 46
"Star-Spangled Banner," 49, 61–62, 116
Stieglitz, Alfred, 128
Stretching exercise
  [after experiential facets], 66
  [for going deep] searching for works with a high IQ, 83–85
  [for going wide] eclectic week, 82–83
  [for going wide] soundtracks as starting points, 82
  of a philosophical sort, 187–88
  searching for omnivores, 74
  works with a high IQ, 104

Stucky, Steven, 177, 178
"Symbol and Reality" (Ruffins), 169–70
synaesthesia, 123, 134

Teaching Hard History framework, 175
Tepper, Stephen, 72
"The People, Yes" (Sandburg), 203–4
triptychs, 95, 108, 111–17, 118–22
triptych strategy, 109–11, 131, 137–38
Turino, Tom, 52
Twittering Machine, The, 138, 142–61, 143*f*, 144*f*

Unchained Melodies, 76–77
Underground (Evans, S. W.), 166, 169, 173
Underwood, Alex, 178–80, 181
Underwood, Titus, 49
Untitled 1953/1954 (Rothko, M.), 119*f*, 122*f*

"Variations on Simple Gifts," 42
Veblen, Kari, 15, 41–42, 46
Vergo, Peter, 137
Visconti, Dan, 76–77
visual metaphors, 1–5, 2*f*, 3*f*, 13
"Visual Music" exhibition, at Smithsonian Institution, 134–35

Wade, Bonnie, 38
Wilson, Sondra Kathryn, 61, 62
Wineburg, Sam, 11, 12, 62, 170, 171–72, 174
Winter, Jeanette, 164–65
Wintory, Austin, 75